Praise for *Evolution Not Revolution*

"*Evolution Not Revolution* tackles the fundamental issue of the high-tech industry—establishing a common decision-making criteria for both technologists and nontechnologists. *Evolution Not Revolution* provides actionable solutions to many of the issues corporate executives must face that I first identified in my book, *Techno Vision*."

—CHARLES B. WANG
Chairman,
Computer Associates International, Inc.

"*Evolution Not Revolution* clearly shows why we are at the beginning of the next revolution in increasing business productivity. Every manager who is actively involved with, or even just concerned about, information technology within the context of strategy setting and execution will benefit from following the mandates of this book."

—BILL ZEITLER
Senior Vice President & Group Executive,
Server Group, IBM Corporation

"Logan dispels many myths while providing an action plan for building market value. He dispenses with the usual preaching about how information technology is good for a company and gets right into the action items required to be successful."

—GERRY ISOM
former President,
Cigna Property and Casualty

"Logan's approach to evaluating the potential business benefits of new technologies has proven itself time after time. *Evolution Not Revolution* will open the eyes and imaginations of executives around the world."

—JOE SANTANA
President & CEO,
Timex Corporation

"*Evolution Not Revolution* will be quoted for many years to come by both senior corporate executives and information technology executives when they work together constructively as a real team. It is the first business book that provides business executives with a real understanding of the unique issues IT professionals face every day in a way that provokes positive action."

—PATRICK J. ZILVITIS
CIO, DEKA Research and former CIO,
The Gillette Company

"*Evolution Not Revolution* should be read by all information technology project managers and consultants to better understand the high-level corporate agendas that motivate business mangers. Too many technology projects are failures because they deliver the initially envisioned requirements, but fail to provide the anticipated business value. As Mr. Logan clearly points out, business needs change. The build-review-improve-build cycle of development proscribed in this book gives business and technology managers a means for collaborating to provide business value."

—KEN SCHWABER
Author, *Agile Software Development with Scrum*

"*Evolution Not Revolution* provides a strategic information technology plan for smaller businesses that can be acted upon immediately. This is a must read for the owner of any private company."

—BARNEY KLEVAY
Owner and President,
Industrial Wheels, Inc.

"Logan's mandate to the corporate world for using advanced information technologies to increase the value of their organizations is just as applicable to government agencies. The leaders of all government agencies will be well served by initiating evolutionary improvement projects based upon the roadmap to success Logan so eloquently lays out."

—C. LAWRENCE MEADOR
Chairman, Independent Panel on the
Central Intelligence Agency In-Q-Tel Venture

"Logan pulls no punches about the executive competencies required to be successful when deploying major information systems. He is a credible authority on how corporations must combine business acumen and technology innovation to improve their market value."

—ANN LIVERMORE
President of Services
Hewlett-Packard Company

Evolution
Not Revolution

Evolution
Not Revolution

Aligning Technology with Corporate
Strategy to Increase Market Value

JOHN R. LOGAN

McGraw-Hill

New York   Chicago   San Francisco   Lisbon   London   Madrid
Mexico City   Milan   New Delhi   San Juan   Seoul
Singapore   Sydney   Toronto

Library of Congress Cataloging-in-Publication Data applied for.

McGraw-Hill

A Division of The McGraw·Hill Companies

1 2 3 4 5 6 7 8 9 0   AGM/AGM   0 9 8 7 6 5 4 3 2 1

ISBN 0-07-138410-3

This book was set in Janson by McGraw-Hill's Professional Book Group composition unit, Hightstown, NJ.

Printed and bound by Quebecor World/Martinsburg.

This publication is designed to provide accurate and authoritative information in regard to the subject matter covered. It is sold with the understanding that the publisher is not engaged in rendering legal, accounting, or other professional service. If legal advice or other expert assistance is required, the services of a competent professional person should be sought.

—From a declaration of principles jointly adopted by a committee of the American Bar Association and a committee of publishers.

 This book is printed on recycled, acid-free paper containing a minimum of 50% recycled, de-inked fiber.

McGraw-Hill books are available at special quantity discounts to use as premiums and sales promotions, or for use in corporate training programs. For more information, please write to the Director of Special Sales, Professional Publishing, McGraw-Hill, Two Penn Plaza, New York, NY 10121-2298. Or contact your local bookstore.

Contents

Acknowledgments

The pragmatic mandates for increasing market value that are described in *Evolution Not Revolution* were first explained to me by pioneering technology executives and I wish to acknowledge their contributions. These true business leaders have spent many long hours showing me what steps they have taken to leverage the benefits of advanced technologies successfully throughout their organizations and the internal political issues that they have had to confront and overcome. Such selfless individuals have objectively evaluated the personal risks of being cutting-edge change agents and consistently made the recommendations and choices that were best for their companies. I have always been grateful for the opportunity to assist in their strategic management efforts and learn from them the strong, disciplined commitments required on the part of leaders to build winner corporations. They have shown by their examples that the most effective market-value building ideas can originate from anywhere within an organization and successfully flow up, down, and across departmental boundaries. I have merely penned their words, summarizing the hard-won knowledge they would like to pass on to their peers throughout the world.

I also very much want to thank the chairmen, presidents, and senior vice-presidents in both the many high-tech suppliers and leading-edge technology-savvy companies I have worked with over the years. We have been in many brainstorming and reality-setting sessions together developing programs to provide a common ground on which business-focused executives and information systems professionals could come together and work constructively as a team. Taking the resulting programs to the managers who run their corporations' operations, we consistently found that the evolutionary approach to advanced technology-based change was much more effective than the revolutionary approach, which others had often tried before us without success. Many of you will recognize yourselves and your companies in this book.

In addition, I must recognize the contributions of the numerous information systems professionals who have challenged me to tell business mangers in an understandable and relevant way about the gritty realities of deploying new technologies. Putting in new systems that nobody in a corporation has expertise with is difficult, nerve-wracking work, fraught with uncertainty and frustration. Successful information systems professionals are very proud of the value they have added to their companies. They want the other members of their corporations to appreciate that acquiring, deploying, and operating the types of advanced enterprise-level information systems that provide a company with competitive advantages requires a very different way of thinking about how to tackle business problems than most traditional managers were taught. *Evolution Not Revolution* is their voice to be heard by others in their companies and I thank them for raising it loud and clear.

My heartfelt appreciation runs deep and throughout this book to all the teachers and mentors who have helped me so much in life. At all the schools I have attended—Harvard Business School, University of Michigan, Linsly Military Institute—there have always been numerous educators who have cared so much about all their students. I have always admired their enthusiasm for teaching the next generation of society how to be better than the last. In addition, every company I have ever worked for has been filled with senior executives who have provided me with their pragmatic wisdom about how to get things done. I hope I can repay them all in this small way by carrying on their efforts by putting in writing for others the valuable management lessons I have learned—just as they taught me the lessons they knew so well.

This book would not have gone beyond the outline stage if it was not for the kind words and encouragement of friends such as Leo Au, Andrew Bochman, Donna Davis, James Gruener, Peter Kastner, Robert Lutz, Larry Meador, Wayne Pagot, Ken and Chris Schwaber, and Patrick Zilvitis. Daniel Greenberg of James Levine Communications was both my agent and security blanket throughout. Without his wise advice and hard work, my original outline would never have become a manuscript. And of course, it would still be a manuscript and not a real book except for the excellent coaching of my editor at McGraw-Hill, Mary Glenn. She has helped translate my unique lingo of techno-business into words that business executives can enjoy, understand, and build upon.

Finally, and most importantly, I owe so very much to the support of my wonderful wife, Karen, and our four fantastic children, Jack, Heather, Brittany, and Megan. Researching this book took me away from our comfortable home far too often and writing it has often disrupted their very busy schedules. This book would never have been completed without their continuous encouragement and strong support. They always show me in their words and actions that the best parts of life really are all about family.

John R. Logan

Introduction

Evolution Not Revolution is a directive for business executives and information systems professionals to work together as a team to increase the market value of their companies. They can and must do this by improving their company's business processes in an evolutionary way. While many business thought leaders recently have been encouraging corporations to undergo revolutions, experience proves that organizations and their customers cannot withstand the chaos that accompanies frequent, radical changes. A far more constructive way to improve the market value of a company is to use advanced technologies as the basis for initiating disciplined changes that will increase a company's revenue growth while allowing it to lower the costs of delivering products and services.

The motivation for writing this book came at the conclusion of a meeting I had with a Chrysler (now DaimlerChrysler) executive. This gentleman was responsible for evaluating, acquiring, and deploying the latest and greatest commercially available technologies for designing and manufacturing Chrysler's next generation of cars. His straightforward objectives were to both cut a year or more off the design process and lower by tens of millions of dollars the tooling costs required for manufacturing new models. Achieving these two objectives obviously was very important for the company and its long-term market value.

This Chrysler executive had the budget to buy one of everything that he might want from the leading high-tech suppliers and the staff to evaluate thoroughly the potential of these advanced technologies within Chrysler. This project was so important to Chrysler that the company located this executive and his group miles from the rest of the organization to work in secret and away from any distractions in a converted old redbrick schoolhouse that it had acquired hastily. This out-of-character-looking high-tech development laboratory did not even have an identifying sign.

Unintentionally, my role in the meeting soon turned into briefing the executive and his staff about the short- and long-term advantages and disadvantages of each of the technologies he could acquire at the time. While I was there to present the benefits of a promising new technology that might help, it soon became apparent that he was very disturbed at the conflicting claims of the different vendors with whom he was working. More frustrating, after months of effort and millions of dollars spent, he could not get the systems he had purchased to work the way the vendors had promised his corporate bosses at headquarters they would.

Abruptly, he ended the meeting with his staff and asked me and his second-in-command to follow him into his private office. We sat down, and he stared at me with a trembling jaw for a full minute. I asked what I could do to help. Suddenly, he started crying from frustration. Here was a loyal forty-something executive who had risen up through the ranks of the engineering and manufacturing departments weeping at a time when he should have been solving a problem that would result in his being promoted to even more senior levels within Chrysler.

Between sobs, he said, "What can I do to make this damn mess work? How do I get these computer systems to work? And even if I can get them to work, how will I ever get the rest of the organization to use them?" Over the years, I have heard the same pleas—but never as emotionally expressed—for help from many executives in every industry and every part of the world.

Evolution Not Revolution has been written for my friend at Chrysler and every other corporate executive who must manage in today's wired business environment. At least once every 3 years for the last 15 years, executives in successful companies have had to direct their organizations and navigate their own careers through a corporatewide information systems technology transition. Rarely have any executives believed that their company has fully supported them through such transition processes.

The individual winners out of each technology transition are those executives who have contributed in their own way to its success. The losers are those who stood in the way of change. *Evolution Not Revolution* is a personal guide for helping all executives manage successfully through technology transitions within their organizations.

As chairman of Aberdeen Group, a high-tech market research and consulting firm I founded, I have had the opportunity to interview and talk with thousands of executives in hundreds of companies around the world about how they have managed the planning, deployment, and use of enterprise-level advanced technologies. This book is based on insights gained from the winner organizations.

Several high-tech market research and consulting firms perform annual global surveys to understand what key corporate decision makers' objectives will be for the use of information systems in the coming year. Invariably, the most common answer that both frustrated business and information systems executives respond with is, "Correlating the corporation's strategic goals with its information technology initiatives." Why has this obvious problem lingered for so long among competent executives who have reached their senior positions by solving problems and building profitable lines of business?

The answer is really very simple: Executives focused on business operations do not necessarily understand what technology can and cannot do at the same time that information systems professionals do not know how to prioritize the types of projects that will have the greatest probability of increasing their firm's market value. Until company leaders can instill within their management culture an ingrained solution to this now-apparent flaw within their organizations, they and their firms will continue to be in danger of losing the technology-based competitive battles of the future. Moreover, as many businesses have discovered over the last several years, losing these often-unexpected information age battles can be fatal for their companies and their careers.

All organizations—from large global corporations to local government agencies—have the potential to increase their value to shareholders and constituents by improving how they conduct business with the innovative use of advanced information systems technologies. All that holds them back is a lack of knowledge about how to manage the processes of technology-based evolution. Hopefully, they will be able to use this book to lead them.

I have found that corporate executives generally view their companies' use of information systems technology in one of two ways. The most common is as a traditional company in which the use of information systems is an overhead cost that must be minimized. The other is as a company in the Competitive Economy for which the creative use of technology to support superior business processes is a potent tool.

Traditional companies have formal information systems departments that senior executives, business unit executives, middle managers, and staff depend on to provide the management and control functions on which their business processes are built. In these organizations, the professional information systems staff as a whole understands neither the company's strategic objectives nor the dynamics of the markets in which they provide goods and services. The management within such companies typically views the deployment of technology as a defensive move. Therefore, managers acquire and deploy relatively *mature* information systems products that provide little or no help in increasing the company's market value and customer satisfaction when compared with their competition.

In Competitive Economy companies, all key decision makers—both those who consider themselves business-operations-focused and those who consider themselves information-systems-oriented—know how to identify and leverage the business opportunities presented by changes in their marketplace through the use of advanced information technologies. These highly competitive and aggressive organizations have advanced the effectiveness of their management capabilities by developing a core competence in collaborating across organizational boundaries to implement *advanced* information systems effectively that allow them to gain operational advantages well ahead of their rivals.

One of the most surprising findings I have learned through many years of research is that even winner companies—those which manage successfully in the Competitive Economy—can lose the management approach to technology that made them great in the first place. At certain critical times, senior corporate executives will focus their attention on adopting advanced technologies to support major improvements in their business processes to gain a lead in their marketplaces. However, the critical actions they took for success too often will be forgotten in a few short years. As a result, all corporations need a road map for every executive to follow for the planning, deployment, and use of enterprise-level advanced technologies—technologies that none of these executives may have seen before—to improve their organization's position in its competitive marketplaces.

Evolution Not Revolution is both a road map for technology-based change and a source for arbitrating disputes about how to make business decisions regarding the deployment of advanced technologies. The 10 competencies a company must have to increase its market value in today's Competitive Economy that are described in this book are also answers to the most common questions that business-focused executives debate endlessly with their professional information systems peers.

Evolution Not Revolution challenges business-focused executives to manage proactively the innovative use of advanced technologies that have the potential to provide their organizations with the ability to win in today's hypercompetitive global marketplaces. And it demands that information systems executives think and act like businesspeople and contribute much more to increasing the operational strengths of their firms.

The conflicts and divisions between the business operations and information systems groups in today's corporations have gone on for far too long. At the heart of the problem is the different perspectives members of each side have about their company's current strategies, goals, and objectives. From this untenable starting point, the disagreements quickly become even more hostile as the two factions maintain strong—but very different—opinions of how their corporations should operate.

To bring business and information systems executives together, organizations must have a common set of management goals and principles for both to follow. Promotions up the corporate ranks must be highly dependent on making decisions that meet company standards for both best operations and sound technology-management practices. No matter what functional or geographic area an executive finds himself or herself in, obtaining superior performance ratings must depend on his or her ability to initiate and manage changes successfully in the organization's business processes using the latest and greatest information systems technologies.

Managers in winner enterprises have been shown to evolve and advance their capabilities over time. Technologists who can run successful business operations and business managers who can leverage technology to their firm's advantage are now known as *technology executives*. Technology executives are the leaders of corporations that will win the competitive battles of global businesses through the introduction of innovative business processes made possible only by the use of recently available information systems technology. Experienced and forward-thinking executives recognize that a strategy of merely following the technology leaders in their industry will cause their organizations to lose ground continuously in the competitive battles for both the highest financial market valuation and the greatest customer market share.

Today's technology executives aggressively use *advanced* technologies to manage to the strategic objectives and goals of their companies. They are using the newest products and services—including the best management practices embodied in these offerings—from high-tech suppliers to increase the market valuations of their companies significantly in comparison with others in their industries. As a result, it is as important for a manager of manufacturing in a midsized metal-bending company to be a technology executive as it is for the chief administrator of a hospital or the director of computer operations at an insurance provider.

In companies whose executives have already made the leap from waiting to be serviced by their formal management information systems department to deploying advanced technologies proactively and profitably, the chairman, the president, the four C's (chief executive, chief operating, chief financial, and chief information officers), and their direct and indirect reports down to first-level line supervisors are either managing as or learning to be technology executives.

Technology executives are key participants in the one enduring economy that has existed for centuries—the Competitive Economy. The Competitive Economy is the business environment in which firms disappear if they fail to meet their customers' needs—and others profit extremely well while delighting their current customers and attracting new ones. Technology executives are part of and thrive in today's Competitive Economy of supplier versus supplier in the daily battles for customers and profitable revenue. On the other hand, technology executives rarely are found in the protected economies that too often result from government policy making.

And why at this time is it so important for corporations and their executives (especially those in traditional companies who still view information systems as merely a necessary cost of doing business) to become more innovative and competent in managing the deployment of advanced technologies? After all, there has been so much publicity about the collapse of the vast majority of dotcom companies that many executives today are initially suspicious of the real value of any and all new technology initiatives.

Below the original overly optimistic (and now pessimistic) media headlines about individual technology suppliers and dotcom startups, something significant is happening in our global economy's infrastructure. Winner organizations in every industry—private sector, government, health care, nonprofits, education, etc.—are changing the way they evaluate and manage the deployment of advanced information technologies. Individual executives who can meet and exceed their organization's strategic goals and objectives successfully through the imaginative, ground-breaking use of advanced technologies are being compensated at significantly higher rates and have greater job security than their counterparts who are conducting business as usual.

Read this book much like you might a primer on a new, proven, and successful career-saving technique that has been field-tested by many others over the last several years. You may already know some of the research findings presented here. Others you may have suspected but have not yet recognized. Many will be management practices that are new to you. Connect the known, the suspected, and the new together, and you will surely have the next great idea for improving the value of your company.

Evolution
Not Revolution

Competency I: Focusing on Market Valuation

"**B**USINESS PLANNING MEETINGS ARE BORING. Why do we even bother to get together? All we do is disagree. Nothing is ever accomplished!" Sound familiar?

Every executive knows the excruciating pain of sitting through marathon management planning meetings. Moreover, these encounters can become absolute agony when the subject is the use of new information systems technologies to improve current business processes.

These same meetings can be turned around into exciting, productive sessions with one critical change. In the center of every conference room should be a large plaque with the inscription, "Increase Our Company's Market Valuation." Whenever a discussion appears to be drifting aimlessly, all the chairperson must do is point to the "Increase Our Company's Market Valuation" sign and ask, "How?"

Increasingly, the answer to "How?" requires the use of enterprise-level advanced information technologies. *Enterprise-level* means computer and communications systems that an entire corporation can rely on to improve both the effectiveness with which it manages its customer relationships and the efficiency with which it delivers its goods and services. *Advanced information technologies* describes products that high-tech suppliers generally have made available only recently to their corporate customers.

Then the next question becomes, "Who?" Who is capable of leading the efforts to apply the latest and greatest information systems technologies to the corporate objective of increasing market value? The answer is the *technology executive*. Technology executives are the 2000's style of managers who are as comfortable evaluating the potential benefits of new technologies as they are running the company's most critical business operations.

Winner Corporations and Market Value

Every technology executive's objective is to build a winner corporation. Of course, the immediate question for many managers is how to define a *winner corporation*. It is a point over which executives have fought and debated for decades.

Winner companies must be defined the way the investment community evaluates public corporations—in terms of both their current market value and their year-to-year increase in market value compared with market indices. A corporation that meets the positive-valuation criteria of investors has the greatest probability of flourishing in the long term; maintaining high levels of customer satisfaction; providing its employees with higher levels of compensation and job satisfaction; working in a responsible manner with its customers, suppliers, and government oversight agencies; and generating above-average returns for its investors.

Increasing the market value of their firms, therefore, becomes the primary decision-making criterion for technology executives and those who follow them. It underlies the entire rationale for why corporations adopt advanced information technologies. While individuals will have many different opinions about how and where advanced technologies should be deployed, if they work together with the common, overriding objective of increasing the market value of their companies, they will be able to improve their business policies and operations most effectively.

Focusing every executive on the ultimate goal of increasing market value by leveraging the capabilities of advanced technologies to improve the business processes of their firms channels their energies in the most appropriate direction.

However, when senior corporate executives review requests for resources to invest in technologies, they generally find that individual departments are more interested in optimizing their own operations than those of the entire corporation. For example, the accounting staff may look for the primary benefits of technology-based change as a means to obtain more accurate, faster-responding reporting systems. The management information systems (MIS) staff may view a corporate executive's request for ways to leverage advanced technologies as an open invitation to experiment with the latest resumé-enhancing computer operating environments. Manufacturing has been known to regard an explicit emphasis on the use of advanced information technology as a way to prepare more compelling capital appropriation requests for upgrading marginally effective departmental production systems. And so on. Demanding that all technology-based initiatives show a means to increase the entire corporation's market value significantly changes the types of projects that will be recommended and approved.

An Aside: Calculating Market Value

The most straightforward way to calculate a corporation's current market value is simply to multiply its stock price by the number of shares of stock outstanding. However, rather than referring to total market value, investors tend to focus on a more commonly reported number—stock price. The movement of a corporation's stock price is directly equivalent to its market value as long as the number of shares outstanding remains the same.

While private companies, government agencies, and nonprofit organizations do not have a public market to provide them with a market valuation, they do have quantitative measures that they can and should use to estimate their relative change in value from year to year.

Obviously, private companies can use their size, profitability, and changes in both to estimate their value in comparison with similar public companies.

Organizations outside the commercial sector have a responsibility to their constituents to establish a quantitative valuation index against which the worth of the services they deliver can be judged. For a college, this might include the number of applicants, the percentage of applicants who enroll on acceptance, the number of seniors accepted by graduate schools, the preparedness of seniors as rated by recruiters, the value of research grants awarded, professor turnover rates, etc. For government agencies, valuations might be based on the amount of work processed per year, cost per unit of work, accuracy of work results, and turnaround time required to respond appropriately to constituent requests or inquiries.

Competing for Higher Market Value

A startling insight one finds from observing publicly traded companies over time is that with the creative and pioneering use of information systems, numerous companies in many diverse industries have increased their market values relative to the market indices. And conversely, without the intelligent deployment of technology-based capabilities, any company can lose market value relative to its direct competitors. This has numerous and significant implications for running a business successfully and building one's own career.

The first and most obvious issue is that building value is a key responsibility of senior management. *Value* is defined as market valuation for publicly traded companies, director-determined valuation for private companies, and constituent valuation for government agencies and nonprofit organizations.

Investors reward fast-growing, profitable companies with higher valuations than slower-growing ones whose margins are continuously in jeopardy of eroding. For example, in the rising bull stock market of 1998–1999, slow-growth, profit-pressured consumer products companies lost value compared with the overall stock market indices and especially in relation to high-growth, high-tech suppliers. While consumer products companies normally may not be in competition for the same customer dollar for their products as high-tech suppliers, they are in competition for the same investors' and shareholders' valuations.

During 1998–1999, senior executives at several leading consumer products companies were shown the door because they had not understood how advanced technologies could and should be used to increase market value. Their companies were now competing in the electronic information age and had the opportunity to increase their effectiveness and efficiency with advanced technologies—but they did not have a plan of action.

The inability of veteran executives who knew the consumer products business well to direct their companies to take advantage of the new opportunities being created by advanced technologies became a career-ending problem. Investors were not putting their monies into these consumer products companies because, they said, they did not have confidence in the current management to alter their operations to take advantage of the new technologies available to all organizations—including their competitors.

The axed executives, without a rational strategy for deploying marketed-in-their-face Web-based technologies to lower manufacturing and other internal costs or a vision of how to use information-based marketing techniques to increase sales, simply had lost the competitive battle for higher valuations in the next chapter of the information age. And yes, technology stocks dropped dramatically from the end of 2000 through 2001 as investors placed less importance on growth and more on profitability for the first time in 8 years. Even so, only the few consumer products companies that are managing with the aggressive use of technology, such as Anheuser-Busch, seem able to beat the market indices.

Table 1-1 shows the largest 20 public companies in the United States as ranked by their market value at the end of 2000. Do not rely on this table to draw conclusions about individual companies —there is a lot of history, including acquisitions and divestitures, different fiscal years, special accounting charges, etc., behind the individual numbers. The growth numbers that are important to the investment community are the growth rates of individual lines of business, and these results are not always readily apparent from the top-revenue lines of corporations that have multiple lines of business.

However, the general conclusion that can be drawn from such a market-valuation table is that corporations with fast-growing, profitable lines of business (such as AOL Time Warner, Berkshire Hathaway, Cisco Systems, Home Depot, and Intel) are rewarded with higher valuations compared with their revenue sizes than those which are growing more slowly and are less profitable. To put this in perspective, we can see that the third largest public U.S. company at the end of 2000, General Motors (GM), with revenues of $185 billion but a market valuation of only 26 cents per revenue dollar, or $48.6 billion, is not even on the top 20 highest market valuation list—it came in at number 50.

Table 1-1   Market Valuations of the Top 20 U.S. Companies (12/31/00)

Rank	Public U.S. Company	Market Valuation ($ B)	Fiscal 2000 Revenues ($ B)	Fiscal 2000 Revenue Growth over 1999	Fiscal 2000 Profits ($ B)
1	General Electric	406.5	129.9	16.3%	12.7
2	Microsoft	288.1	23.8	9.1%	10.0
3	Exxon Mobil	286.3	206.1	28.1%	16.0
4	Pfizer	246.2	29.6	8.0%	3.7
5	Citigroup	225.5	111.8	14.8%	13.5
6	Wal-Mart Stores	210.8	191.3	15.9%	6.3
7	Intel	195.2	33.7	14.8%	10.5
8	American International Group	176.6	46.0	13.1%	5.6
9	AOL Time Warner	173.1	7.7	34.6%	1.2
10	IBM	167.2	88.4	1.0%	8.1
11	Merck	166.0	40.4	23.4%	6.8
12	Cisco Systems	147.3	23.9	59.6%	3.1
13	SBC Communications	142.1	51.5	4.0%	8.0
14	Johnson & Johnson	129.7	29.1	6.1%	4.8
15	Verizon Communications	126.7	64.7	11.2%	10.8
16	Coca-Cola	118.6	14.8	2.4%	2.2
17	Bristol-Myers Squibb	115.0	18.2	-9.9%	4.7
18	Philip Morris	106.0	63.3	2.5%	8.5
19	Berkshire Hathaway	100.6	34.0	41.4%	3.3
20	Home Depot	96.6	45.7	19.0%	2.6

Source: Forbes 500.

While size matters in establishing a corporation's market value, *projected* growth and profitability are the most significant factors in determining current value—and are even more important than size when the investment community decides on the appropriate *changes* in valuations it should make.

In 2000 AOL Time Warner entered the top 20 for the first time because the company demonstrated high growth in 2000, and many investors projected high growth rates for its multiple lines of business into the future. In addition, companies such as Microsoft, IBM, and Bristol-Meyers Squibb that had only single-digit or negative growth rates in fiscal year 2000 were awarded relatively high market valuations based on the investment community's projections for higher growth rates in the near future (1 to 3 years out) on top of already relatively high profitability levels.

On the other hand, many 1999 high-tech members of the top 20, including Oracle, Lucent Technologies, Dell Computer, Hewlett-

Packard, Sun Microsystems, and Texas Instruments, fell out of their previous high standing and did not make the 2000 top 20 because the investment community believed that both their growth rates and the profitability of the sum of their lines of business would decline substantially from previous years. Clearly, market valuations change as the investment community adjusts its perceptions of a corporation's future growth and profitability prospects.

The threadbare argument that only high-tech suppliers need to have a vision that shows insightful business technology planning falls apart when it is made to the investment community. After all, investors have witnessed such diverse firms as Enron, originally a distributor of natural gas, redeploy its physical and intellectual assets to become both a provider of broadband communications right of ways and a highly effective electronic broker and market maker of natural gas, pipeline services, and multiple other supposed commodity items. It should be noted, moreover, that Enron shot up from being the seventeenth largest company in the United States in 1999 to seventh in 2000. Financial services companies, such as Charles Schwab, Fidelity, and Wells Fargo, have learned to take advantage of the latest Web technologies to grow their businesses profitably by reaching customers they had not even identified 5 years previously. In addition, the list of technology-based successes goes on as airlines have increased customer loyalty, automobile makers are communicating more clearly and directly with their prospects and customers, oil companies have improved their internal production efficiencies, and retailers have added "clicks and mortar" operations.

The hard reality is that senior executives are competing today for relatively higher valuations than other companies with comparable revenues, assets, and profitability, not just against other firms in their own industry. To win this battle, the investment community is demanding both a credible strategic vision for profitable growth and proof of an ability to execute against that strategy. And one key component of any winner strategy must be taking the actions necessary to obtain a competitive advantage based on the aggressive use of advanced information technologies. A strategy based on deploying advanced technologies to both gain market share and lower production costs is key to being successful in the critical area of obtaining and holding investor confidence.

This same competition for increasing market valuation through the use of advanced information technologies extends beyond the private sector and into both the public and educational arenas. One does not have to look beyond the U.S. 2000 presidential election to see that political candidates now believe that they must demonstrate their technology vision and acumen to gain the confidence of the public. Dedicated government agency heads report that they must show credible plans for improving the services they are chartered to provide and increasing their internal efficiencies at delivering core services with the use of technology if they are to hold onto their positions and obtain the funding they believe their departments deserve. Moreover, the heads of educational institutions, from kindergarten through graduate school, without an information systems technology-inclusive 5-year plan for the future simply are not going to gain the necessary support from oversight boards, parents, and students to remain in their leadership positions. All must become technology executives if they wish to be successful.

Finally, from a personal career perspective, the executives in charge of a company that is losing value run a high likelihood of being removed from their positions. Either the board of directors will ask them to resign, or a more successful rival will acquire the company and eliminate their redundant positions. Increasing market value through the use of advanced technologies really does become a matter of corporate survival.

The Market Valuation Golden Equation

There is nothing magical about obtaining a higher market valuation than other firms in an industry category. It is really a quite simple formula that we call the *golden equation.*

The golden equation states that having the largest market share of the industry's target customer base *plus* obtaining the highest profitability compared with all other suppliers to the this target customer base *equals* a winner corporation with the highest-in-class market value. Sounds simple? Yet, when other firms are striving for the same goal and not all the members of your corporation understand that working toward the objective of increasing the firm's market value should be their ultimate objective, managing to the golden equation can get very complicated.

Increasing Corporate Value

The predicament that executives face continuously when strategizing about ways to advance their corporation's market value is how to increase *both* revenue growth rates and profits. However, the serious problem they face is that these actually are two conflicting goals.

Investing in growth opportunities lowers total company margins in the short term. The tradeoff, however, is that while *not* investing in a line of business generally results in higher margins over the short term, this tactic also will result in lower intermediate- and long-term growth rates. Figure 1-1 illustrates how two companies with identical revenues and unit sales at a specific point in time might be managed—one for current profitability and one for future growth.

Figure 1-1   Income statements for growth versus profitability.

	Near-Term Profit-Focused Company	Near-Term Growth-Focused Company	Reason
Revenue for previous year	$100	$100	Same price per unit and same number of units sold the previous year
Cost of goods sold	$ 60	$ 60	Same quality and productivity in the previous year
Marketing and sales	$ 20	$ 25	The growth company added salespeople and advertising
Research and development	$ 2	$ 5	The growth company put R&D into new product ideas
General and administration	$ 3	$ 5	The growth company added new facilities and information systems
Gross profit — earnings before taxes and interest	$ 15	$ 5	The company managing for profitability has the higher profit, but what about next year?

Technology executives have evolved from both traditional business executives and professional information systems managers because they want it all. And they have learned that they can obtain above-average growth rates and profitability through the skillful deployment of advanced technologies throughout their companies and ahead of their competition.

When technology executives are faced with a choice between higher growth and higher profitability, invariably they will choose growth. My colleagues and I have found consistently that the typical technology executive's objective is to obtain higher valuations over a long-term career with a firm. After technology executives have achieved a significantly larger market share than a competitor being managed for current profitability, they believe that they will have the ability to obtain significantly higher profitability even while pricing at levels so low that they threaten the competitor's very existence.

To summarize, the investment community views a winner company as one that can obtain both higher growth rates and higher profit margins than other companies supplying similar products and services. Such a company is considered a double winner if it is in an industry that has higher growth rates and margins than the majority of other industries that make up the global economy.

Growth, Growth, and More Growth

Focusing on the use of advanced information systems technology for growing revenues faster than the competition is critical for today's executives in the Competitive Economy. A rapidly growing business is given a higher valuation than one of similar size and profitability that is not growing as fast. And the higher the corporation's *projected* growth rate, the higher is the relative valuation. Investors generally will forgive a company's financial losses for a limited period of time if they see that these losses are the short-term penalty of building for very high growth rates that eventually will be translated into larger, more profitable business operations.

Growth is so important because standing still, or maintaining the status quo, is unacceptable. No-growth companies run the risk that at some point in time their core business will erode as consumer tastes change. And if maintaining position is dangerous, how much more so is the other option—outright decline. A company with declining revenues is one that surely must have a lower market value in the future than in the past. To reemphasize, the concern is that a corporation that has flat revenues (even with excellent profitability) has a greater probability of experiencing declining revenues and profits in the future than one that is growing.

As a rule of thumb, most investors want to see double-digit growth rates in each of a winner corporation's lines of business—even mature or commodity-like businesses. And in faster-growing industries, winner companies should obtain growth rates that are 50 percent above the industry average. Growth-rate targets must be a key focus for building market value—they provide a common objective for all the executives in a firm to achieve. If corporate executives cannot see a way—especially with the wealth of new technologies that comes to the market each year to help them—to achieve these growth rates, the company simply does not have the potential to be classified a winner.

In large conglomerates, lines of business that consistently miss their growth targets are prime candidates, first, for management shakeups and, second, for divestiture. In other words, if it appears impossible to achieve high growth rates in a line of business by the current owning corporation, the line should be sold to another company that has the unique competencies required to spark higher growth.

Therefore, setting growth objectives backed up by realistic plans to achieve these goals is a critical—if not the most important—focus of management's charter to increase market value. Technology executives have found that eventually the drive for growth based on the deployment of advanced technologies so permeates a winner corporation that it becomes an inherent part of the culture.

Using New Technologies to Grow Existing Businesses

The mindset of technology executives is that growing existing businesses starts by imagining how to add value to a company's offerings using information technology. Since widespread acceptance of the Web, the number of ideas for increasing growth rates available to companies today is staggering. One leading way to achieve this objective that is being used by many winner corporations is to deploy advanced Web-based technologies both to better identify prospects and to communicate with customers.

However, in addition to Web-based marketing efforts, an often more strategic and long-term approach is to use information technology to add value to a company's products and services. The next evolution in products and services should be the addition of easily available information that assists the owner or, in the extreme, the product or service changes from something physical to purely electronic.

The book, music, and video industries contain many examples of organizations in the process of strategizing how to increase their growth by distributing their products as electronic content directly to consumers rather then as physical goods stocked in intermediary bricks-and-mortar warehouses and retail stores. With today's technologies, publishers can provide free samples of their products, such as a clip from a CD soundtrack or a chapter of a book, over the Internet to entice prospective buyers. From a revenue-producing perspective, they now can sell selected parts of their products on demand. A consumer may want only one song from an album and will not pay for the entire CD, or a consumer may want to create a custom CD with specific songs from different artists in the sequence that he or she finds most pleasing.

Publishers may be able to expand their potential consumer markets through wider electronic geographic distribution and Web-based marketing to nontraditional prospects for their content. To use an extreme example, one could imagine selling individual recipes from a cookbook authored by Julia Child to a corporate chef in China who has been told with little notice to prepare a Western-style meal that was requested by one of the visiting executives from America before a key negotiating session. Moreover, note that in this "what if" scenario, the timeliness of delivering the recipe and preparation instructions is as important as the ability to provide measurements in English and metric standards—a trivial conversion for a computer. In addition, the publisher might use language-translation technology to allow the chef a choice of dialects in which to read the written version of the recipe. And a National Public Television film clip of the meal being prepared by Ms Child might accompany the whole package.

In addition, there may be ways for publishers to expand their revenue opportunities by licensing their content for electronic distribution by others. A parent of a prematurely born infant might wish to review medical textbooks on premature birth but be unable to afford the high cost of such books. However, an insurance or pharmaceutical company could license the relevant chapters from the medical publisher and make them available for free (or on a per-chapter pay-by-use basis) to encourage the parent to use its products in caring for the child.

While I might have let my imagination wander in the preceding examples, a real-life illustration of harnessing virtual value to create real value that has been deployed for some time to increase sales of existing products is help-desk technology. General Electric's (GE's) Home Appliance Division is a casebook example of a company being able to differentiate its traditional physical products by adding information. GE understood that the best way to sell its next appliance was to support the last one better than the competition. GE does this well by having support representatives armed with help-desk application software available to consumers and contractors. Each of its built-in home appliances has a toll-free telephone number attached to it that allows anybody who uses it to ask questions of a support representative. The help-desk software provides the support representative with the knowledge to sound like an expert on all use and maintenance topics concerning any appliance. The support representative types in the caller's question on a terminal, and the most likely solution to the problem or answer to the question will appear quickly.

Where this help-desk capability is very important is in appliance sales to home builders. Typically, an appliance manual will be lost either by the contractor or by the first homeowner. However, even subsequent home buyers have a sense of confidence that they can obtain operating instructions or trouble-shooting support for their built-in appliances by calling GE directly with the attached telephone number. The result is that GE has grown its business faster than one would expect in the stodgy appliance industry by earning the loyalty of its target customer bases—home builders and experienced home buyers—at the expense of its competitors.

The art of growing an existing business with technology is to determine well before the competition how incremental informational value that creates a compelling reason to buy a company's product over alternatives can be added—and then to know the target customer base well enough to determine if additional profitability can be obtained by charging a premium price for a product that is now perceived as more valuable and desirable.

A Starting Point

Business executives might use the following checklist as a very basic start for developing possible ways to use advanced technology to increase the growth rates of existing businesses:

- Can we use new technologies to establish better marketing communication programs for our most likely customers and prospects?
- Can we add value to our offerings with better support?
- Can we improve our distribution system to get the right product to the right customer at the right time?
- How can we add information value to our offerings in ways that our competitors have not yet done?
- If we have content, can we repackage it and sell it to customers who in the past might not have had access to it or rejected it for cost reasons?
- Can we turn our offerings into electronic content that can be delivered anywhere in the world at the speed of electrons? If not, could we license appropriate content from a content provider and resell it for a profit?

Profitability Must Accompany Growth

While growth is paramount, growth without profits is fool's gold—it looks valuable but is not. Investing in growth is only justified when the business can make higher profits in the future.

In the weirdness of the dotcom mania, many companies (many of which have now failed) seemed to believe that they could grow indefinitely before demonstrating profits. However, the successful dotcoms and the dotcom divisions of traditional companies are the ones that could all show that, after a reasonable period of time investing in the most strategic aspects of their businesses, they were making operational profits.

An excellent example of profitable technology-based growth is Staples, the office-supply superstore. Staples' Internet-based sales division became an extremely large and profitable portion of its total operations in just a few years. While Staples originally had planned to set it up as an independent company that would issue its own stock, its role in the company's operations was so critical that Staples eventually integrated the dotcom group with its traditional business operations—just as this online operation was approaching $1 billion in annual sales and substantial (but undisclosed) profits.

Using technology to fuel increases in revenues requires senior executives to set specific profit-margin goals in conjunction with growth goals and then test these objectives realistically against the investments required for growth, the necessary technologies, pricing realities, anticipated cost of goods sold, and other factors.

To again set a rule of thumb for increasing market valuation purposes, in slower-growth industries where the corporation does not expect to go to the capital markets for additional funding for growth, operating profits before taxes and interest payments should be at least the same as the planned growth rates. That is, if a company plans to grow revenues in the upcoming year at a 12 percent rate, it needs to work against a plan that calls for achieving at a minimum a 12 percent gross operating profit margin.

In higher-growth businesses, especially in emerging industries where the company expects to require continuous amounts of new funding during its investment phase, planned gross operating profits will be different during each phase of the company's product offering's life cycle. Corporate planners typically will project growth, profitability, and investment requirements for the upcoming 3 years. Of course, these 3-year planning horizons will be updated on a regular basis—often every 3 months. Key to building investor confidence is showing a history of both managing profitability (or short-term losses) successfully against a plan and being able to improve the plan even when confronted with market changes.

The way winner-driven companies set profit goals is, first, they demand to obtain the highest gross margin or highest return on assets employed of any business in their industry and, second, they want that profit to be 50 percent higher than that of their best-performing competitor. That is, if the best-performing competitor has a profit margin of 6 percent, the winner wants 9 percent.

By setting specific profitability goals, all of a company's executives have a common objective they must achieve. The only way they will be able to achieve or exceed such a goal is by working together as a team.

Setting firm profit goals and compensating managers to achieve them constitute one of the most important management techniques for bridging the divide between conventional managers and information systems professionals in order to force individuals of both extremes to grow into technology executives.

Being the Largest Is Best

The most logical way for a business to achieve its highest-in-industry profitability goal is to be the largest firm in terms of market-share revenues. As the largest firm in a customer-defined market, a company generally will have access to higher levels of cash flow to reinvest appropriately in its business so that it can become even more dominant.

The ultimate objective of growth is to be the largest and most profitable player in an industry and with a definable customer group. This is why winner conglomerate corporations, such as GE, spend so much time making sure that their portfolio companies are either number one in their markets or at least have a pragmatic plan to become number one within a reasonable amount of time. It is also why some companies that are focused only on one customer group make strategic acquisitions to grow themselves into the leading position within that customer set.

Using Technology to Increase Profit Margins

There are three fundamental ways to increase profit margins with existing products. The first is to increase the product's price (or the complementary tactic, reduce its discounted margins through the distribution channel). The second is to increase sales volumes without proportionally increasing overhead costs. And the third is to cut costs, including components, labor, development, support, overhead, marketing, and sales.

Technology executives seeking to increase the market values of their firms explore all three of these approaches on a regular basis and from the perspective of how new, advanced technologies could be applied to each. The three winner tactics for a consumer products supplier would be (1) to increase the perceived value of its existing products in consumers' opinions in order to reduce discounts, (2) to be fortunate enough to have sales volume grow as word-of-mouth (also known as "buzz") recommendations result in purchases by new customers, and

(3) to identify and start working with new component suppliers who would supply better-quality components at lower prices that can be assembled with less labor. And yes, shipping costs also would drop substantially in this dream scenario.

Note that different companies have obtained all these results over the last several years through the innovative use of advanced technologies. Value has been added by providing better customer support, as in the GE appliance help-desk example discussed earlier. Buzz has been created by the entertainment industry by launching Web sites in advance of product (movie, recording, and book) launches. Price-driven commodity component suppliers are more likely to bid on orders from manufacturers anywhere around the world when they can communicate electronically instead of sending expensive sales representatives. Moreover, advances in logistics software have revolutionized the science of distribution and lowered shipping costs.

What should be apparent is that to increase profit margins, a corporation needs to use advanced technologies to improve *continuously* on *all* aspects of this very important objective. One cannot, at an arbitrary point in time, demand that the organization's executives focus on increasing profitability based on the latest "gee whiz" technology that has been reviewed in a business publication. The Competitive Economy approach demands a never-ending effort to evaluate how new technologies can be deployed to increase profit margins.

Dropping Prices Often Lowers Market Value

Unfortunately, a tactic that companies that have increased their profitability through the deployment of advanced technologies all too often follow is to drop their prices to the point where profit margins for their business remain the same as before it made the investments.

The objective of lowering prices is to drive competitors to barely break even or to lose money when they attempt to remain competitive in price and value. When this situation develops, many people wonder where the anticipated financial returns from investments in technology advantage went. The technology-leading company does not see higher profits, and its competitors are forced to invest in new information systems just to stay in business at an unsatisfactory profit level. When this situation arises, as it often does, company executives and the investors that follow their industry often question the real value of technology investments. Yet, in today's Competitive Economy, the lesson technology executives have learned from this industry dynamic is that it is better to be the leader and winner in the use of advanced technologies than the less capable competitor who must struggle mightily just to survive.

Acquisitions for Growth, Profitability, and Risk

Many successful corporations find that they cannot improve revenue and profit growth fast enough from internal operations to increase their market value sufficiently to keep their shareholders happy. Their next logical step is to obtain growth by acquiring other companies. An acquisition often allows a company to enter new markets quickly or provides it with additional revenues from within its current markets.

In either case, the acquiring company hopes to spread its fixed overhead costs, including the cost of maintaining an information systems department, across a larger revenue base for the purpose of decreasing the percentage of general and administrative costs to revenue. If executed successfully, acquiring other businesses and cutting the costs of duplicative functions will result in an increase in gross margins as a percentage of revenue.

If a company is considering acquiring another one to increase revenues, the least risky approach is to do so in such a way that it will increase the offerings it can provide to its existing customer base. Therefore, companies that want to leverage and optimize their information systems advantages typically only consider acquiring businesses that have essentially the same customers as their current core businesses. There are many examples, especially in the banking and financial services industries, of corporations acquiring others that service the same customers and using advanced technologies to add financial, marketing, distribution, and/or management support to increase the value of the combined enterprise dramatically.

To understand the commonality between a company's current customers and a potential acquisition candidate's customers, organizations need to survey their target customer base continuously. There are numerous advanced information technologies, such as online survey questionnaires and powerful analysis applications, that can assist a company in cost-effectively learning more about its customers and their overall product acquisitions.

A strategic question faced continuously by successful corporations is whether to build or buy the new lines of business that will increase their market value beyond its current levels. While building a new line of business allows a corporation to leverage its existing core competencies and existing strengths, it is also a slow process that is ripe for failure due to internal roadblocks and dissension (especially if it might take revenues away from existing businesses), poor judgment, and just plain bad luck.

Buying another corporation's seemingly successful business is acknowledged as high risk. Yet acquiring another business is a quick way to enter an attractive, growing market. It is faster than building a business from the ground up. Moreover, while the risk of an acquisition failing to meet its projected financial and operations objectives may be as high as 70 percent, according to business researchers, many corporate executives believe that the risks involved in attempting to build a new business from the ground up and becoming a major industry player within a few short years may be even higher.

Technology executives generally focus on evaluating acquisition possibilities that serve the same customers. However, to go two steps further, during the acquisition-evaluation process, a corporation's executives first should assess objectively, clearly, and in the most concrete way possible how they can use information systems to add significant value to the company they are considering acquiring. Then they should appraise the most likely impact of the acquisition on both its suppliers and its end-user customers.

An excellent example of the serve-my-current-customer-better approach to acquisitions is EMC Corporation. EMC focuses its business on supplying high-end data storage devices and premium support services.

When EMC recognized the limitations to the growth of its core storage hardware business, it developed a strategy to enter the related business of offering storage-management software applications and solutions. It acquired small storage-management application software providers whose offerings would appeal to its own installed customer base as opposed to larger ones whose acquisition prices were much higher and whose products were more generalized to meet the needs of non-EMC customers. EMC then integrated the acquired companies' products with its own and supported the combined offerings with its best-in-class global support operations. The result was that EMC evolved quickly from being a seller of large storage hardware boxes to also being a leader in storage-management software and support solutions, a product category in which it is competing aggressively to be number one.

However, the key to this successful acquisition strategy was that the customers who purchased EMC hardware were the same decision makers for storage-management software. And EMC had already invested in the technologies to know who they were, how they purchased, and how to provide them with the high levels of support they required. It was relatively easy for EMC to add value to its customers through its software company acquisitions.

Avoiding Acquisitions that Distract

In the past, many corporations have chosen to acquire their suppliers or their customers in an effort to increase their profit margins. While these tactics often were successful in the manufacturing economy, where companies competed on production and distribution efficiency, they have backfired most commonly in industries where the competitive battles are won by numerous companies that are networked together electronically so that they can act together as a coordinated business ecosystem. Why? In a networked ecosystem, numerous individual managers employed by different companies must collaborate and coordinate their own company- and business partner–focused actions to leverage change ahead of competitive ecosystems.

In an old-line integrated manufacturing company, any change disrupts the efficiency and performance of business processes on which individual middle managers are evaluated. Therefore, their natural inclination is to slow the pace of change and shape changes to the advantage of their own areas of responsibility—even if the totality of these actions weakens the competitive position of the entire corporation over time. Having learned from history that manufacturing and distribution integration benefits are fleeting in a world continuously undergoing change, corporations that know how to use advanced technologies for coordinating their efforts with their suppliers and customers prefer to increase profit margins by focusing on exploiting their own unique competencies rather than on acquiring their suppliers and customers, muddling up these companies' operations, and eventually causing a drop in overall profit margins and market valuations.

Avoiding distractions and remaining focused on what a company does best have been taken to the point that many high-tech suppliers, such as Hewlett-Packard's inkjet printer division, contract out the majority of their manufacturing requirements and depend completely on other organizations for product distribution—all in an effort to increase profit margins. And most companies that have learned to use advanced technologies to coordinate the efforts of their suppliers and customers efficiently would never even consider acquiring other members of their business ecosystem.

TheV/E Factor

As technology executives in many different companies have been building new information-based business capabilities, an interesting phenomenon has occurred in the art of setting corporate market values. Corporations that can demonstrate an ability to use advanced technology to strategically leverage their businesses and can communicate their plans for future market-valuation-enhancing improvements are rewarded with a higher price-earnings ratio—and therefore market value—than those which do not. This additional market value is often called the *V/E factor*—the vision-to-earnings ratio. That is, investors believe that organizations that have a core competency in aligning their business and technology strategies have the potential to grow both revenues and profits faster in the future. A company with a very high V/E ratio is frequently called *overvalued* by skeptics who do not believe that the corporation will be able to execute as current investors hope—and it is referred to as *undervalued* by those who are buying its shares in hopes of seeing dramatic increases in profitability in the future.

For the last several decades, managing the deployments of successive generations of information technologies to gain substantial and ongoing competitive advantages has been an art. Companies that have done it well and have increased the efficiency and effectiveness of their business processes have gained superior positions in their marketplaces. This is a simple fact that no objective observer will argue with today, although it has been debated hotly many times over the last two decades.

In stark contrast, corporations that historically have believed that information technology is merely a cost of doing business that should be minimized and whose only benefit is to automate activities that were done by clerical staff have fallen behind in their industries, in the opinions of their customers, and in the eyes of the investment community.

However, many senior executives—often without any previous information technology education or experience—in such varied sectors as government, universities, transportation, hospitality, financial services, utilities, manufacturing, professional services, retail distribution, and so on have understood the investment community's and their customers' requirements for a forward-looking vision of how they will use technology to make their organizations more efficient and effective over time. Therefore, they have prepared themselves personally with the knowledge of how to manage the planning and deployment of enterprise-wide information systems. These winner technology executives are now either leading winner corporations or in the process of turning mediocre ones into winners. They are personally able to add the V/E factor to increase the market value of their firms.

Growing Market Value Increases
Employee Compensation and Retention

Just as important as investor capital for the long-term health of a company is human capital. The hard reality of corporate life, however, is that a company that cannot increase its market value over time will not be able to keep the brightest and most motivated executives and employees for the decades of service that it wants and needs them.

Today's most productive employees want to and should be compensated over the long term in the form of company stock ownership through stock options. An increasing market value makes these options valuable. Winner firms gain the momentum of a highly constructive cycle of attracting the best individuals who perform well to increase the company's value, which then attracts even more talented individuals to join the firm, and so forth.

Successful executives understand the direct relationship between a company's market value and its human resources management. Companies must increase their market values and share these benefits with the employees who are building the wealth (as well as with the outside shareholders) if they wish to attract and keep the best. At this time, most industrial economies are experiencing an astonishing shortage of skilled, loyal executives, professionals, and frontline workers. To attract and retain the most desirable employees during good and bad economic times, a company must demonstrate that it is willing to reward such individuals based on their ability as a group to increase the company's market value.

A hard-charging company that demonstrates an unwillingness to offer the dedicated technology executives it wants to retain over the long term the ability to share in the wealth they are helping to build will soon be relegated to the same tier of undesirable employer as companies that do not offer health care benefits. This research finding is clear—the most highly sought after talent will move to the companies they believe can help them create their own personal wealth over the short and intermediate term through distributing a percentage of the increases in its market value to them as well investors. Typical "hyperachieving" technology executives want the rewards of increased company market value throughout their careers—not just at the end.

What relevance is a retirement pension plan, promising what seems like a relatively risky possibility of a payout up to 40 years or more into the future, to this type of highly sought after individual in his or her twenties? Such individuals want the cash generated through sharing in the market appreciation of their company when they need it.

What happens, however, if the company's stock price drops due to reasons beyond its control, such as a slowing global economy or an unexpected new government regulation that changes the economics of its industry, and already issued options appear to be worthless for many years to come? Shouldn't the company's employees also be made to feel the pain of its investors? The technology executive's answer is, "No!"

Investors can sell their shares at any time and move onto the next investment they believe will give them a better return. For a valued manager to do the same means leaving the company for one with better prospects. If this happens, the firm would face the destructive situation of losing its most talented employees—those others find most desirable to hire—just when the company needs them the most. Losing its most valuable human capital is a sure way for an organization to eventually suffer a drop in value against the indices with which it judges itself.

So yes, stock options for employees do have to be repriced if there is a significant drop in value. However, they should be repriced intelligently to reflect the company's value over time versus the index against which it measures itself. A company's board of directors is sending a serious message to its technology executives when it reprices stock options. To make sure that this message is clear and understood by all, any repricing action also requires a detailed explanation about the board's reasoning for making an adjustment and its expectations for the company's valuation relative to its benchmark indices going forward.

Remember, focusing all members of a company on the corporation's market value by tying the firm's market value to their own personal wealth is a clear-cut and bold way to send the message that increasing market value is the number one objective. And if the deployment of advanced technology is the most effective means to increase both corporate value and personal wealth, be assured that the organization will heartily embrace technology-based improvements.

Lessons Learned from Experience

A corporation is judged as being a winner based on its market value and how its value changes over time in comparison with market indices. Corporate executives have the opportunity today to use advanced technologies to improve the financial results necessary for increasing the market value of their firms. The areas in which they must use enterprise-level advanced technologies to be winners include boosting growth rates, improving profit margins as a percentage of revenues, increasing returns on assets employed, and evaluating acquisitions that will increase revenues obtained from the firm's current target customer base. Growth must be accompanied by profits for a company to be considered a winner.

Requiring that all requests for new information systems demonstrate an ability to increase the corporation's market value creates a common and advantageous decision-making criterion for selecting advanced technology-based initiatives. Research shows that when evaluating which new technologies to deploy within an organization, there typically is a divergence of opinion between departmental managers who want additional information systems tools to better run their specific operations and corporate-level executives who want to improve the effectiveness and efficiency of the entire company. By focusing all the managers on market value creation, companies are able to make better decisions faster.

Having the largest market share within a company's target customer base is the best position from which a business also can become the most profitable and obtain the highest market value within its peer group. Corporate executives need to be customer focused in their acquisition and use of advanced technologies to obtain the greatest benefits.

Using information technology to add value to a corporation's products and services to grow both revenues and profitability is a key strategy of technology executives. Many long-established firms have found ways to use advanced technologies to increase the value of their offerings in the opinion of their customers. Technology executives have plenty of leeway to use their imaginations in devising ways to add value to existing products through leading-edge deployments of advanced technologies.

Applying advanced technologies to reduce costs and increase customers' perceived value of the firm's offerings should be an ongoing, methodical process—not merely a one-off project that is started at an arbitrary point in time.

When a market-leading company that has used advanced technologies successfully to increase both its market share and its profitability initiates a price war that lowers its margins, many observers will question the value of technology investments. Blame the management decision to compete on price, not the technology that provided the firm with the capability to do so.

Acquisitions generally are considered to be highly risky and rarely meet their original financial and operational goals. Yet these risks are lessened when the objective of an acquisition is to obtain more products and services to offer to a company's current customers and the acquiring company can add significant value with its information systems capabilities. When a corporation decides to enter a new line of business, acquisitions of successful companies may be less risky than attempting to build a new business from within the organization.

Businesses need the best people to increase their market value. Executives who are savvy enough to blend business operations and technology management skills want and expect to be compensated for increases in the market values of the corporations that employ them. As a result, the use of stock options that are priced appropriately is key to attracting and retaining such talented executives.

And yes, market values can be increased with pragmatic, profitable business model–based visions of how corporations will use technology in novel, beat-the-competition ways in the future. However, corporate executives must execute successfully against their visions if they wish to maintain the confidence of the investment community.

Competency 2: Managing with "Emagineering"

T H E ABILITY BOTH TO IMAGINE how the world could be and to make that creative vision a reality is the basis of innovation. We are all born with the instinctive ability to both imagine and then to turn the visions of our dreams into physical realities. Parents tell stories of observing with great pride their preschool children drawing events that have occurred only in their imaginations. The same imaginative drawing instincts we display as children both can and must be extended to help executives manage successfully in today's fast-changing information-based economy.

People do not lose their imaginations as they grow older. If we look at the remarkable outpouring of originality and creativity in the arts, literature, and hobbies by those between the ages of 18 and 108, it is obvious that many people grow their imaginations as they gain more life experiences and wisdom. Successful, happy individuals truly increase their abilities to imagine what could be over the years. They instinctively learn how to make connections that, while they may not be obvious, draw on their many life experiences to imagine how new things could and should be created.

Imagination Is a Key Value-Building Talent

Business innovations are the direct result of the imaginations of numerous people working together toward a common objective. While one individual generally is credited with being the visionary and motivator for significant economic innovations (after all, the retelling of history is simpler and faster when we can ascribe the results of the efforts of many to one), the reality is that major innovations come from the shared vision and actions of numerous individuals working toward a common goal.

For an historical example, let's review the development of the printing press. Johann Gutenberg is credited with inventing the printing press. However, the key innovation of mass producing books required not just Gutenberg's vision, drive, and design genius but also the assistance of financiers, parts suppliers, employees, distributors, content providers, and of course, customers who wanted books at a price they could afford. And isn't it fascinating that the spirit of imagination-based innovation motivated all these stakeholders in medieval times to act on their collective vision of the mass production of books? In reality, the printing press, like all great technology advances, was born in both the imaginations and supporting actions of a group of individuals—not just one—collaborating together.

Gutenberg's team practiced an early form of a term coined by the Walt Disney Company several hundred years later: "imagineering." The term *"imagineering"* is used most commonly by Disney to describe the methods that it instituted to create some of the most entertaining attractions the world has ever seen. Disney originally developed its "imagineering" skill sets to assist a relatively small group of talented artisans with a wide-range of skills working collaboratively on one-off projects intended to build machines that give the illusion of moving and talking, such as Disney's display of former U.S. presidents.

In the same vein, Gutenberg and his associates could imagine what the value of producing books in high volume might be, as opposed to having them copied individually by scribes. In addition, Gutenberg had numerous skills gained from the numerous crafts in which he had been trained that provided him with the supporting knowledge necessary to build both the first press and hand-set type. Gutenberg's team's actions embody the core values of "imagineering"—imagination (a vision) combined with the capability and will to make that vision a reality.

To build market value, corporate executives need to combine their imaginations and their deep pool of experiences to visualize how to grow their firms' revenues and profitability. However, they also must have the appropriate tools to do so. The relatively straightforward skills of "imagineering" alone are not enough to be successful in business. In today's Competitive Economy, the latest and greatest information system technologies applied appropriately are the richest source of implementing the innovations that can turn insightful visions into profitable realities.

"Emagineering": The New Management Competency

Many successful executives have shown a consistent ability to innovate. They have led their organizations in the launch of unique business capabilities based on advanced technologies. The results have been an increase in the market value of their companies compared with that of their competitors. Researching their efforts, we find that they take a disciplined approached to planning and implementing technology-based change. We call this new management competency "emagineering"—a term these pioneering executives appreciate.

"Emagineering" is an enterprise-level approach to managing the acquisition, deployment, and use of advanced information systems technology to continuously improve and enhance an organization's business processes with the ultimate objective of increasing its market value. "Emagineering" focuses on the use of advanced technologies both to increase the external *effectiveness* with which a company services its target customer base and to improve the internal *efficiency* of the business processes with which it operates to create customer value. The principles and processes of "emagineering" have been developed by organizations in both the public and private sectors to expand and improve on their operational capabilities.

The beginning *e* in "emagineering" stands for the requirement that individuals at all levels within a business must now be knowledgeable about the capabilities and limitations of their *e*lectronic information systems—both computing and communications. While an individual reading a book, magazine, or instruction manual typically could care less how it was printed, a corporate executive or frontline worker obtaining information from an electronic display needs to know the source of the data, what they were based on, when they were created, how they can be changed, what actions can be performed with them, and when they will be irrelevant. Literacy in the electronic age requires a full understanding of the capabilities and limitations of the medium that delivers information on which so many daily operational decisions are based. This knowledge leads to a stable foundation for building technology-based changes to increase market value.

The *magine* in "emagineering" stands for the ability of a company, its suppliers, and its investors as a group to accurately identify a specific market that in the future can be dominated by the firm as a result of its foresight and ability to meet emerging customer needs using advanced technology tools better than its competitors. To build new businesses or significantly improve current business processes to make organizations more effective and efficient requires executives first to *imagine* the realistic options available to them through the deployment of innovative business processes based on advanced technology, then to identify which are viable, and finally, to prioritize action plans by each option's potential to create the greatest increase in market value.

The *ering* in "emagineering" refers to the business-career requirement that executives must be competent in managing the efforts required to evaluate, acquire, deploy, and operate the enterprise-wide technology infrastructures that underlie the creation and operation of today's advanced information systems. Thus *ering* is the big-picture view of engine*ering*—focusing on the management of capturing the business benefits that can be gained from advanced technologies as opposed to being conversant in the technical details of every information system component. Executives who practice "emagineering" are able to apply their experience and competence to the skillful acquisition and deployment of technology from a high-level engineering-management perspective to create beat-the-competition business processes. And beat-the-competition operations are those which are the most efficient and effective in meeting the needs of the company's target customers.

Technology executives (whom we will describe in much more detail in Chapter 3) are those individuals who have mastered the art and science of "emagineering" and can lead and direct their organizations based on this relatively rare competency.

The "Emagineering" Approach to Strategy Setting

Executives who manage with "emagineering" know that once-a-year formal strategy planning exercises in isolation and by themselves simply are not effective in today's fast-moving and hypercompetitive world. The reality is that most senior executives of well-established firms are far too removed from their competitors' customers—the best source of information for planning how to grow a business by gaining market share and increasing profitability. And most junior managers, unfortunately, substitute intuition, internally politically correct proclamations, and press clippings for reality in their planning assumptions.

Yes, properly deploying technology as the catalyst for planning new business processes requires having the correct strategic goals and objectives from which the organization can execute. However, technology executives manage with the wisdom that successful strategies must be organic. That is, the company's strategy needs to be changed as market conditions change or as the organization better recognizes its actual abilities to execute its current strategy. As a result, technology executives will refer to the strategies of their companies as "disposable" to convey throughout the organization that any strategy, no matter how influential, will be adjusted and improved continually as business conditions evolve.

Successful companies rarely initiate strategic revolutions. Only companies on the brink of disaster or where the owners want to "cash out" engage in dramatic shifts of strategy. Ongoing, incremental improvements to a company's strategic goals and objectives will lead to greater success. Therefore, "emagineering" is based on a strongly held belief that continuous monitoring of the results of a company's strategy and a willingness to improve it whenever business conditions change provide far superior returns than conducting a formal strategy-setting exercise once a year and then implementing a radically different business strategy the next day. "Emagineering" management clearly encourages continuous strategic evolution through the ongoing improvements to a company's operations that can be obtained by deploying advanced technologies.

Creating and Building on Disposable Strategies

One of the most important aspects of "emagineering" is its approach to strategy setting. In classic companies, especially natural resource suppliers and heavy equipment manufacturers, strategies had to be set for the long term and were difficult to change. In many corporations, this allegiance to the long term created an almost religious zeal to communicate internally and maintain a commitment to in-place strategies that had worked well in the past even when it was obvious to all that they were not working in the present.

In successful companies, suboptimal strategies are discarded gracefully and regularly without creating distrust on the part of employees, customers, or suppliers. More to the point, a company operating in a highly competitive business environment that does not adopt a new strategy on a regular basis is considered a potential loser for not reinvigorating itself proactively.

One result of the "emagineering" approach to strategy setting has been a growth in the strategy guru business. When one includes venture capitalists, market analysts, university professors, retired industry (and government) executives, consultants, and journalists, there has never been a time when business executives could chose from such a broad range of strategy experts. Even for those who dismiss their commentaries as entertainment from noncommitted gadflies, strategy gurus with a technology slant can act as catalysts for executives who need to regularly reevaluate their key assumptions about the proper strategic options for their own businesses.

Companies that are aggressively changing how they do business based on "emagineering" have shown that their professional information systems technologists are often the final translators of planned strategies into actual strategies. That is, strategies often are established while the supporting information systems are being put in place. Why? As the deployment project teams make changes to overcome whatever obstacles they might encounter and improve on their original plan as they test and implement new technologies, they are creating the reality of the company's strategic plan. Once new information systems are operating and accepted internally and by the company's business partners, the corporation often will then declare its next new strategy based on its actual capabilities.

Recognizing that the most senior executives do not know what they do not know about the capabilities of information technology, a company should be prepared to create a sequence of multiple, sequential, disposable strategies. The current strategic plan will be disposed of quickly when it is improved on or as business conditions dictate a change.

The disposable strategy process starts with a strategic initiative created by the organization's most senior executives. It is common today that this initial strategy may be influenced by inputs from several different types of external gurus. This is the "cheerleading" aspect of modern-day strategy setting—the gurus will all cheer the corporation's executives on to see the external environment as they do. However, the first disposable strategy must be the executives' own vision of how they believe the business can best prosper based on its strengths and ambitions—not merely a restatement of the most persuasive of the outside strategy experts' pronouncements.

This initial disposable strategy then needs to be tested against the technology realities that are required for its execution. Can the company's information systems professionals and outside suppliers of product components and services execute to the strategy in terms of functionality, budget, and time requirements? Even more important, can the technologists improve on the strategy with capabilities beyond what the executive team had considered? Experience with "emagineering" has shown that the information technology experts can add significant value to corporate executives' initial strategy when they both understand the market positioning and critical success factors the senior management team has identified—and when they are aggressively encouraged to help.

To help increase the probability that execution will match strategy, the organization's senior information systems executives should be required to write the second disposable strategy. While building on the initial disposable strategy, their strategy should be created with an emphasis on what advanced technologies can be put in place to support the business operations vital to the success of the business.

A case in which the information systems group's strategic input saved a company is seen in the power supply industry. (Power supplies are the black boxes inside computers and other electronic equipment that transform the power from a wall socket into the type of power the device requires.) A supplier of traditional fixed-capacity power supplies that competed on both price and breadth of offering (over 3600)—but could take as long as 6 weeks to ship the specific product a prospect wanted—was losing market share to a startup that was using a new technology to create a new type of power supply. This new, proprietary technology allowed the challenger to ship a limited number of power supplies, but each product had the capability to provide numerous different capacities. While the startup charged a premium price over the traditional supplier, potential prospects found that if their needs could be met by the startup's components, a part would be shipped to it immediately. The incumbent supplier's traditional management, in response, had planned to implement a strategy that would both reduce price even more and increase the number of products and their variations that it offered.

However, when this more-of-the-same strategy was communicated to the information systems group, it proactively countered with a strategy whereby the company could use advanced technology to transform its manufacturing process from a batch system that only made each family of products once every 6 weeks (hence the overly long delay for components that were not in inventory) to a new process that would allow the company to build to order and be able to ship any product in its catalogue within 4 business days. Suddenly, the firm's executives had a viable option to compete more effectively against the startup on the criterion of customers' desire for speedy delivery.

However, keep in mind that the strategy envisioned by the information systems group also must be considered disposable. In this Delphi-like "emagineering" method of creating either a new or significantly different strategy for the corporation, the other functional areas of the company need to review the disposable strategy for impacts on marketing, personnel, manufacturing, finance, sales, customer support, legal, and all other core areas of the organization. The Delphi method is used most commonly in forecasting in situations where initial projections are created by one group, given to another group for refinement, and then passed on to yet another group with all the changes noted. After all groups have had their first inputs, the process is repeated until the organization runs out of time (at which point the final report includes all changes and the rationales from the initial projections) or there are no more changes.

At the end of this disposable strategy-building process, the business does not have a final, long-term strategy. What it does have is yet another iteration in the strategy process that it should consider as being disposable if it is proven to be either inferior to that of the competition or the organization is unable to execute effectively on it.

A strategy that is failing for any of three reasons—(1) it does not increase market value significantly, (2) it is inferior to the strategies of direct competitors, or (3) it cannot be executed effectively by the organization—needs to be either discarded or modified as soon as possible. Since the business and technology environments in which firms operate and compete are changing continuously and rapidly, organizations must create a culture that includes the belief that any current strategy is disposable and at the first sign of weakness will be discarded. Moreover, in today's rapidly changing business and technology environments, "emagineering"-knowledgeable executives all manage to the rule that every corporate strategy will have a finite life and needs to be updated sooner rather than later.

Evolving from Where You Are to Where You Want to Be

It should be obvious by now that imagination is key to "emagineering" competence. Constructive business imagination most often comes from visualizing logical but unorthodox changes to current industry practices and policies. Each wave of advanced technology provides technology executives with new tools with which to envision such evolutionary advances.

Even successful startups build on the skills of their founders to make incremental changes to current industry-standard products and policies—they do not just create a new business without any previous reference point or history. And after winner startups are successful at meeting the needs of one customer group better than their entrenched competitors, they build on their expertise to expand into other market areas where there is latent demand for their unique offerings.

One example in today's information world of using imagination successfully and then building and executing against disposable strategy after disposable strategy is AOL Time Warner (AOL), formerly America Online before its acquisition of Time Warner.

The early 1980s technology roots of AOL go back to the days of general-purpose minicomputer timesharing. AOL's original strategy was to provide a for-fee service for playing computer games. An individual with a modem-equipped personal computer (PC) and a credit card could log onto AOL's computers in Virginia and play the games it offered, usually competing against other gamers scattered around the world, but all connected to the same computer.

Luckily for AOL, it is located in a region of the United States that is the headquarters of many of the companies that were pioneers in using computers in the global transmission of news. Many of the employees of these firms joined AOL in its earliest days.

A natural evolution of AOL's initial gaming offerings was the creation of a service to meet an as-yet-unseen need—a portal for PC users who wanted access to such capabilities as e-mail and news feeds without the inconvenience of being forced to learn the techno-idiosyncrasies of the then industry leader, CompuServe. With the skills of its second round of employees, AOL had the business knowledge and technology capability to launch such a service.

Ever since AOL expanded beyond games to become the most popular online service for mainstream consumers, it has been on a mission to increase the value of its content and services on a global scale. Even the mid-1990s rise of the Internet, providing access to greater amounts of content at a lower price than AOL offered, did not slow down AOL as it both took the good parts of the Internet into its core and smoothed over the rough edges as a real value-added service for its customers. The result is a successful corporation that has grown, despite its critics, by knowing its customer base thoroughly and courageously taking one logical step after another to meet their changing needs. The excellence of AOL's incremental strategy setting and good-enough execution has been well demonstrated now that it has completed one of the largest acquisitions ever by buying Time Warner. However, remember that AOL started merely by providing online games and was built into the giant, winner media company it is today one evolutionary step at a time by focusing on delighting its target customers.

Executives must use their imaginations to envision the evolutionary steps that will make their companies winners and improve their positions in comparison with the competition. Following the proverbial "Hail Mary" approach to strategy setting (say a prayer and then initiate a radically new strategy) generally is as unsuccessful in business as the "Hail Mary pass" is in American football. Competence in managing the use of advanced technologies to create and execute superior, evolutionary strategies gives an organization a powerful advantage over competitors who still treat information systems as an overhead cost—not a capability with which to grow revenues.

Tightly Coupling Strategy and Execution

In an ideal world, a company would have a perfect strategy that would be reinforced constructively by an organization that executes on all the interdependent business processes of the strategy flawlessly. The logical result should be an increase in market value. The corollary also would be true in an ideal world—a terrible strategy coupled with awful execution would lead the business owners to abandon both as soon as possible.

In the real world, corporate strategies and their execution lie somewhere between perfect and terrible. And it is difficult to recognize where the problems that should be corrected to achieve perfection lie. Is the strategy correct and the execution too poor to allow it to succeed, or is the strategy defective and the organization executing it in an excellent fashion to keep the company viable? (Figure 2-1 presents a description of the strategy-execution matrix.)

Since so many winner corporations today are counting on the use of information technologies to make their overall strategies successful into the future, a business's strategy and the information systems aspects of its execution must be coupled tightly.

Experience has shown that if the technology required to implement a strategy does not work as planned, the strategy is flawed and needs to be rethought. As an example of a brilliant business strategy based on flawed technology, United Airlines in the mid-1980s invested in the appealing idea of allowing travelers to make airline, car rental, and hotel reservations with one phone call to United. (Yes, this was before the Internet.) To implement the strategy, United acquired both one of the largest car rental companies and a prestigious hotel chain. The next task in executing the strategy was to tie the reservations systems together and connect them with airline seat, car, and hotel room availability.

Unfortunately, after spending tens of millions of dollars on the information systems side of the project, United had to admit that it would not work in the near future. Needless to say, the most senior executives at United were asked to leave.

The irony of this case was that independent experts identified the fatal technical problems in the proposed information systems early on

Figure 2-1 Strategy-execution matrix.

	Very poor	Excellent
Excellent	Business continues to operate for some time even as alternative suppliers grow larger and stronger — eventually will result in the enterprise no longer being viable due to competitively small size	Success all around — basis for building a long-term dominant company and strong customer relationships
Very poor	Quick failure — allows all participants to rapidly move on with their lives	Corporation does not grow as fast as competitors who always appear to be copying its initiatives — continuous frustration on the part of the company's management and employees until the business is no longer viable due to competitively small size

Operational Execution of the Corporation's Strategy (vertical axis)

Quality of the Corporation's Strategy (horizontal axis: Very poor → Excellent)

Corporations need to determine objectively where they currently are located on the strategy-execution matrix and then use "emagineering" to move to the upper right.

Note: Descriptions are for companies at the extreme corners of the matrix. Most organizations will be closer to the middle.

during the design phase of the project. However, because United's management neither had built the internal "emagineering" competency necessary to oversee the project itself nor established a communications channel to coordinate its strategy rollout with its execution progress, it was unaware that the execution would fail until it was much too late.

The difference between the success of America Online and the failure of United Airlines lies in the establishment of an "emagineering" mechanism to tightly link the feedback loop between an advanced technology-based strategy and its execution—and objectively and quickly evaluating which aspects of both would meet (or exceed) the corporation's intended objectives and which would not.

Technology executives who have been successful with "emagineering" report that they have outside experts from different disciplines whose opinions they have learned to trust over many years evaluate their strategy versus its execution approximately every 6 months. The project assignments are quick, and the allocated time to conduct the studies is short, often under a week for experts who are familiar with the business. The reports are also expected to be direct and to the point—primarily providing the expert's rating of where the company is on the strategy-execution matrix and the expert's opinion on how and why the company's position has changed since the last review. In addition, the outside experts often act as an objective early warning system by informing the organization's executives of changes in the business and technology environments that they may not have yet recognized or whose significance they need to better understand.

The Skills of Winner Organizations

While knowing how to manage the deployment and operation of advanced technology to survive and be successful in today's competitive environment is a requirement, not an option, technology executives also must have many additional capabilities. To put "emagineering" in the proper perspective, it is the foundation on which a winner strategy and superior operational capabilities can be built—but technology by itself is not a complete business solution. Technology executives also must have the business and management skills and attitude required to capture the maximum benefits possible from their technology-based initiatives. For a company to obtain the benefits and objectives of "emagineering"-oriented planning and management, it must have the following six core competencies and skills:

1. Operational acumen to know how to transform the company's products, services, distribution channels, and resource-acquisition methods successfully to meet the changing preferences of its customers
2. Marketing skills to establish loyalty bonds with current customers (see Chapter 9 for a more in-depth discussion of using advanced technologies to create loyalty bonds), seduce new customers away from traditional competitors, and create new

classes of customers that the business has never before attempted to reach

3. Negotiating and communications talents to build a common vision of the future with the best supplier and distribution-channel business partners both to create the most effective business ecosystem possible and to preempt competitors from gaining strong and highly supportive allies

4. Financial "smarts" to change in a manner that maximizes the company's economic returns

5. Management discipline (see Chapter 8 for an in-depth discussion of how critical this competency is for deploying new technologies successfully across a corporation) to execute on time and across all organizational boundaries

6. Information systems management skills to identify and implement the wide range of possible technical components into a stable, secure, flexible, and expandable operational information systems architecture—on time and within budget

Importantly, to build and manage an "emagineering" culture successfully requires *all* these skills. Each is as important as the others. This is a demanding requirement that few organizations have had the capability to master—but those which have are now the winners within their customer bases and against their traditional competitors.

Many senior executives will review this list and respond by saying, "Our firm has the capability and strengths to do four of the six, but not all six. Isn't that good enough?" From the failed experiences of those who have attempted to execute against a partial list of these critical competencies, the answer is resoundingly, "No!"

One of the reasons that so many disruptive startup companies have been successful against well-established adversaries is that they build their executive teams around these six skill sets. Historically slow-to-change companies tend to promote executives who can improve the firm's ability to manage current operations smoothly—not dramatically change the way the organization operates internally and externally. Yet, in today's Competitive Economy, winner companies such as General Electric and Citigroup have shown that even large, traditional corporations can acquire the skills required for "emagineering" to dominate their markets and handily beat aggressive startups.

Lessons Learned from Experience

A key management talent in today's Competitive Environment is the ability to imagine how a company should evolve to better meet the needs of its customers to become the leader in its industry through the use of enterprise-level advanced technologies. Technology-based imagination is not the misused term *thinking-out-of-the-box*, where dreams too often blur reality, but the underused concept of *expanding-the-pie*, where visions of the future are based on the concrete realities of what is possible.

"Emagineering" describes an information systems technology-oriented management approach to increasing market value. It is based on the best practices of the many organizations that have deployed advanced information systems technologies successfully as the basis for improving their business processes so as to increase their market values. To be successful with "emagineering" management, a company   must (1) want to be the winner within its customer base, (2) be willing to make the changes necessary to put into practice evolutionary improvements in its business processes and policies, and (3) have an accurate knowledge of what advanced technology products can and cannot do.

One of the most important aspects of "emagineering" is its approach to strategy creation. Strategies must be developed by taking into account what capabilities advanced technologies can give a company and must be updated as soon as business conditions change or technology benefits increase. To give employees and business partners confidence that a company will evolve to take advantage of new opportunities, "emagineering"-based strategies are referred to as *disposable*. The traditional view that a corporate strategy should be set for the long term is unacceptable within the context of "emagineering" management.

One of the key tools of "emagineering" is the use of the strategy-execution matrix. To maximize market value, business executives need to improve their strategies and the execution of those strategies continuously. It is advisable to bring in objective, knowledgeable outside advisors to provide a dose of reality about a business's true progress over time on the strategy-execution matrix and compare the relative positions of direct competitors.

Successful startups are created based on the strength of their founders' and early employees' "emagineering" capabilities and skills. Most of the high-tech firms that have come to prominence over the last 20 years, such as AOL Time Warner, Cisco Systems, Dell, eBay, E-Trade, I2, Microsoft, Nokia, Oracle, Palm, SAP, Sun Microsystems, and many more, were started and grown through the skills of "emagineering." While each of these firms had numerous competitors at the outset, the winners were managed by technology executives who were competent both in the art of business and in the science of technology.

The benefits of "emagineering" are not limited to startups and high-tech suppliers. Executives who follow "emagineering" practices at such companies as American Airlines, Brigham and Women's Hospital, Citigroup, Charles Schwab, Dow-Jones, Enron, Fidelity, Ford Motor Company, L.L. Bean, Mobil, W.W. Grainger, Wal-Mart, Washington State University, and Wells Fargo Bank have improved how their organizations do business. True, not all the managers in these firms are enterprise-level technology savvy, but many of their leaders are. These and many other organizations have provided the basis on which this road map of "emagineering" management has been created.

Traditional organizations and executives can master the management approach described by "emagineering." "Emagineering" does not just work in high-tech suppliers and startups—it can add value to any type of organization, including private companies, government agencies, educational institutions, and nonprofit organizations.

Competency 3: Leading with Technology Executives

Aᴿᴱ ᴛʜᴇsᴇ ᴛᴇᴄʜɴᴏʟᴏɢʏ ᴇxᴇᴄᴜᴛɪᴠᴇs sᴘᴇᴄɪᴀʟ?
Are they geniuses or workaholics? Where does a company find them?
The answers are, "No," "No," and "In your own company and through
normal recruiting."

Any successful corporate executive can become a technology executive. All that is required is a desire to grow professionally and a hunger
to be a member of a winner organization. One of my favorite technology executives is the head of information systems for a major bank who
never ceases to submit business plans to the management team for
entering new businesses based on new technologies. Another is in
charge of human resources and has never taken a formal computer science course in his life. However, from his position on the company's
executive operating committee, he never stops demanding that his
firm's management consider every possible way to use the latest technologies to create entirely new and unique product lines, launch innovative, aggressive Web-based marketing programs, and implement more
efficient business processes.

The Technology Executive

The progression of today's technology executive over yesterday's organizational manager is that the technology executive actively seeks to put in place more effective and efficient business processes based on new, often barely out of the laboratory technologies.

Traditional managers are expected to be proficient in the core skills of planning, controlling, and measuring the results of existing operations. Technology executives have advanced beyond merely the traditional skills taught in business schools 20 years ago and are also highly expert in leveraging advanced technologies to improve the operations of their companies continuously for the purpose of increasing market value.

However, not everybody is born as or yet trained to be a technology executive. In addition, an organization that has only a few technology executives will not be able to build the management consensus needed to initiate the information-based projects necessary to increase its market value significantly. This is why adopting the "emagineering" approach to management—ensuring that all executives are savvy to the electronic age, can imagine how to improve the position of their company, and are capable of actively supporting the enterprise-wide deployment of new technologies—is so important. "Emagineering" provides a road map for all executives to follow to help them grow into the role of today's technology executives.

The greatest pressure to become a technology executive is on the most senior managers of public companies. Their investors continuously demand both that they increase the market values of their corporations and that the percentage increases be larger than those achieved by comparable companies. This pressure flows down the organization. It soon becomes a requirement that any manager who wishes to be successful in the organization also must develop the capabilities and competence of a technology executive.

Individuals who plead for an exemption from being actively involved with information systems because they were liberal arts majors in college with a phobia toward all subjects that even hinted at a need to understand technology are making a career-limiting decision. Following the principles of "emagineering" that are described throughout this book, they, too, can become technology executives.

Wal-Mart is the textbook example of how business managers can become technology executives. Wal-Mart has used advanced technologies to provide its executives, from the chairman down to individual store managers, with the information they need to be more nimble than their retail competitors in carrying the products their customers want while incurring lower costs and obtaining higher profits. Wal-Mart buyers track sales of individual items by store to understand which new products consumers want and which products and designs are falling out of favor. Operations managers use technology to determine when to restock stores and with how many units, when to order additional products from suppliers, and what the optimal delivery methods are to the store.

Store managers are expected to use Wal-Mart's information systems to customize the items they carry and display prominently in their stores based on the demographics and buying patterns of their specific customers. For example, while the Wal-Mart store manager in Phoenix, Arizona, may still be ordering bathing suits in October, his counterpart in New England will be promoting heavy winter jackets. Successful Wal-Mart executives understand the source of the information on which they are making daily decisions and know how to manage with the possibly missing or out-of-date data that often are provided by their suppliers. In addition, Wal-Mart is well known for improving its business processes based on the recommendations and insights of its store and operations managers, who have learned to perform as technology executives within the Wal-Mart organization.

By building an organization of technology executives—very few of whom have formal computer science educations and backgrounds—and allowing them to lead the evolution of the company's strategy and operations, Wal-Mart has become America's largest retailer. Its knowledge of its customers and its delivery efficiency have made it the market value leader in its industry.

Many high-tech technology executives started their careers as information systems specialists—often computer programmers writing lines of code. Over the last 25 years, professional information systems technologists who have made the leap to become technology executives have constituted the backbone of successful high-tech startups. One does not have to look any farther than Bill Gates at Microsoft and Larry

Ellison at Oracle to see evidence supporting the fact that these two technologists who learned the dynamics of business and took advantage of change are the top contenders for richest person in the world.

Within corporations, it is time and again information systems professionals turned technology executives who can recommend powerful strategic initiatives, more effective and efficient business processes, and even potential new lines of business. For example, major money center banks truly do rely on their information systems professionals to act as technology executives to outmaneuver the competition both for attracting customers with unique products not available from others and for providing these customers with an extremely high level of service at a relatively low internal cost. In the financial services industry—as well as most other industries today—any information systems professional who cannot make the leap to become a technology executive has limited upward career opportunities.

In contrast, many people have been surprised how Sam Walton, founder of Wal-Mart, and Jack Welch, the legendary leader of General Electric, both businesspeople first and foremost, were able to manage the deployment of technology within their corporations to set them apart from the competitors. Each understood the benefits that could be obtained from doing business better than competitors by applying innovative technology solutions to everyday business issues—and both are now regarded as the best of a pioneering group of technology executives.

Today's technology executives are a diverse group. They can come from any background and may be any age. They can be located anywhere within a business. What they all have in common is a business understanding of how to use technology to contribute to the success of their organizations in every way possible.

While Johann Gutenberg became an early technology executive through hard work, instinct, foresight, personality, and luck, companies today do not have the luxury of waiting for their key managers to miraculously turn into the next Gutenberg. Therefore, it is imperative that they begin the educational and training processes required to assist motivated individuals in their advancement toward becoming technology executives who will take the "emagineering" approach to increasing the value of their firms.

Technology Executives Create Operational Excellence

Successful "emagineering" requires having technology executives located throughout the corporation. This is a simple thought but an extremely difficult objective for most organizations to accomplish.

Having technology competence as a company requires much more than having an experienced and expensive professional information systems staff. It also means having "emagineering" competence. This means that all senior company executives and managers—both staff and line—must be capable of contributing to the business's ability to leverage the latest information technologies to better serve its customers and outdistance the competition. Striving for technology competence must be part of the corporation's culture and every executive's performance requirement.

After a generation plus of using information technology at the enterprise-level throughout corporations, many business executives are still uncomfortable with evaluating new technologies and participating in the management of information systems. Moreover, while almost all use a personal computer (PC) today for e-mail, spreadsheets, Internet access, and word processing—both at work and at home—they are ill prepared to make the knowledge leap from personal computing to enterprise-level computing.

At the same time, many enterprise-level information systems professionals seem to have a difficult time grasping the business requirements for achieving operational excellence based on use of the very advanced information technologies they know so well. Unfortunately, they are not as helpful to and supportive of the business-focused executives they work with in their companies as they could be. And *helpful* means explaining the business benefits and systems capabilities and limitations of the multitude of new advanced technologies introduced into the marketplace every few months. And *supportive* is demonstrated by objectively creating and communicating the business and financial cases for adopting or rejecting (at least for the time) possible technology-based options.

To increase their market values, corporations must take the actions necessary to encourage and compel all their executives to become technology executives. Line-of-business and departmental managers who are charged with running a company's business functions profitably mistakenly believe that they have different goals than executives who have been given the responsibility of proactively supporting the business with information technology. Not realizing that their goals are the same—combined with dissimilar cultural, educational, and experiential backgrounds—creates the typical company "businessperson versus technologist" divide. Moreover, this division often is exacerbated over time by a combination of misunderstanding and lack of empathy.

The best analogy about how the business versus technology culture has come about may be the story about the young man who attended a prestigious Ivy League university. In the first semester he utterly failed his economics course. Ashamed and discouraged, he left college to work at a financial firm on Wall Street. He did remarkably well at the firm, rising from mail boy to become a successful and wealthy principal over the next 25 years. At that time, his son decided to attend the same Ivy League school and, by chance, was enrolled in the same professor's economics class that caused his father to flee academia. On Parent's Day, our hero wandered into the now-much-older economic professor's classroom to find both his son's most recent test and the professor. Examining the test, he looked up at the professor and exclaimed, "This is the same test I flunked 25 years ago. You have an easy job professor!" The professor coolly looked askance at him, however, and replied, "No I don't. I have to change the answers every year!"

The same phenomenon happens between line-of-business managers and professional information system technologists. Those executives who want to focus only on business issues and be fully supported by a professional information systems staff are frustrated at every annual planning session when they ask the question, "How should we achieve operational excellence through technology?" and are provided with answers that are significantly different from what they received the preceding year. And the technologists are mumbling in the restrooms, "What do the business types mean by *operational excellence* this year?"

Technology executives have found that the best means to build organizational consensus for achieving operational excellence is through *continuous* collaboration between responsible line-of-business and information systems executives. Limiting management exchanges to formal planning meetings between these two groups in which the wrong questions are asked and inappropriate answers are provided— the standard format for managing enterprise information technology in traditional companies—is unacceptable in the information-critical Competitive Economy.

Teaching Business-Focused Executives to Be Technology Executives

Can even the most recalcitrant traditional corporate executive who believes that PCs are merely fashion accessories become a technology executive? If he or she wants to, yes. Company after company is filled with stories of executives becoming change leaders once they had a solid intellectual foundation on which to both understand and make decisions about the use of information systems. Experience has shown that organizations that immerse their business-focused executives in the issues, art, and science of enterprise-wide information systems are the first to take the lead within their industries in increasing the market values of their companies by leveraging the new opportunities opened up by the latest and greatest technologies.

To bring business executives to the point where they can collaborate with other corporate executives constructively—those with both business and information systems backgrounds—using the principles of "emagineering," firms need to establish formal, required training programs. They will then have the basis to identify star performers—those who understand both the company's business objectives and how advanced technology can help meet those objectives. Finally, firms need to assign their high-potential executives, no matter whether their backgrounds are in business or information systems, to positions that will provide them with the opportunities and challenges necessary to rise up the organizational structure.

The best training programs for executives who come primarily from business backgrounds include gaining a better understanding of and insights into

- The firm's current information systems architecture, capabilities, limitations, cost to maintain, and currently identified improvement projects.
- How the company's information systems' capabilities compare with those of the most relevant competitors. Special emphasis should be placed on understanding the difference provided by

information systems between firms in terms of customer benefits, managing supplier relationships, and attaining low-cost internal business processes.

- Case studies of how other companies in different industries (and not just high-tech industries) have managed the process of increasing their market values by adopting and leveraging advanced technologies. It is key that these sessions go beyond polished success stories and include examples of how and why many organizations have failed at acquiring and deploying advanced technologies in order that executives can see the seeds of potential problems in some of their own management practices.

- The different approaches that leading corporate-level technology suppliers such as Accenture (formerly Andersen Consulting), Ariba, Cisco Systems, Compaq, Computer Associates, Hewlett-Packard, I2, IBM, Microsoft, Oracle, SAP, Sun Microsystems, and others are recommending for improving business processes with their most recent product and service offerings. Leading-edge suppliers of advanced business applications will urge executives to think beyond the boundaries of their own companies and to imagine how to establish networked business ecosystems. Such ecosystems include a company, all its suppliers, their suppliers (and their suppliers, and so on), its distribution channels, and the final consumers. With the use of advanced technologies, all the participants in a networked ecosystem can communicate with each other to create superior products and services as well as deliver them faster and at a lower cost. (See Chapter 6 for an in-depth discussion of business ecosystems.)

- How and why following "emagineering" management can provide the company with a significant competitive advantage in both strategy setting and operational execution.

Is any of this training difficult to absorb? No. Any business executive who has kept up with the state of the company and is aware of current business trends will be able to understand it. Neither different educational backgrounds nor age will stop dedicated business executives from making the leap to becoming technology executives. With a well-constructed educational program, all that is required on the part of any individual is a willingness to devote the effort and time to understand how and why the deployment of advanced technologies can benefit the company.

Growing from Information Systems Professionals to Technology Executives

On a parallel track with training executives with a business background to become technology executives, companies that apply "emagineering" successfully make their information systems executives part of the management team. Organizations that sincerely want technology executives throughout their structure do not relegate their professional information systems executives to the role of being necessary but merely tolerated departmental cost-center managers.

Information systems professionals tend to learn best how to become technology executives when they have leaders whose examples they can follow and who support them on a daily basis as they grow their understanding of the company, its strategy, and the industry dynamics of the markets in which the company competes. Moreover, while formal training works well with business-focused executives, information systems professionals who want to move up to the role of technology executive often learn best by actually carrying out projects as part of a team of supportive corporate executives.

Companies that have not used advanced technology aggressively in the past have found that to start the process of growing their professional information systems staff into technology executives requires recruiting senior information systems leaders who are as capable and dedicated to increasing the company's market value as they are to managing the technology underpinnings that automate the firm's business processes. Focused recruitment is then followed up by placing these information systems leaders on the appropriate operating committees with the specific responsibility of continuously suggesting ways to improve the market value of the entire corporation and its individual lines of business. They must not be allowed to fall into the role of official whipping post for all the perceived computer-related (both at home and at work) and business-process problems the other members of the committee bring to their meetings.

The three primary roles for the head of the formal information systems group—usually with the title Chief Information Officer or Vice President of Infomation Technology—become

1. Chief agent of strategic information-technology-initiated change at the senior executive level

2. Senior executive in charge of technology-based changes that cut across organizational boundaries
3. Overseer of quality and cost control for the firm's installed information systems

These roles emphasize the chief information officer's responsibility to proactively search out ways to use advanced technologies to increase the corporation's market value while delegating the tasks of running day-to-day operations to responsible managers.

To grow members of the professional information systems staff to think more like technology executives, one must educate them about how their role in the company is evolving. In most traditional companies, the information systems department is expected to meet two very contradictory objectives. The first goal is to automate business processes so that the company stays abreast of the competition in terms of cost and time efficiency. The second objective is to minimize the cost of the information systems themselves in order to keep overhead-to-revenue expenses below or, at worst, on par with the competition.

As long as information systems executives think primarily in terms of information systems costs, they will not be able to make the leap to becoming technology executives who are most concerned with market value. Therefore, the culture—or, as it is popularly known, mindset—of the individuals who manage information systems within a company must be made to conform to the "emagineering" approach of managing to increase market value before the organization can gain the maximum benefit from them as technology executives.

Experience has shown that the more information systems professionals communicate with technology executives who understand how to manage the deployment of advanced technologies for the benefit of the company, the faster they too grow into the technology executive role. They learn about the business and how it is conducted during these one-on-one sessions. An excellent technique to ensure that information systems professionals meet with technology executes is to assign them the task of educating these role models about the different ways that advanced technologies might be used to improve how the organization operates.

In addition, information systems professionals should be expected to be knowledgeable about and brief corporate executives regarding how the company's competitors are using new technologies. This is especially important when competitors are using advanced technologies to appeal more effectively to customers and prospects as well as to lower their costs of producing and delivering products and services. Both the corporate executives and information systems professionals will progress on the path toward becoming technology executives as a result of these sessions.

Information systems professionals also will learn about how to increase the value of their corporations by assisting technology executives with the complex details of planning for the implementation of new information systems and business processes. The most successful implementation projects are led by technology executives—whether they are experienced senior executives or rising stars within the organization—not by managers focused on information systems. Being a major contributor to a successful team effort to deploy advanced technologies for gaining a competitive advantage—not an impediment or merely a technical functionary—is a much better way for an information systems professional to advance to becoming a technology executive than attending numerous formal training programs.

Actions Speak Louder than Words

Technology executives understand that taking action is critical to success. One can talk about business and technology changes reinforcing each other and imagine how the world might look in the future for an entire career. These are fruitless exercises, however, if a company and its executives are not dedicated to taking the actions necessary to turn such insights into a higher market value for their business.

In contrast to AOL, let's examine AT&T, where imagination and an accurate and widely communicated vision of the future have failed to help an American institution become a leader in the information age. AT&T has, since the late 1970s, espoused its vision of the network as central to the information age. Its senior executives clearly recognized that high-speed, high-quality two-way data, voice, and video transmissions among businesses and homes could be one the fastest growing, largest, and most profitable business opportunities of our times. With its huge customer base, physical infrastructure, and access to capital and technical knowledge, AT&T clearly was positioned to be the dominant player in establishing the fabled information highway in the United States—and then filling it with content and dictating which standards must be met to attach to it.

Yet, when one judges industry leaders by any measure, such as market value or customer loyalty, AT&T presently is just another struggling player that has for the most part failed in executing its grand strategy. Having tried to do everything at once and having made little headway on its own, it can now be seen blundering from one partnership with a then-current industry winner to another with a seeming inability to become a superior or highly profitable player in any emerging market segment. In fact, the industry joke is that when a hot technology supplier partners with AT&T, the firm's founding management team must have decided that its glory days would soon be coming to an end.

The result is that now AT&T is seeking ways to increase its total market value not by integrating the different services it offers (as originally planned) but by breaking up its different lines of business into independent, publicly traded companies—just as it increased shareholder wealth over 20 years ago when it split off its regional telephone operating companies.

How within 15 years could AOL, starting as one of many suppliers of interactive gaming services, become larger and more important than AT&T in the information world? This current situation was not based purely on a lack of vision and imagination at AT&T—AT&T executives clearly described the information world we now live in well before most other industry leaders. And AT&T certainly had access to greater resources of all kinds than AOL over most of the last 15 years.

The difference between these two firms lies in their use of technology executives to lead change. While AT&T had a few technology executives at its highest level and a few dispersed throughout the organizations, it simply did not have enough in the right places. AOL, on the other hand, has been composed almost entirely of technology executives.

AOL was able to execute the business and technical engineering skill sets of "emagineering" successfully, often overcoming tremendous hurdles and industry pundit cynicism. For example, when AOL pioneered the use of a relatively low monthly charge in the United States of approximately $20 for unlimited use of its services, it quickly had to hire thousands of employees and deploy tens of thousands of new pieces of equipment to support the overwhelming demand for its offering. Yes, service was poor for many months while the company was in the midst of this dramatic growth spurt, but within a year and due to the capabilities and dedication of its technology executives, it had implemented its vision.

AT&T, on the other hand, even with its strategic foresight and vision of how the world could and would be, did not understand the customers both it and AOL were competing to win. And even if AT&T had understood the prospective customer base's buying criteria, it is very clear that AT&T's executives, unlike AOL's, did not have the courage and skill sets required to initiate and engineer such a disruptive transformation of both the industry's business policies and its own information infrastructure.

Technology executives are expected to initiate actions that have a high probability of increasing the market values of their companies. The reason that strategy setting is not overemphasized by technology executives is that too many staff members can become overly comfortable with talking about what their organization *should* do, like AT&T, as opposed to *implementing* new technology-based extensions to their existing operations in the aggressive and successful manner of AOL.

Experimentation: It Takes Fast Misses to Make Big Hits

Technology executives using "emagineering" must follow traditional scientific experiment discipline when evaluating new ways to improve their companies with advanced technologies. Why? Because any enterprise-level information system changes have the potential to have a major and unexpected impact—either positive or negative—on the organization.

One of the reasons "emagineering" has come about is because companies no longer have the luxury to always conduct pilot tests of new ideas. In fact, regional pilot tests, the traditional testing standby technique, are impossible with the *worldwide* Web and enterprise-wide integrated application suites. Any public test of a marketing program conducted on the Web is available immediately to the worldwide population of Web surfers, and all employees must use *enterprise-wide* applications before it can be demonstrated whether they work or not.

Therefore, technology executives have learned that they must use experiments with both advanced technologies and the business processes they support to better understand what the results of actual deployment might be. Experiments are controlled efforts that can either prove or disprove a hypothesis about new technologies or new business processes. Quickly gathering data from the experiment and analyzing the results are extremely important. Experiments have a predefined start and stop time in order that they do not grow out of control and into standard company processes and procedures before the results are understood fully.

A simple internal information systems department example of an experiment might be to provide a limited number of senior executives with wireless Internet connections to the company's financial reporting system to determine if it will help them make business decisions when they are at home or traveling. An external test might be offering every tenth visitor to a retailer's Web site a 20 percent discount to determine if this increases the number of sales, the sizes of the sales, or the profitability of the organization.

Technology executives must begin an experiment by designing it using the principle of interconnections, that is, how to improve on what is already in place. Then they will design the experiment to test their hypothesis of how an improvement could be made. They will then conduct the experiment with their target audience—often letting the members of the group know that they are part of an early test program. Most important, they must observe the results of the experiment closely and analyze their implications.

Managers who guide "emagineering"-initiated projects tend to follow a rational methodology of sequencing their experimental efforts into four reporting phases:

1. They identify the *issues* that the experiment is to address.
2. They report their *findings* objectively to the responsible executive leaders and teams on a regular basis so that there are no major surprises at the conclusion of the experiment.
3. They correlate the issues being addressed with their findings to document the *conclusions* of the experiment.
4. Most important, they weigh all the findings of the experiment to establish the *implications* for the organization's business processes and achievement of its strategic objectives. With the results of the experiment in a comprehensive format, the executives

responsible can see clearly what their recommendations should be as to whether or how to proceed.

By conducting experiments in a controlled and disciplined fashion, technology executives can conduct numerous small ones, especially those which use the Web for improving customer interactions, in a relatively short time. Successful results must be communicated quickly and widely so that the experiment can advance swiftly to the stage of a new standard business process. Experiments that turn out poorly can be redirected or dropped quickly before they run amok and damage the business and its relationship with its customers.

Within a few weeks of the deployment of new information tools, technology executives need to know honestly and objectively if the new systems capabilities have added value—how and where. They can do this by establishing and running experiments on their use. If the newly provided functionality did not meet its objectives with customers, prospects, and internal staff, the technology executives need to know why and either revamp the delivery mechanism or stop the initiative immediately.

High-tech suppliers conduct experiments in conjunction with their installed customer bases all the time. These experiments typically are called *beta tests*. Microsoft, for example, designs and runs experiments as one of its most important business practices. Microsoft is continuously developing new versions of its Windows operating system and Office product in order to provide its customer base with both greater systems stability and greater functionality. One of the last steps it goes through in the development process, before mass producing and packaging millions of CDs with the software, is to ask its leading-edge customers to participate in a beta test.

Microsoft will provide its most loyal customers with what is referred to as a *beta version* of the new software—being careful to communicate that the product may not yet work as intended. Microsoft methodically records the feedback from loyal customers who are willing to participate actively in the experiment. Based on its analysis of what its beta customers report, Microsoft has the opportunity to fix problems or market unexpected benefits before it releases the new offering to the general public. Microsoft and its customers both win from the process of experimentation because

Microsoft can ship a better product than it would have been able to do otherwise.

Experimentation: Risk and Reward

It is important to recognize that the process of experimentation goes against the traditional management rule of simply providing the triage necessary to keep an obviously failing business process operating for another few years. Experimentation is also the opposite of the general approach of simply paying no attention to those business functions which are working well enough but not better than the competition even if they are critical to the business.

Experimentation is an aggressive technology executive practice for improving smoothly running operations. In the manufacturing-dominated economy, the general rule was, "If it is not broken, don't touch it." In the Competitive Economy, the general rule is, *"If it is working fine and is a critical system or process, improve it as soon as possible."*

Experimentation was and generally is strongly rejected in business cultures that are not faced with aggressive competition. Middle managers in such organizations are discouraged from making changes, taking chances, or experimenting. Their task is to focus on running existing processes as efficiently as possible. Rewards are given either for not breaking the system or merely making incremental productivity improvements through better management techniques.

In firms that do not understand "emagineering," any proposed experiment may require several management layers of approval over many months or years. If the experiment does not meet its projected objectives smoothly and by quickly overcoming internal resistance, the sponsoring manager often finds that he or she has taken a career-limiting action (CLA). Moreover, if the experiment is a major success, the responsible manager will be lucky to get any more than a nice, "Attaboy, this will put you in the running for the next promotion when a higher slot opens up." No wonder experimentation is not a normal practice in traditional companies!

However, when the advantages of new technologies are considered, "emagineered" customer-focused improvements can lead quickly to designs for experiments. In addition, with the tools provided by recent advances in Internet and database technology, these experiments can be set up and launched relatively quickly and inexpensively.

On a personal level, even managers responsible for failed experiments at companies that must compete based on change will gain the desired resumé designation of "experienced" and are sought after anxiously for the next experiment based on what they have learned previously. Managers of failed experiments in leading-edge companies may even be given a promotion for showing the initiative to propose the experiment, for the ability to carry it out, and for the integrity to report the disappointing results objectively. In addition, successful experimenters will get promotions, company-wide recognition, probably a bonus, and even more stock options in the hope that they will not jump to another corporation and take along their newfound experience.

Technology Must Be Correct for Experimentation

There is one significant caveat about technology executive-led experimentation: Even if the proposed new business processes are an obvious market-value-building improvement, the technology needed to build the experiment may not yet be available. Although there has been a tremendous amount of progress in information technology over the last 40 years, advances are coming continuously out of the laboratories because there is so much more still to be done.

Senior executives need to recognize that high-tech supplier marketing and technology realities are two different animals that never should be confused with each other. Fortunately for information systems professionals, over the last several years, nontechnical executives have learned this hard fact of the high-tech world personally through experiencing their home PCs crashing—even after the manufacturers assured them that their products were both reliable and easy to use. Alternatively, they may have been enlightened suddenly when they realized that their brand-new, "Internet-ready" cellphones or personal digital assistants (PDAs) could not perform conveniently as the wireless Internet connections that were promised.

Nontechnical company executives must recognize that one key aspect of any experiment is to truly determine if the technology products on which the experiment is built can perform (and at what cost) as their suppliers claim.

Failed Experiments—So What?

What happens when a company deploys advanced technologies aggressively in an experiment that fails either for technology or customer-rejection reasons in the opinion of its customers who participate? Typically, nothing!

For example, Sun Microsystems, like many other high-tech suppliers, releases products (both hardware and software) continuously from its laboratories for its early-adopter customers to try. Sun's accompanying marketing campaigns rather consistently promise that each new product quickly will become another mainstay of the Unix computing world. Yet, compared with key competitors BEA Systems, EMC, Hewlett-Packard, IBM, and others, a relatively high percentage of Sun's products do not live up to their marketing-created expectations. This does not seem to bother Sun's customer base, however.

The information technology professionals who buy from Sun are known for their appreciation of having the opportunity to acquire and evaluate (otherwise known as "play with") new technologies. Even when Sun's experiments fail, the fact that it tried something new actually increases the loyalty ties it has with its most strategic customers.

The Sun example and numerous others like it initiated by aggressive companies who consistently attempt to serve their customers better are not unique. Customer acceptance of failed experimentation is an important difference between the culture of today's information-knowledgeable customers and that of their predecessors.

Today, corporations and technology executives can fail in their attempts to provide a stronger linkage and provide more services to their customers without doing serious damage to their reputations. However, if they do not both *experiment* and *communicate* that they are trying to use technology to improve their product offerings and customer service, their customers will feel that they are not being supported properly and are much more likely to begin evaluating competitors' offerings.

Merrill Lynch, the large financial services firm, found out about this new fact of business life, much to its chagrin, in the consumer brokerage world. After making repeated public attacks over many months on the evils of Web-based stock trading, Merrill Lynch realized that it too had to offer this service or watch many of its best customers defect simply because they had no expectation of ever being offered online trading. As soon as Merrill Lynch *announced* its about-face and stated when and how it planned to offer trading over the Internet, the pressure from its established customers subsided immensely.

Successful Experiments Create Competitive Advantages

With enough skill and luck, a company's technology experiments have the opportunity to create major competitive advantages. Successful experiments that are deployed widely can create substantive barriers to competitors and increase a company's market value.

Amazon.com (Amazon) provides an excellent example of experimentation success. Amazon made the connection that its customers would like the benefits they could obtain by moving up from the "e-tailing" industry's standard shopping cart function to Amazon's proprietary 1-Click process. Rather than go through the time-consuming shopping cart checkout procedure, Amazon's customers who have already registered with or purchased from Amazon can have 1-Click activated for all their visits to its site and, with their credit card and shipping information stored previously, buy items with simply one click of the mouse.

This Amazon-developed buying process is both convenient for customers and assists Amazon in reducing the number of created-but-uncommitted orders. Sixty-five percent of Internet customers suffer buyer's remorse during the typical much-too-painful shopping cart checkout process and simply log off before making a final order submission—a consumer action 1-Click substantially minimizes. Amazon attempted to prevent other e-tailers from using 1-Click by patenting its innovative business process. What a great result from an experiment!

Planning and executing numerous experiments based on the interconnections of how a business currently communicates with its customers and how it would like to in the future, especially with the combination of its Web site, front-end customer-touching applications, and e-mail marketing campaigns, constitute an important principle of "emagineering." Experiments that result in so greatly delighting customers to the point that they integrate the corporation's business processes into their own business processes are the most successful. These experiments are the ones that create the strong ties within a company's ecosystem that provide stability and higher market value.

The Technology Executive Challenge

For "emagineering" to work and increase a corporation's market value, it must be executed with skill by technology executives. This is much easier said than done because technology executives are expected to blend the skills of both strategy setting and operational execution.

From a technology executive perspective, there are two extremes in management styles. At one extreme is the *builder*. This type of executive wants to build new businesses and/or create larger, more profitable businesses out of existing ones. Builders tend to be characterized by searching continuously for discontinuities in the current business environment that they can leverage for their company's advantage. They believe that their organizations and they themselves will be rewarded handsomely by entering new business areas successfully or initiating radically improved business processes.

The other management extreme is the *administrator*. The administrator wants to run his or her organization for maximum efficiency using the business processes currently in place. The administrator, for example, focuses on improving customer service against well-established metrics, such as time spent with the customer and customer ratings. The administrator finds change positive only when it can be used to improve on the metrics that he or she relies on to evaluate his or her own personal performance.

The builder revels in change; the administrator wants stability on which to improve business efficiency and effectiveness. Naturally, the management style of most executives lies somewhere between these two extremes. "Emagineering" efforts recognize that there is value to both the builder and the administrator. The building phase of "emagineering" focuses on making changes—creating the best strategy for the corporation and initiating the appropriate changes in business processes. The administrative side highlights actions for continuously improving the efficiency and effectiveness of the business—the execution of the strategy.

The personal challenge for technology executives is to recognize when to build and when to administrate—when to set strategy and when to execute against an excellent strategy. This can be difficult. Timing is critical, as is communicating to the entire organization which one of the modes of operation is most important at any point in time.

In addition, winner companies almost always have developed through a self-selection process a group of *coaches* who reside throughout the organization. Coaches—those who can assist others in understanding how and why a company is changing and help them in conforming to the change—are extremely important in their ability to provide balance between the business's building and administrative phases.

One of the world's largest technology suppliers went through a period a decade ago when an administrator was president. No matter how hard he tried to improve on the traditional metrics for success of the corporation, its market value continued to decline as its offerings and business policies became less relevant to even its most loyal customers. Fed up with a deteriorating market value, the board of directors brought in an outsider who had an excellent reputation as a builder. Based on his previous experience, the builder immediately invested in and expanded the scope of the company's customer service and support groups, a business area for which there was tremendous demand but one that the old administrator had relegated to his second tier of priorities as he focused on traditional hardware and software products. The new president also threw out many of the company's old measurement metrics, such as revenue by country, in favor of more relevant ones, such as global gross margins by named accounts in the same vertical industry and revenues from entirely new accounts.

The market value of the company increased many times over the next 5 years. However, this result did not come solely from the new builder and his handpicked executive team. Those intimately involved in this successful turnaround could see the power of the invisible, unidentified network of coaches—individuals in place from the operating committee down to local sales offices—who executed with excellence on all new strategies and business policies. The coaches were able to motivate highly capable employees to move from a heads-down administrative mode to a proactive builder stance in the way they approached their business responsibilities each day. And when the new president simply failed at specific initiatives to increase market share with certain proprietary technologies and products that were rejected by the marketplace, the coaches did a superb job of damage control to keep even those customers who had followed the president's guidance to their detriment loyal to the company.

Coaches also can motivate employees in other companies that are part of the same ecosystem. On an informal basis, supplier and customer representatives with an established loyalty bond attempt to coach each other on how their companies could and should work better together.

Technology executive coaches often show up at industry seminars as speakers to describe to executives in other companies in their ecosystem how they would like to see the different parts of the ecosystem use new technologies to coordinate efforts and work together more closely.

Industry awards for achievement often are given to technology executives who are then expected at the awards ceremony or as part of published interviews to explain in a coaching manner to their peers in other organizations how they were able to obtain notably superior results.

The challenge technology executives must overcome to manage successfully with "emagineering" is to understand when and how they should blend the different qualities of builder, administrator, and coach (Fig. 3-1). To manage successfully in the world of networked ecosystems, technology executives need all three skill sets. The successful builder must be prepared to be an administrator after a new line of business is created. The excellent administrator must know when and how to employ the techniques of creative destruction (see Chapter 7 for a discussion on the why, when, and how of creative destruction) to transform current but out-of-date business processes into industry-leading operations. The best people work energetically—whatever the goals and objectives—for coaches who inspire and mentor them to perform to their full potential. A generation of professional managers and employees brought up in the prosperity of the last quarter of the twentieth century simply will not perform to the organization's goals for supervisors who try to microcontrol and evaluate all their actions—they plainly perform much better when coached.

Builder, administrator, and coach are often roles that did not fit into many slow-to-change organizations (especially government agencies), where almost every employee was charged with simply processing a relatively stable type and amount of work each month. On the other hand, this model has developed and flourishes at many of the leading universities that manage their own information systems groups. And winner corporations and technology executives have followed it consistently.

Figure 3-1 Attributes of a successful technology executive.

Builder

- Engage in creative destruction of current business processes and products to improve the enterprise

- Recommend and establish new lines of business and customer-support services for the organization

Administrator

- Execute current corporate strategy and operate current business processes as efficiently and as effectively as possible

- Continuously improve current business processes in an evolutionary manner

Coach

- Assist superiors, peers, and subordinates in understanding and adjusting to change

- Explain why and how the company is changing to other members of the ecosystem—and challenge them to change as rapidly

Lessons Learned from Experience

What traditional managers will find extraordinary about the new breed of technology executives is their abilities both to manage business operations skillfully *and* to direct the deployment of advanced technologies to improve the efficiency and effectiveness of their organizations' overall business. Often there is a real and substantive cultural division between those managers responsible for running business operations successfully and those charged with implementing and supporting the business's information systems. This division, which is a major obstacle to achieving and maintaining an organization's potential operational excellence, has been created and widened over many years. Technology executives, through their knowledge and abilities to build consensus, are the bridge across this divide.

Technology executives do not just thrive in high-tech suppliers and startups—they can add value to any type of organization, including private companies, government agencies, educational institutions, and nonprofit organizations. They can be located anywhere throughout a firm but are especially valuable managing the most important business-process functions.

Because the business world is always changing, traditional managers—no matter how well they know their organizations' business or their own current job functions—are becoming less important to the success of their companies than technology executives. Those traditional executives who typically focused on long-established management functions that required no significant knowledge of enterprise-level information systems must become much more knowledgeable and expert in how to evaluate and implement new business processes based on advanced technologies if they are to advance to the stage of the technology executive. Managing with the principles of "emagineering" to build corporate market value is critical to making the transition to becoming the technology executive of tomorrow and building the long-term value of your organization.

Traditional organizations and executives can master "emagineering." Mastering the management of enterprise-level technologies as part of the executive function is an individual requirement. Executives who have made the transition to become technology executives can expect to see their incomes grow at a faster rate and to a higher level than their traditional executive peers. Managers at firms whose relative market value is dropping and are unable to manage as technology executives are more often in fear of being let go as their corporations attempt to shrink themselves to what they believe will be the proper size for survival.

Professional information systems technologists must develop a greater understanding of both the business realities and market dynamics facing their companies if they wish to advance in their careers. They must be able to proactively recommend business process changes based on advanced technologies to improve the market values of their corporations if they want to progress to the stage of becoming a true technology executive.

Winner corporations create and maintain a high level of business-technology competence within their management teams. This requires educating line-of-business executives about the current information systems capabilities within their company and how best to use them. In addition, line-of-business executives need to be evaluated and promoted based on their ability to improve their areas of responsibility with advanced information technologies as well as on conventional performance criteria.

Senior information systems executives must communicate continuously with the company's management team about ideas for using advanced technologies to increase the corporation's market value. Communication and collaboration among business and information systems managers are critical for creating an infrastructure of technology executives throughout an organization.

Many organizations that have not promoted technology executives to lead them and consequently have failed at making the transition in changing the way they manage advanced technologies are suffering the consequences. These consequences include being acquired by (or the nicer term of "merged with") others, such as AOL acquiring Time Warner, eBay acquiring the old-line (but not online) auction house Butterfield and Butterfield, and QWEST acquiring U.S. West. These acquired firms literally lost the battle for survival as independent entities. Others, even those once considered invincible, such as Xerox, Proctor and Gamble, General Motors, and AT&T, have seen their relative market values drop as they continue to be unable to leverage new technologies skillfully to increase their marketing effectiveness and internal business efficiency.

Technology executives are constantly initiating technology-based experiments for improving their firms' operations. Experiments require an intelligent, customer-focused process design, an identification of the issues that need to be addressed, an objective assessment of the findings, an analysis of the implications of the findings, and the drawing of conclusions about the results of the experiment. After an experiment is launched, technology executives need to evaluate the results of the experiment quickly so that they can determine whether to proceed with, modify, or drop the experiment. Technology executives have a simple motto, "Make and bury your mistakes quickly so that you can get to your successes quicker."

Customers expect their trusted suppliers to initiate business-process experiments based on advanced technologies for the purpose of serving them better. They will criticize a supplier's lack of trying to use advanced information technology to better support them much more than a well-intentioned effort that fails.

To manage successfully in a business environment of technology-initiated change, technology executives must be a combination of builder, administrator, and coach. The art of managing with "emagineering" becomes knowing how and when to emphasize each of these three different but complementary skill sets.

Competency 4: Loving Your Customer

W<small>INNER COMPANIES KNOW THEIR CUSTOMERS.</small>
And with this knowledge, they do everything they can to take care of their customers better than any other firm.

Executives within companies that are profitably growing market share spend an incredibly large amount of their time creating products and policies to better support their customers. They think about how each decision they make will benefit their customers. They talk about their customers with affection.

Wherever possible, technology executives also want to be customers of their own firms. The president of a leading chain of bakeries, for example, goes out every Sunday morning to one of his stores to buy bagels to experience the pleasure of being a customer of his own company.

Critical to the success of any startup company is selecting and targeting the right initial customer set for its products and services. For managers in well-established corporations, it is critically important to know accurately the firm's customers and be able to anticipate correctly how their needs will change in the future. The company that can best service its target customer base will have the highest market share, and this is imperative for obtaining the highest market valuation of any firm in the industry.

Know and Focus on Your Target Customer Base

An essential principle of "emagineering" is that a company can build the highest market value in its industry by using advanced technologies to be the best at understanding and servicing its customer base. An organization's focus with "emagineering" first must be on better meeting the needs of its current customers and then on capturing potential customers that are being served by competitors. Simple and smart!

Only after a firm knows and understands its customers and their overall buying patterns thoroughly will it have the solid knowledge on which to launch new product offerings intended for their use. As all experienced corporate executives know, the most successful new product launches are those which are aimed at a company's traditional customer base and are related to its core business. Think of Disney starting with short cartoons, expanding into full-length movies, producing television shows, marketing videos of its movies, opening theme parks, launching a chain of retail stores, creating live theater shows, and becoming the core of a global entertainment corporation. All its new businesses actually were product evolutions of the original cartoons, and all were aimed at generally the same target customers—families wanting to be entertained by fantasy. The "emagineering" approach to starting new businesses is similar—only now technology executives focus on building new product variations through the innovative use of advanced technologies.

By focusing on its customers first, a company gains the knowledge necessary for building the appropriate business processes into its back-office operations. The most promising back-office improvements according to technology executives are those designed to improve how the business can support its strategic customers most profitably. New efforts that strengthen the customers' ties with the business at the front end then can be extended to make the back-office processes more efficient.

As illustrated in Figure 4-1, technology executives believe that all corporate value and critical information flow from its target customer bases (and its competitors' customer bases) down into the organization and then into the business ecosystem in which the company participates. The purpose of back-end internal information systems is to support the demands and needs of the target customer bases and service the businesses and individuals that make up these customer bases better than any alternative supplier.

Figure 4-1 "Emagineering" overview of the world.

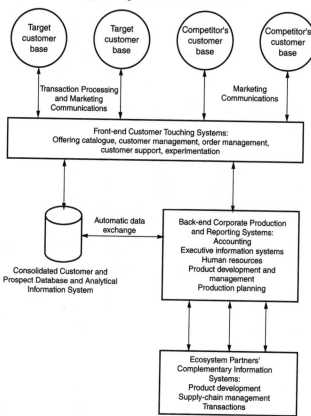

Improving the efficiencies of the back-office processes before front-end customer-supporting processes, as too many traditional executives have erred in doing, most often results in a wonderful system that simply does not provide the business with the maximum benefits possible. After all, a customer will never see and in most cases should never care about its supplier's internal operations. Therefore, focusing on increasing the efficiency of internal back-office processes at the expense of customer-delighting enhancements will result in a competitive disadvantage when the company is faced with an "emagineering"-driven competitor who understands that "It is all about the customer!"

Let's analyze a well-publicized example of "emagineering" at work to closely link successful, effective front-end customer-facing information systems with efficient back-end production systems. The story of how Michael Dell began this now-behemoth personal computer (PC) business by custom assembling PCs in his dorm room for other students has now become legendary. However, when Dell Computer Corporation first became a national business, it was perceived as merely another mail-order supplier by most observers. Entrenched competitors such as Compaq, IBM, Digital Equipment Corporation (now part of Compaq), Hewlett-Packard, NEC, and others gave Dell minimal chance of surviving in the long term, believing that both their own dealers and lower-priced "garage shop" PC assemblers would snuff it out in a classic squeeze-the-company-in-the-middle play. When Dell's growth continued unabated, the competitors decided that the company's strength must lie in its extensive mail-order cataloging campaign (remember, this was in the pre-Internet age) and advertising prowess—so they attempted to emulate Dell in those areas. Again, they had no success at slowing down Dell's tremendous growth. How could such titans of the industry fail to outmaneuver little Dell?

What Dell was doing, which the other PC suppliers did not, was focusing all its attention on the *end-user* customer. IBM, Compaq, Hewlett-Packard, and the others had decided that the distribution channel was their customer. Dell decided that its customer was the end user—usually the owner of a small or medium-sized business.

To support its end-user customer, Dell built an information support system capable of tracking each PC it shipped and what software applications and peripheral devices the user added. When a customer called Dell with a problem (of which there were many during this early period of the PC industry), a technician could look immediately into Dell's customer and trouble-shooting databases. Usually the Dell service representative had a solution or, if there was no work-around, could tell the user why he or she could not do what was requested with the existing system and suggest a new, more capable one.

This front-end customer-support effort created tremendous end-user loyalty for Dell that none of its competitors, who used distributors, could match. Moreover, the simple reason why its PC-manufacturer competitors could not build an end-user customer database is that neither they nor their distributors actually knew who the ultimate end users were.

Dell customer loyalties translated into word-of-mouth referrals (a much stronger motivator for instigating buying actions than advertising) and repeat business as users upgraded to more powerful machines needed to run the newest application software.

By tailoring front-end systems to maximize its connection with customers, Dell gained market data that enabled it to design and build the back-end systems that would allow it to assemble PCs to customers' exact orders both quickly and cost-effectively. The competitors, without a clue about what end users actually were planning to buy in the future, were building batches of the exact same PCs using advanced back-end production planning and scheduling systems. However, their fatal flaw was that without a direct linkage to the final customers, they were efficiently building too many types of the wrong PCs—usually the ones that end users wanted 3 to 6 months earlier but not in the future.

With its up-to-the-minute database of direct purchases, Dell could analyze trends in purchasing preferences before its competitors, who obtained their end-user buying behavior information both late and through the filter of their distributors. Additionally, this customer-trend information advantage allowed Dell to better manage its inventories of parts components—the highest-cost portion of the PC business. All this led to better financial results than its competitors were achieving and permitted Dell to continue its profitable growth and increase its market value dramatically.

While the successfully "emagineered" business strategy just described was developed by Dell during it's startup phase, the same requirement to identify, understand, and support a company's target customer base—its strategic customers—is key to successfully establishing the "emagineering" approach within any company at any stage of organizational maturity.

What is so new about today's information world is that all of a company's customer and prospect information can be captured, shared, analyzed, and communicated more cost-effectively and in ways never before possible. This leads immediately to more productive ways to define potential target customer bases, the customer groups that compose them, and penetration rates by market segment for the firm's offerings.

Target Customers Change Over Time

The overriding objective of "emagineering" qualitative research—as opposed to quantitative—is to find out what leading-edge and early-adopter customers want from their suppliers before the competition offers it. High-tech marketers have found that new buyers within a specific target customer base may change many times over the often-short product life cycles of their offerings. As illustrated in Figure 4-2, they may begin selling to experimentalists within corporate data centers. *Experimentalists* are the customers who have the budget, time, and inclination to try newly developed advanced technologies as soon as possible, even before they are mature enough for wide distribution.

However, for the high-tech supplier's offering to be successful, the marketers need to be able to communicate the benefits substantiated by the early-acquiring experimentalists to "emagineering"-driven leaders.

Figure 4-2 A high-tech supplier's view of its target customer base.

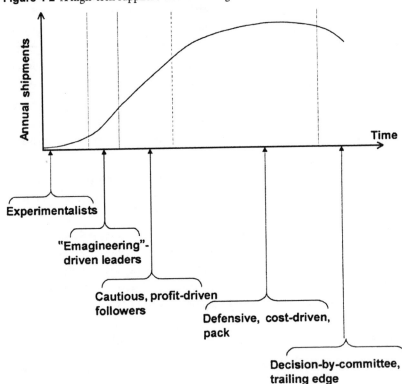

• In this planning exercise, the high-tech supplier has projected its annual shipments versus time by correlating when prospects with different buying profiles will begin their acquisitions combined with follow-on orders from earlier customers

"Emagineering"-driven *leaders* are savvy consumers who understand technology—in other words, technology executives. If this group begins acquiring the high-tech supplier's offering and deploying it with good results, the product will earn positive "buzz" within the industry. The high-tech marketers can expect sales to grow at an increasing rate as cautious, profit-driven *followers* tag along behind their traditional leaders.

Even with the same offering and selling to the same target customer base—data-center managers in this example—the high-tech supplier's marketers have had to change their approach to communicate to three different groups of decision makers. Moreover, before the offering is retired, the marketers will identify more potential groups with different buying agendas but all within the same target customer base.

Without an accurate, ongoing method of gathering information about how first-time buying criteria are changing, the high-tech supplier would not be able to market the offering effectively throughout its entire product life cycle. It would provide many openings for competitors to take advantage of in its marketing and product-improvement programs. It could expect that these competitors would gain share by exploiting unidentified flaws in its product-management efforts.

A successful product rollout in nontechnology industries will follow the same pattern of progressing from early adopters to trailing-edge customer bases. While the characteristics of buyers within different markets vary, what remains constant across industries is the dynamic of continuous change in buying groups. Therefore, every winner corporation will monitor changes in its target customer base continuously in order to avoid being left behind as its customers move ahead.

Learn Your Customers' Needs—then Act

The next marketing agenda item then becomes to determine which target customer bases the company should pursue actively, which customer bases will seek it out regardless of the firm's marketing efforts, and which it should ignore for the time being.

The science of "emagineering" is to use analytical applications to define the business's different target customer bases by common buying behavior, demographics, and any other significant characteristics. Then each segment of the target customer base can be scrutinized for profitability and growth rates. Technology executives understand that an organization has the ability to make the best marketing decisions when it defines multiple customer bases that it wishes to service based on their commonality.

The art of "emagineering" is to develop and execute marketing programs to obtain more revenue and increase profitability from specific target customer bases. This requires knowing the target customer bases well enough to propose intelligent, creative experiments.

An excellent example of knowing a target customer market well enough to take a leadership position with an experiment is American Airlines converting its frequent-flyer upgrade coupons to electronic records while archrival United Airlines stayed with paper. In the marketing war between these two airlines, each wants to own the largest share of full-fare travelers. Why? Each airline's analysis of its customer base shows that passengers who are willing to pay the full posted fare, normally traveling on business, are the most profitable—even though they also change their reservations most frequently. These customers appreciate being treated with extra comforts whenever possible and will select airlines based on the availability of such perks. However, their employers typically allow them to pay full-fare prices only for coach seats, not for business or first class. Therefore, both American and United offer paper coupons (either for free or at a nominal price) to allow individuals who purchase full-fare coach tickets to upgrade to business and first class on an as-available basis. However, harried executives with business—not traveling logistics—on their minds often misplace or lose the paper coupons.

Recognizing the frustration of customers at not having upgrade coupons with them when they needed them, American stored the upgrades as electronic credits in its global computer system so that they would always be available on demand at check-in. United either did not think of this or did not have the information infrastructure necessary to experiment with this capability. For whatever reason, it could not quickly match American's customer service in this area. Electronic upgrade records may seem like a "little thing" compared with more traditional competition points for airlines, but American's clever extension of its passenger information systems—along with other initiatives—has contributed to American's capture of a greater share of target high-profit customers at United's expense.

To do it justice, United also deserves its due. As one of the first airlines to put its membership rewards program benefits online, it gained customer loyalty and share at the expense of other airlines—and much of this loyalty remained even after the others caught up and United experienced extraordinary flight disruptions in 2000–2001.

Both American and United have shown excellence in the marketing art of "emagineering." Both airlines implemented novel marketing programs that neither their customers had seen nor competitors had launched before. Good art is the result of doing something new and imaginative in a form that is appreciated by those who are touched by it. This definition fits the first-strike marketing programs based on advanced technology of both American and United in their most recent fights for high-profit frequent business travelers.

Continuously Monitoring the Company's Customers

Technology executives intrinsically understand that servicing the key customers of their companies is of the utmost importance. This means not just meeting customers' basic requirements but also delighting them with unanticipated benefits. A winner organization wants its current customers to be so happy that they will tell others how satisfied they are with the use of its offerings and the support that it provides. The "buzz" generated by delighted customers is the best means of increasing market share in the long term and inducing consumers who were not even targeted originally to try a firm's offerings.

Therefore, organizations managing with "emagineering" spend considerable resources on continuously measuring changes in their target customer base's attitudes and buying behavior. They measure buying criteria and supplier evaluation changes among their customers, prospective customers, and competitors' customers. Vital to success for technology executives is having a continuous feedback loop that tracks the target customer base's size and characteristics, buying preferences and behaviors, and how these are changing. Against this information flow, corporate executives must monitor in detail share changes and preferences in both their and their competitors' positions.

To be of real value to technology executives, the feedback loop must be designed and operated to understand the cause, effect, and time-delay issues that result from the initiation of "emagineering" projects. This means that the loop must be able to measure the impact of initiatives based on the use of advanced technologies in the perspective of other business environment dynamics.

Analyzing the results of the company's own "emagineering"-initiated actions provides short-term feedback and does not take into account competitive counterinitiatives or intermediate-term changes in economic conditions and customer preferences. Therefore, monitoring customer changes over longer periods of time is necessary to detect and measure underlying trends to which the company must be prepared to react and leverage.

Customer feedback loops should be used by organizations of all types, including business-to-business suppliers, business-to-consumer suppliers, nonprofit charities, large and small businesses, and government agencies. All that is necessary is to identify individuals who can respond credibly to research surveys.

Using advanced technologies, the information that is gathered can be stored, analyzed, and acted on at the enterprise-level, not just by line of business or isolated in an individual department. When key customer information is available to the most senior executives of a corporation, they will have the leading indicators they need to make the moves necessary to meet customer needs before their markets move away from them.

The following is a general listing of customer characteristics that technology executives might wish to monitor—and why:

1. *What are the respondent's background, position, experience, and responsibilities?* How customer demographics change over time can be extremely important. For example, Ford Motor Company recently discovered that a new release of its low-end Escort appealed not just to price-conscious shoppers but also to an unexpected and large prospect group—young males who wanted to customize their car dramatically.

2. *What products or services similar to what the firm offers has the respondent purchased, used, or influenced the acquisition of over the previous year?* Is the respondent a customer, a competitor's customer, or a prospect? Does the respondent influence others in their buying decisions or merely use the offerings quietly?

3. *What are the most important driving factors motivating the respondent to use, or possibly use, the firm's offering?* For example, do members of the target customer base buy, say, canned soup because they believe that it

is highly nutritious compared with other foods, they find it faster to prepare than alternative luncheon items, or they use it as a premade sauce for cooking? How does this change through the seasons of the year or correlate with where the respondent lives? Use advanced analytical systems to correlate motivation with type of respondent.

4. *What are the decision criteria used for selecting an offering? Why? How are these related to the key factors motivating purchase and use?* Does the respondent value price over quality? Can technology executives determine how these motivational factors change when the economy is improving versus when it is in a downturn? Gillette, for example, claims the quality position in shaving devices but states that it loses market share in many countries when the unemployment rate goes up.

5. *How does the respondent perceive the comparative value offerings of all the alternative options available? Are these perceptions based on firsthand experience or communications from third-party influences? How have the different competitors' offerings and value propositions changed over the last several months?* Using all the buyer's decision-making criteria—ease of purchase, low price, quality of product, supplier reputation, previous experience with the product, design of the product, customer support reputation, etc., map the firm's position against that of competitors. Try to reposition the company's offering to meet the changing requirements of the majority of buyers in the target customer base before the competition. For example, when the major soda suppliers found that their leading-edge customers were buying bottled water and urging their friends to do so, they quickly developed strategies to meet this emerging market dynamic ahead of new entrants as well as their traditional competitors.

6. *What sources of information does the respondent use to keep abreast of and learn more about the company's offerings?* The organization's marketing executives need to know what the most credible channels of communication are, especially when electronic communications are changing so dramatically how firms and their customers are establishing two-way dialogues. Automobile dealers have faced this challenge over the last several years as customers have gone to the Web to obtain the type of pricing information that provides them with stronger bargaining positions.

7. *What could the company do to add greater value to its offering?* If possible, the company should describe to the respondent enhancements

that it is considering making or ones that it thinks its competitors might be considering making to gauge the respondent's receptiveness in terms of relevance and desirability. The best new product ideas come from customers—and these ideas change over time as the business and its competitors improve their offerings.

8. *What additional messages would the respondent want to send directly to the chief executive officer of the corporation conducting the survey?* Customers often will praise an organization as well as criticize it when given a chance. Open-ended questions whose replies are categorized with advanced-technology tools provide executives with many insights into the future direction of their target customer base and what it expects from the company.

Naturally, the questions used in each company's feedback loop must be customized to meet the company's specific needs. In addition, individual firms will have their preferred research methods, such as telephone, mail, focus group, advisory panels, or in-person surveys.

The fundamental requirement for knowing the company's customers well enough to gain market share, however, is to monitor *changes* in the customer base *continuously*, leverage any and all opportunities, and communicate these changes electronically throughout the organization.

Gathering Qualitative Information as Well as Quantitative Data

Most of the installed customer and prospect marketing information support systems in traditional companies are passive. That is, they collect and store quantitative data based on individual transactions or interactions, such as an initial request for product brochures or a sales call, but are not designed to alert management about fundamental customer-preference changes. Straightforward historical information does not provide the knowledge necessary for anticipating significant consumer trends.

Corporate marketers need to obtain much more qualitative information—facts that cannot be quantified reliably in traditional computer databases—from their customers concerning what economic and business issues they are facing, what factors may put them into a buying mode, what alternative solutions to the firm's offerings they are considering, what constructive advice they have for the company to improve its offerings, and so on. Much of these data are in the form of stories told as opposed to numbers recorded. However, it is the richness of qualitative data that, when combined with the quantitative (numbers) data collected by customer-facing information systems, can provide executives with the full-view marketing insights they need.

With the information age characterized by large amounts of personal opinion swapping over omnipresent cellphones and through e-mail (especially with the convenience of the "Forward" command) and rapid dissemination of information through broadcast messages, customer groupings are more uniform than ever. As a result, sample sizes for obtaining qualitative opinions and buying behaviors can be much smaller than a decade ago and still be accurate. Many companies have found (as hard as it may be to believe for statistics students) that proactively and correctly polling in-depth as few as 20 demographically similar users—that is, users who constitute a market *cell*—can lead to greater insights into a business's customers and where they are going than sampling hundreds of users and asking them what purchases they have made recently.

The rapid communication of information also means that customer opinions and preferences can change much faster than in the past. Therefore, corporations that rely on older information systems that were well known for providing statistically accurate reports based on reams of quantitative data will soon find that their knowledge of their customers is out of date and that acting on it will lead to making incorrect decisions.

In the world of "emagineering," which assumes rapid change, qualitative research is more important than ever. Qualitative research provides answers to the important strategic questions of why and when customers are changing their buying behaviors. Qualitative research becomes technology executives' telescope to see into the distance and prepare for customer change before it can become overwhelming.

Methods of Gathering Qualitative Information on Emerging Trends

Traditional means of gathering forward-looking marketing information are based on telephone, mail, and face-to-face surveys; focus groups;

customer advisory panels; and sales representatives' customer stories. Now, with most business customers and consumers being "wired," important marketing data about emerging trends can be collected proactively from additional sources and turned into actionable information more quickly with advanced analysis tools.

To know their customers better, technology executives have taken on the objective of getting their customers to go online regularly and tell them honestly both about themselves and about what they like and do not like about their companies' products. There are many methods to do so. For example, many high-tech companies have found that an effective method for obtaining current information on what their customers think about them is to establish user chat areas on the Internet. Business staff members monitor the typed conversations of users and prospects in an electronic chat room, respond to comments when appropriate (politely, and without a defensive manner), and provide follow-up answers to questions when asked. The information obtained from chat room sessions is summarized and forwarded to the appropriate marketing executives on a regular basis.

Consumer goods companies, such as beverage and cereal manufacturers, are offering incentives such as coupons and giveaways to customers who will visit their Web sites and participate in market surveys. Their reasoning is that their wired customers represent the leading edge and can give them the first clues as to how consumer tastes and buying behaviors are changing. Their unwired customers are most likely to follow these leaders.

Another approach to proactively gather marketing insights is to have a short survey appear after a prospect or customer has finished visiting a company's Web site. The results of such completed surveys, analyzed in conjunction with the individual's actions at the Web site, can quickly tell marketers which messages and product offerings are being received positively by prospects and customers.

A tactic used widely by many companies and in many industries, such as *Business Week* (a unit of the McGraw-Hill Companies) in business magazine publishing, is to create a virtual customer advisory board with demographics parallel to the company's target customer base and poll the members (or subsets of its members when appropriate) regularly regarding their opinions on the corporation's offerings. While this approach often uses traditional, general question-and-answer responses that could have been conducted using paper instead of computer screens, with e-mail these surveys can be conducted quickly and cost-effectively to learn what customers think about many more current, specific aspects of the business and its offerings. Providing rewards to participants and allowing for anonymous responses can increase both response rates and honesty levels appreciably.

A technique at the core of many proactive intelligence-gathering programs is to send large numbers of e-mails based on purchased lists to find competitors' customers and ask them about what they like about the competitor and do not like about your company. This effort is likely to result in a relatively small percentage of responses—but a large number of unexpected insights. The technique should be used judiciously, however, because many e-mail users consider mass e-mails (even those sent for research rather than for advertising purposes) to be "spam"— irritating, inconsiderate, junk e-mail. Other e-mail recipients, however, will be pleased to have been given an opportunity to voice their opinion on a subject with which they have experience. As with any direct-mail campaign, the more targeted the mailing list, the better are the customer responses.

An additional method is to engage a firm that specializes in Web-based surveys and focus groups to perform its magic in identifying the appropriate individuals to survey and coaxing them to participate in an online market research session.

Finally, a relatively new practice is to track the Web sites customers have visited in addition to the company's. However, this last method is losing favor rapidly (and rightfully so) due to invasion-of-privacy concerns.

Analyzing Your Target Customers

In the past, most executives assumed that they knew the answers to many of the most important questions about who their customers are and what they are thinking based on their customer visits or the results of periodic market research efforts. However, experience has proven that instinct and quantitative reports alone are not enough to determine what the majority of customers will want in the near to intermediate term.

In the Competitive Economy, corporate executives are recognizing that what end-user customers will tell a supplier's representative typically is polite (unless there is a major problem) but often quite different from what they really think. Therefore, corporations must use information systems that correlate what customers say they are going to do with what they actually do in order to accurately assess changes in their marketplaces. In addition, corporate executives of global companies have found that their customers around the world represent such a diversity of needs that they must have a methodology for sorting through both the common and conflicting requirements.

By using applications that analyze customers' transactions, many banks have been startled to learn that only 20 percent of their retail customers account for over 80 percent of their profits. Operationally, this means that 80 percent of a bank's customers are close to breakeven or actually cost the bank money to attract and service. The same type of analysis has been used in many other industries over time and shows similar results—a fraction of a firm's customers frequently account for the vast majority of its profits. The use of advanced technologies for performing customer—as opposed to product—profitability analysis has shocked many corporate executives into reexamining who their top customers really are and how to best market to and service them.

Sophisticated analysis applications can now group customers by common buying patterns and behavior. Armed with this information, businesses can identify and deliver appropriate messages more cost-effectively to their "most likely to buy a specific product" target customer bases. In the extreme, firms are terminating their business relationships with customer groups that are simply too expensive to service and support. Fidelity Investments is one pioneering company that uses its extensive knowledge of its customers both to pinpoint its mailing campaigns to the most likely prospects and to drop specific high-cost, money-losing customers from its telephone support systems.

However, customer analysis systems cannot be static and also help a business grow profitably. They must be complemented by customer relationship management (CRM) systems. CRM systems create a database of all customer interactions—not just purchase transactions—from the first contact with a prospect onward. If the customer is another business, such systems also track the multiple individuals within the customer organization who act as different points of contact for the supplier and their roles in the purchasing process.

The clear conclusion is that enterprise-level advanced technologies can assist corporations in storing, analyzing, and reporting data that provide a comprehensive description of their customers and how they are changing. Having this capability is a base-level requirement in the information-age Competitive Economy for making the crucial decisions that will allow a company to obtain and maintain the largest share of its market.

Customer-Focused Goal Setting Is Key

Knowing and analyzing the company's customer base now provide a firm basis for setting customer-focused goals. And having the company's goals the same as those of its customers is the only way to move customers to love the company for the long term.

Costco, the large warehouse club retailer, has found that its target customers want high-quality products at the lowest prices possible. These customers expect to spend well over $100 per visit and will trust that they will be offered everyday prices that are lower than other retailers' sales prices. They do not want to be treated to piano music, carpeted aisles, or pushy sales assistants while they are in the store, but they do want wide aisles and big carts. They do not want a wide range of merchandise to select from, but they do want a continuously changing lineup of goods, including products that are not available from other local retailers.

Knowing its customers, Costco has set operational goals that meet their particular needs. It operates on less than a 10 percent markup to assure customers that they are getting excellent value. New products line the entrance area that every customer must pass, and employees busily hand out samples of new foods in the grocery section. Waterford crystal, filet mignon, home entertainment centers, top-of-the-line personal computers, out-of-season fruits, and brand-name tires—all items that appeal to those with money to spend—are available. And yes, Costco maintains a database of customer purchases by item, date, and store to better learn what its customers actually will buy. By offering its target customers what they want and continuously improving its operational capabilities, Costco has built an excellent reputation with a specific group of customers who are very loyal to it. They believe that Costco's goals and their goals are the same.

Another approach to obtaining customer-focused operational excellence is to set a quantitative goal against which line managers can be measured. A well-known initiative for using measurement systems successfully to achieve customer-focused results is General Electric's Six Sigma quality program. The Six Sigma program set a concrete goal for the maximum number of defects that GE would accept in both its own and its suppliers' products. To achieve this goal, processes required for creating GE products were redesigned to meet Six Sigma objectives, even if they increased labor and capital costs or limited output quantities. In other words, GE management made clear that costs could go up and orders could be backlogged, but the quality goal had to be met to satisfy customer expectations.

Inteconnetions: The Art of Loving Your Customers

Once a company has profiled and prioritized the customers it wants to service, one of the most critical, creative, and difficult aspects of "emagineering" comes into play. The technology executives must answer the pressing questions of what new products, services, support offerings, and business-policy improvements can they make to obtain greater revenues by meeting both the stated and implicit needs of these target customers. The three critical follow-on questions include

- How fast will the target customers demand or accept changes in the business's offerings and policies?
- What first-strike capabilities can the corporation make that its competitors cannot match for at least 2 to 3 years?
- What actions are the competitors taking that might cause the company's own traditional customer base to desert it if the company does not counter quickly?

The objective of this aspect of the "emagineering" effort is to connect where the company is *today* with where it should be *tomorrow*. Executives who have been assigned the task of applying their imaginations and experience to planning the future of their company and its industry should brainstorm a series of interconnections based on answers to the preceding questions. "Emagineering"-based interconnections should be natural progressions of the current business made possible by deploying advanced technologies—not major leaps of strategy. Think evolution, not revolution.

The primary goal of "emagineering" interconnections is to use technology to make a successful business even more successful. The secondary goal is to assist executives in thinking about ways to focus on new target customer demographics and possibly to create new lines of business. In addition, the reason technology executives call these forward-looking plans *interconnections* is to assure the rest of the organization that the ongoing deployment of new information systems to increase market value and act as a catalyst for corporate improvements will not degenerate into the basis for never-ending management flip-flops.

An Amazon.com or an eBay could be founded because traditional executives in the book retail and auction industries did not make the imagination-based interconnections between their core businesses and how newly developed technology could be used to serve their existing customers. While a few visionaries may have imagined the possibilities, they did not get the needed support from their organizations to move forward and take advantage of the new opportunities that were being created during this period of rapid technology change and customer stratification.

Amazon.com and eBay, by contrast, built their entire businesses from the ground up by using recently developed technologies to satisfy the unmet needs of a specific but as yet unrecognized group of customers. The leaders and visionaries of these corporations did not need to get support from any other parts of their organizations—the organization itself was the vision. Once they were successful with one class of products sold to one target customer base, they then grew dramatically by building interconnections that allowed them to expand both their product offerings and the number and types of target customer bases to which they would attempt to appeal.

We can learn a lot about how to create successful "emagineering" interconnections from the short, well-publicized history of a company that is still either a future global business giant or disaster in progress—Amazon.com. Amazon.com (Amazon) is a company that overcame the key challenge of first identifying a significant underserved target customer base—one that book retailing industry veterans did not even notice as potentially significant—and then, in just the last few years, expanding its revenues through the skillful creation of customer-focused interconnections.

Amazon's initial target customers were computer geeks around the world who could not get the technical books they wanted at their local bookstores, especially in Europe and Asia, but did have access to the Internet. A unique market dynamic of this target customer base was that with numerous new books in the field of computer science being published each week, out-of-date mail-order catalogues could not possibly meet their needs, nor could they haunt the local bookstore due to their hectic workloads.

However, Jeff Bezos, Amazon's founder, was not the only entrepreneur to identify the market opportunity to sell computer science books over the Internet. Amazon had to build its infrastructure and support services to be the best at serving its target customers' wants before the other 20 or so startups that were focusing on the same opportunity. Quite frankly, Amazon executed this task excellently.

On the other hand, leading established book retailers, such as Barnes and Noble and Borders, simply did not recognize computer professionals and enthusiasts as a growing and significant market with needs that were different from those of their traditional buyers of bestsellers, classics, and how-to books. Even if they had, it is doubtful they would have changed their business processes to meet this one-of-many market group's unique needs. Why? They would not want to discourage potential customers from going to their stores—such an action would be the exact opposite of good retailing practice. In addition, they did not have the technology and business expertise to build a high-quality, customer-touching online store.

Starting from its one specific target customer base focus of computer science book readers, Amazon was able to branch out to capture the numerous other types of customers who buy at traditional bookstores as well as expand its systems to meet the needs of consumers in parallel areas such as CDs, videos, video and software games, and others.

Amazon, like Dell, initially was misunderstood by both its competitors and individuals in the customer bases it was not focusing on capturing. These groups believed that Amazon must have become a significant player in the book industry because it was offering lower prices on books than alternative suppliers.

The key point that noncustomers did not understand about Amazon-the-industry-disrupter is that with shipping charges, its prices were comparable with what one would have to pay at a bricks-and-mortar bookstore—if the bookstore had the book. However, since the bookstore often did not have the computer science book the prospective customer was interested in buying, certainly did not advertise what the most popular computer science books were, rarely featured what it thought would be the hot books of the week, and could not be visited in a few spare minutes from the office or home, these traditional retailers did not meet the unique service—as opposed to price—needs of the emerging marketplace of computer science readers.

Having the lowest price has been a relatively minor characteristic of successful Internet retail ("e-tailer") operations. The real advantages of winner Internet retailers come from meeting the convenience needs of their target customer bases and then building even more convenience features over time.

In retrospect, Amazon's vision of creating interconnections from the then-current general book retailing business model to a better one for computer science readers seems logical and straightforward. In reality, it required understanding its target customer base's unique and unmet requirements accurately as well as having an appreciation for what information technology could and could not do at every point in time in order to execute successfully against the vision.

Until the advent of Web-browser technologies on PCs, Amazon simply could not have been established. After the technology to build Amazon's customer-focused information infrastructure was available in the marketplace, creating Amazon's Web site and improving it continuously—typically without the benefit of following the pioneering paths of others—required its technology executives to truly understand and be willing to act to meet the changing, expanding needs of their customers.

The Difficulty of Maintaining Customer Focus

While the art of "emagineering" interconnections seems logical, it is different from how too many traditional executives approach the process of expanding their businesses. The reason is that there is always a temptation at the beginning of any strategy project to plan for big—really big—changes. The "it must be BIG" syndrome is evident when strategy meetings are held and the number one question is invariably, "What business should we be in 3 years from now?"—not "How can we serve our customers better tomorrow?"

For large, profitable global corporations that are arrogant enough to feel confident in their answers to this question, the next logical question will be, "Whom can we acquire or partner with to get into that business quickly?" Yet few such acquisitions provide a benefit to the corporation's customers.

For example, when General Motors (GM) acquired Electronic Data Systems (EDS), there was an assumption that EDS would overhaul GM's back-end processes, resulting in both lower internal overhead costs and shorter development cycles. Yet both these objectives proved too far removed from directly servicing GM's target car-buying customers to add much value to GM. As a result, GM's executives soon lost sight of why they had acquired EDS. EDS executives worked diligently on GM's internal back-office processes with no visible benefits to typical automobile buyers. (One of EDS's proudest achievements early on that it talked about publicly was how it had streamlined the processes for and lowered the cost of managing the insurance benefits GM provided to its employees. It is doubtful that this really increased GM's customers' delight when buying a new car.) EDS and GM middle managers were clashing continuously over different objectives and work cultures without a common ground on which to work together. As a result, the planned-for beat-the-competition benefits of the acquisition never materialized.

Eventually GM realized that it was better off buying services from an independent EDS than trying to integrate EDS's in-house information systems organization into the existing GM structure and spun it out of the corporation.

GM thought "big." It let its imagination work overtime when it envisioned the benefits of acquiring EDS. GM's executives probably thought that by bringing EDS in-house as a wholly owned subsidiary, they would never again have to do the hard work of evaluating how advanced technologies should be deployed in conjunction with new, customer-delighting business processes or make the tradeoffs necessary to lower their internal information systems costs. As the results show, they were terribly wrong.

In comparison, when PepsiCo or Coca-Cola makes an acquisition, the key question appears to be, "What will our customers want to drink over the next 2 to 3 years?" These companies use advanced-technology products to analyze their customers' buying behaviors and evaluate what types of drinks are emerging as winners in the opinion of their most likely to lead the pack customers. If their customers are drinking more fruit juices, they will acquire a leading brand. If it is bottled water, high-end coffees, or sports drinks, they evaluate these potential growth opportunities. Moreover, when they make an acquisition, they use their extensive asset of information systems to add value to the marketing, manufacturing, and distribution processes.

A Repository of Ideas

Building customer-focused interconnections is a continuous process—not a once-a-year planning session. It requires a corporation to build a repository of ideas and options that matches different types of customers against the opportunities now available to improve both subtly and significantly the company's products, services, and support for them. These serve-the-target-customer-base ideas can come from many sources—from current customers, from prospects who choose a competitor's offering, from distributors, from suppliers, from industry pundits, from the media, and even from friends and family.

Experiments generally are built on what appear to be the most promising business ideas. However, no ideas should ever be discarded—even ideas that seem to be totally ludicrous at first may have tremendous value when analyzed from a different perspective. Who would have thought that the world would prefer to drink sweet, black, fizzy water over most other beverages until Coca-Cola pioneered its concoction in countries around the world? Or that a talking mouse could win the entertainment dollars of billions of individuals until Disney created an entertainment empire around Mickey Mouse? Ideas that may appear foolish or worthless to internal executives often prove smart and valuable to customers.

An excellent example of a company that seems to never run out of ideas on which to build experiments is Dow Jones. Starting well before the Internet became popular, Dow Jones has experimented continuously with ways to distribute both its own content and complementary information from other sources to its target customers for a fee. Some experiments are successful; many are not. However, its ongoing process of experimentation based on ideas in its repository helps retain the loyalty of its key customers. And loyal customers are those who love their supplier as much as their supplier loves them.

Lessons Learned from Experience

Using advanced information systems, companies can now know objectively and comprehensively who their customers are as well as their wants and needs from their businesses. Any "emagineering" effort that strays away from a single-minded focus on methods and capabilities to improve customer relationships directly based on this knowledge has a high probability of failing.

Using new technomarket research techniques, companies can cost-effectively gather more qualitative and quantitative marketing information about their customers than ever before. It is vital to gather qualitative input from leading-edge customers to determine how their preferences may be changing and combine this with quantitative data to determine if they really took the actions they said they would. Analysis software can be used to verify such correlations and to identify accurately customer groupings and common buying behaviors that are not readily apparent.

Customers must be analyzed and grouped based on their profitability to the company. The company can then focus its attention on better understanding the particular needs of the most profitable customer groups and act to service them better. Unprofitable customers should be either dropped or provided with less service and support.

A company's target customer base is not static. It changes over time as new businesses or individuals enter the base and others leave. To respond to these changes, a company must monitor its customer base continuously to understand what groups of buyers are included, their buying behaviors, their attitudes about all the suppliers in the market, and their suggestions as to how the company could service and support them better. Advanced information systems should be used to analyze this market data—much of which will be qualitative in nature.

A company's operational goals and objectives should be the same as those of its customers. That is, what customers want a company to provide it with should be the same products, services, and business policies that the company wants to provide. The greater the alignment of customer and company goals, the more likely the company will have the largest market share of its chosen target customer base.

To better service its customers and meet their changing needs, technology executives focus on creating evolutionary interconnections between the products and services their companies currently provide their customers with and what offerings they can and should make available in the future. Advanced technologies have been proven to allow companies to more quickly make the incremental changes necessary to remain aligned with expanding customer requirements.

Never minimize the difficulty of keeping executives focused on knowing and better serving their companies' customers. The daily task of running business operations distracts most corporate executives from thinking about their companies' overall customer bases. Advanced technologies should be used to update on a regular basis all corporate executives about who their customers are and how the mix is changing. After this profile-of-our-customer information has been distributed properly, companies should actively solicit suggestions from employees throughout their organizations about improvements they could make to better support their customers.

Knowing the company's most important customer types and creating a repository of ideas of possible interconnections between how they are serviced today and means by which they could be better supported in the future lay the foundation for "emagineering"-based change.

Competency 5: Demanding Customer-Focused Internal Operational Excellence

O NE OF THE GREATEST FLAWS in most businesses' information systems today is the different goals of front-end customer-focused applications versus back-end production applications. Front-end customer systems generally are designed to safely capture customer transactions to be acted on in the future, and the back-end systems are designed to produce goods to go into a warehouse or schedule a service as inexpensively as possible.

All one has to do to observe this issue is order a product over the Internet. One places an order with a leading supplier, and it is generally confirmed with an e-mail from the company within seconds. This is great. However, you have only been dealing with the front-end customer-touching system. The back-end production system may not schedule pickup of the items on your order for another day. In fact, the supplier actually may be out of stock on your order but could not tell you at the time you placed your order. As a result, experienced Internet buyers know to wait until they receive a second e-mail from their online retailer telling them the product has been shipped and providing a tracking code before they can feel confident that they actually have made a purchase. The same separation between front- and back-end systems occurs in every industry, including manufacturing, banking, transportation, hospitality, etc., and is not just limited to Internet-initiated transactions.

Technology executives understand that one of their tasks is to make back-end production business processes complementary and subordinate to front-end customer-touching applications. "Emagineering" the tight linkage that makes internal production systems responsive to customers is critical to obtaining the *operational excellence* required to be a winner corporation.

Operational excellence has two components. First, it requires *operational effectiveness*—the external face of a business, that is, how well it works with customers and prospects. The second component is *operational efficiency*—producing the right product at the right price and delivering it to the right location at the right time.

Operational Effectiveness

The technology executive's definition of successful *operational effectiveness is meeting the needs of the company's target customer base better than the competition*. Operational effectiveness starts by ensuring that customers and prospects are delighted each time they communicate or conduct a transaction with the company.

Improving operational effectiveness requires first gathering as much knowledge as possible about the business's target customers, as described in Chapter 4. Once gathered, target-customer information must be made available to all the appropriate members of the organization so that they can make better operational decisions. When a company ensures that both business-focused and information systems managers have a common understanding of the company's customers, the organization substantially increases the ability of these groups to work constructively together.

Knowing the customer better is accomplished by monitoring interactions—both transactions and communications—with customers and prospects, analyzing the results of these exchanges, obtaining market research insights as to where the customers are going (as opposed to where they have been), and then projecting buying trends and probable future changes in market dynamics. Armed with this information, corporate executives can proactively manage their business operations to meet the target customer base's continuously changing needs and preferences more effectively. Positioning a company and its offerings to where the market is going, not where it has been, using advanced technology is a key to long-term success.

There have been many breakthroughs in recent years in the use of advanced technologies to increase a company's operational effectiveness. For example, today's best Web sites provide a personal Web page—a "my [Company Name]" page. This page is personalized for the user, whom the Web site individually acknowledges when the customer logs on after presenting a unique identification code. At a portal site, the personal page may contain information about the price of specific stocks the user is tracking or recent news about a favorite sports team. For an authorized business buyer entering a vetted supplier's Web site, the personal page may include the status of current open orders and the discount prices on items covered under a master purchase agreement.

Another example of operational effectiveness and how it is related to operational efficiency is the ability to customize products and services for specific customers. For example, Ben and Jerry's makes many flavors of ice cream in a batch process—all the cream, milk, sugar, flavorings, and mix-ins are turned into different flavors of ice cream at one of its factories in Vermont. However, as the ice cream flows out the production line, Ben and Jerry's has learned that it must be flexible enough to package it in different-sized containers for different types of customers. In the United States, where consumers have large freezers, the ice cream is shipped in its trademark pint cartons. Its subsidiary in Japan, where households have small refrigerators with tiny freezers, requires packaging in small single-serving cartons. On the other hand, the warehouse clubs in the United States demand that Ben and Jerry's ice cream be packaged in 1-gallon containers so that they can differentiate their offering from those of traditional retailers and sell at a lower unit price. And of course, Ben and Jerry's retail stores demand large 5-gallon containers for stocking and scooping efficiency. To achieve operational effectiveness excellence, Ben and Jerry's must be able to customize how it packages its base product without ever penalizing any group of customers. And the customer orders must drive the production process, not the other way around.

To achieve customer-delighting capabilities requires that the organization's internal information systems support its customer-touching systems. These internal systems should be invisible to the outside. However, the "emagineering"-created benefits—especially market nimbleness and the foresight to change offerings and policies to match what customers and prospects want before they start evaluating alternative suppliers—will be highly visible.

Operational Efficiency

Internal *operational efficiency* comes from improving the business processes over time for producing, selling, and delivering products, services, and support as measured by

- *Cost*—Lower is better. While industrial engineers have spent decades taking the costs out of the direct manufacture of goods, there are still plenty of costs that can be taken out of the delivery of services, administrative overhead, product movement through an ecosystem, direct selling of complex products, etc.
- *Cycle times*—Faster is better. Cycle-time efficiency improvements include the ability to deliver a product or service more quickly when requested by a customer, to respond rapidly to a customer request for information (such as clarifying a billing detail or a new product feature), and to develop new products in a shorter period of time. Note that one of the most significant improvements ever in consumer banking cycle times was provided by the technologies underlying automatic teller machines (ATMs). With the use of ATMs, a bank could accept a deposit or disperse cash within seconds of receiving a customer's request to make a transaction.
- *Quality*—Higher is better. Examples of higher-quality products include those which have more functionality than expected and last longer, more personalized and helpful customer services, and suppliers that proactively support the maintenance needs of their customers by fixing potential problems before they occur.

- *Requirements for dedicated assets*—Fewer is better. Each year companies want to produce more goods while lowering their required minimum levels of raw materials in inventory, finished goods on hand, and work-in-progress. They should at all times want to have fewer days accounts receivable outstanding—it is always best when the customer pays in full even before the product is delivered (think of your typical mail order catalogue, where an order is charged to your credit card days before it is shipped) or a service is rendered. And the ability to operate out of fewer physical locations is always viewed as a positive improvement by executives responsible for operations. Along the same line of prudent management, educational institutions generally would like to be able to deliver higher-quality learning experiences for students while spending less money on constructing buildings and equipping laboratories.

Efficiency improvements are the productivity gains that businesses always should be attempting to create within their organizations. The phrases "Work smarter" and "Do more with less" accompany the quest for greater internal productivity. Each new generation of information technology promises significant productivity gains—and many, when deployed intelligently, have delivered on the promise. In the 1990s, even academic economists sitting "way too far" from the workplace were able to correlate the first significant productivity increases in decades with industries that had intelligently adopted advanced technologies.

There are three types of operational efficiencies that advanced technologies can be used to improve. The first, and most significant today for increasing market value, is corporate-level efficiencies. "Emagineering" efforts are based on the concept of changing business processes to gain new corporate-level efficiencies. The second type of efficiency gain comes from individual productivity increases. Personal efficiency improvements mean doing the same task better and faster. Here, "emagineering" is used to determine how to get the right information to the right person at the right time so that that individual can make a better decision quicker. And the third efficiency gain, which will be the most important in the future, is business ecosystem efficiency improvements.

"Emagineering" Corporate Business-Process Improvements

Obviously, moving toward operational improvements on all fronts at the same time is an organizational impossibility. No organization has the necessary people and capital to work on more than a few projects simultaneously. Even if a company did have the money to tackle numerous concurrent projects, its managers and staff would not be able to work competently in the chaos of continuous process and policy changes. No matter how carefully prepared and detailed a business's change plans may be, too many process and policy errors would surface when the different but interrelated projects went live.

Recognizing that it is only practical to have a relatively few significant operational improvement projects going on at one time, technology executives have developed a straightforward method for prioritizing projects that are intended to improve a corporation's back-end processes. *Potential back-end operational improvement projects must be ranked by their level of impact on the target customer base.* That is, technology executives ask what activities the organization performs do its customers place a high value on and what projects should be initiated to improve the processes to deliver this value.

For example, in the upscale watch industry, the combination of design and functionality are extremely important for selling new timepieces successfully to customers. The ability to deliver watches that the target customer base believes look distinctive and can display more than just the time of day is critical. Therefore, projects for improving the speed of design processes and analysis of customer feedback regarding new models have a high priority. On the other hand, lowering cost is vital in the mass watch market. Suppliers to this market will move manufacturing and distribution cost-savings projects to the top of their priority list ahead of those which merely speed up the design process.

Figure 5-1 is an example of the normal process and its tasks for developing a new consumer product. Developing a new product requires a tremendous amount of intraorganizational and ecosystem collaboration (parts suppliers, distributors, customers) as well as the completion of a large number of specific tasks. Moreover, each task may have a large number of subtasks that often are technology-dependent. For example, the prototype creation task may require such tools as computer-aided design (CAD) and computer-aided engineering (CAE) to complete the subtasks of both designing the proposed new product and using preproduction computer simulations to test its durability to heat and pressure.

Improving a process is accomplished most typically by the continuous upgrading of the necessary task activities. Each task has the potential to be improved on by being made more effective or efficient. In addition, as the tasks are improved, so are operational results of the business process they support. For example, manufacturing companies

Figure 5-1 New product development business process.

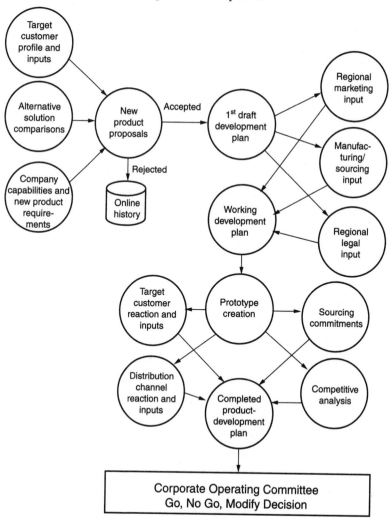

tend to upgrade their CAD equipment and software every 2 to 3 years. These regular technology upgrades improve the efficiency of the professionals who use the systems to meet their organizations' objectives for the design tasks.

However, technology executives will, when possible, redesign an entire business process when advanced technologies make it possible to do so. U.S. state governments, surprisingly, provide an excellent example of such an effort. In recent years, they have totally revamped how tolls are collected on many state-maintained turnpikes.

For years, the task of collecting tolls has been mostly manual. In the 1970s an attendant would hand a driver a paper ticket when entering a turnpike, and the driver would pay the required fee in cash to a toll taker when exiting. In the 1980s the task of handing the ticket to a driver was automated with the installation of ticket dispensers. This improved the efficiency of the task by lowering its costs—machines are less expensive and better suited than people for accomplishing such a basic and repetitive task.

In the late 1990s the entire toll process was rethought based on advanced technology and new business processes. The various turnpike authorities issued drivers who established an account with them a transponder—technically known as a radio-frequency identification device (RFID)—to place on their car windshields. An RFID sends a signal that can be read by receivers at a turnpike's entrances and exits as a car approaches. Once a receiver captures the RFID's identification number, it then sends a transaction message to a central computer. The computer calculates the driver's toll when the car exits and updates the owner's account. If the driver has authorized the turnpike to charge the tolls against a credit card, the transaction is then forwarded to a credit-card processor for payment.

The new system increases the effectiveness of serving the turnpike authorities' customers—drivers—by eliminating the long lines that can occur when they are backed up waiting to get a ticket or to pay and the inconvenience of paying with cash. It increases the efficiency of the turnpike authorities by reducing the need for toll takers as well as ensuring a higher level of toll-collection accuracy.

Experience has shown that the most significant beat-the-competition efficiency improvements come from changing business processes—not merely speeding up existing tasks.

Coordinating Interdependent Departmental Processes

Technology executives understand that the different departmental operations within their corporations that touch the customer must be tightly coordinated if they are to achieve their goal of operational excellence. Let's go back to the example of Dell Computer Corporation to illustrate the "emagineering" efforts required to establish first-class, consistent front-end operations—even when these operations must rely on multiple back-end support processes delivered by separate departments.

When Dell realized that its initial strategy of building a higher-quality product and supporting it with industry-leading service while charging a premium price over other direct-market personal computer (PC) suppliers was well received by small and medium-sized businesses, it had to build interdependent departmental business processes to support its excellent market position. Such processes included

- Preinstalling a broad range of software applications on customers' PCs at the factory because there was no dealer in the value chain to do so and the customer probably did not have the technical capability—and certainly did not want to incur the expense and hassle—of installing multiple programs. This new process had to be integrated with both the customer-ordering and hardware-manufacturing processes.

- Quickly building all hardware to order on a scale larger than any other computer manufacturer had ever attempted. This activity was necessary to support the customer-delight experience of providing each buyer with exactly the unique product he or she wanted and delivering it faster than a local dealer. To achieve this goal, the customer-ordering process had to flow directly into the production-scheduling and parts-procurement processes, and each of these had to be able to be updated daily.

- Aggregating all known technical problems, including component-interaction conflicts from different hardware and software component suppliers, building a knowledge base of Dell-unique problems, and making this information available to a well-trained support staff in an easy-to-understand script. In addition, the support staff had to have this information instantaneously available to it 24 hours a day, 365 days a year to provide anytime support. The engineering, procurement (supplier relationships), and customer-service departments all needed to coordinate their information-gathering and dissemination processes to create this unified, corporate-wide knowledge base.

- Establishing the fastest product design-to-manufacture cycle in the industry in order to earn a reputation among its target customer base as the "hot PC company." This was especially important to value-conscious small and medium-sized business owners, who wanted to buy at the beginning of the life cycle of each PC generation in order to obtain the longest possible useful life from their PCs. To maintain a first-to-ship reputation, all customer-touching processes—from order entry to customer support—had to be updated in a coordinated way at the time each new product was released.

- Identifying the current and projecting the future buying behaviors of Dell's target customer base and delivering the appropriate marketing and advertising messages. This required combining the customer-ordering processes with the market-analysis processes.

It is important to recognize that while it was difficult for Dell to put all these interrelated business processes in place, once they were in place, they gave Dell competitive advantages so significant that other PC suppliers could not capture market share from Dell in its target customer space. To participate in the small and medium-sized business PC market, Dell's competitors have had to create unique value propositions to attract buyers who want different products and services than what Dell offers.

One of the reasons Dell's business processes, as described above, have brought such success to the company is that they were built across organizational lines and in a hyperlinked manner: A change in one process or the data and information against which the process operates has been supported throughout all the other processes. For example, a significant new chip release from Intel, such as introduction of the Pentium processor, or Microsoft's release of Windows XP requires Dell to make substantial changes in the information contained in all its business processes.

An emphasis on using advanced technology for improving the efficiency and effectiveness of customer-focused interdependent business processes sets winner companies apart from their traditional rivals who are always striving to catch up.

The Best Employees Demand the Best Technology Tools

Winner corporations want both enterprise-level operational excellence and personal operational excellence. An important reason that many corporations renew their information systems assets on a regular basis is that the best employees want and need the best tools and the knowledge of how to use them correctly. Just as soldiers know they have a better chance of survival and victory when they have superior weapons than their enemies, so do employees know intuitively that they cannot win the competitive battles for customer loyalty and high market valuations if they do not have superior information systems.

Here is a great story to help better understand this finding. It was widely reported that Bill Gates, the chairman of Microsoft and a genuine technology executive, was shown an IBM software laboratory in the late 1980s while negotiating plans for Microsoft and IBM to collaborate on the (now long forgotten) OS/2 operating system. Gates was appalled to see that the IBM programmers were using 3-year-old, dated PCs, whereas Microsoft's top programmers enjoyed the newest, most cutting-edge, and fastest systems available. Gates was told that IBM would not upgrade its programmers' computers until they had been fully depreciated—a 5-year period back in the information systems business dark ages of the 1980s. At that moment, Gates knew that he could beat IBM at the game of developing software for the PC. His reasoning was straightforward (and accurate): No self-respecting, talented programmer who really understood the personal computing operating environment would ever join IBM's development group with its antiquated PCs. Moreover, the programmers on IBM's development staff would take longer to produce the same-quality output as Microsoft's because of IBM's slower and less functional PCs

Gates' insight—that the best people must be armed with the best information tools—holds true for executives and staff in every company that is part of the Competitive Economy. Aggressive sales executives need access to comprehensive customer relationship management (CRM) tools. Insightful marketers need business intelligence (BI) systems to tell them what, when, and where customers are buying their products and those of their competitors in the global markets in which they all compete. Manufacturing and distribution executives and planners simply cannot be best in class with the use of a last-generation spreadsheet planning system when advanced supply-chain management (SCM) tools will allow them to optimize inventory, facilities, and employees both within their companies and with their ecosystem business partners. Top-notch administrative assistants demand scheduling and other office tools that allow them to continuously coordinate the activities and projects of the executives for whom they are responsible.

Technology executives are highly motivated to provide their direct reports with the information systems that will allow them to outperform their peers in competitive companies.

Knowledgeable People Achieve Operational Excellence

The typical product or service company is organized by grouping specialists together. At such firms, the salespeople all work with other salespeople, the engineers work with other engineers, the accountants are located with other accountants, and so on. Each department is rewarded by how well it achieves its own goals. Occasionally, managers are moved between departments and lines of business both to attempt to provide their perspective across the company on issues and to increase their own personal knowledge before being promoted to the rank of corporate-level executives. While companies go through phases where they reorganize or create some financial incentives in an effort to alleviate the hindrances to internal improvements created inherently by specialized functional organizations, they eventually revert back to the traditional functional structure for efficiency reasons.

Experienced technology executives recognize that most employees work best in the areas in which they are both most knowledgeable and experienced. In the real world, it is impractical in the long term to ask a "top gun" sales rep to lead the new product marketing department or a creative marketer to increase manufacturing productivity. Encouraging managers and staff to remain in those functional areas in which they are the most skilled and have a critical number of peers and superiors to both challenge and assist them is the most effective and efficient way to operate a corporate organization in the long term.

However, by formally grouping the outputs of each functional organization into interrelated business processes that are supported by advanced information systems, corporations can gain the best of both specialization and interdepartmental collaboration.

To improve collaboration for working toward common objectives, all departments must be educated on a regular basis about the company's primary target customer base: what it likes and does not like about the company today, how the senior executives believe its buying behaviors may be changing in the future, what the competitive environment dynamics are, and in which customer-focused growth areas the company should be participating in the future. With this knowledge, most of which can be communicated to employees in 2-hour sessions conducted twice a year, technology executives generally can gain the necessary organizational support for initiating and improving the collaborative, coordinated business processes that are necessary for operational excellence. The agenda for a typical meeting to educate employees about what they need to know for achieving operational excellence would include

1. A description of the company's key customers.
2. An analysis of how these customers' buying behaviors have changed in the past and how they are anticipated to change in the future.
   a. What they buy.
   b. Why they buy.
   c. Where they buy.
   d. When they buy.
3. A description of what the customers like about the company and its products.
4. A description of what customers do not like about the company and its products.
5. An analysis of how the company's competitors are positioned and why they win customers and the company loses.
6. An analysis of what roles are played by the company's distribution channels, market influencers, and other third parties in the customers' decision-making process.
7. An analysis of what new classes of buyers may begin evaluating the company's offerings in the future.

8. A description of what actions the company believes it must execute successfully in the future to obtain the largest market share among its target customers.
9. A list of suggestions and feedback from the employees.

Providing employees instant electronic access to corporate data about customers and operations and fast PCs with which to work is a mere information systems issue. Giving them the knowledge necessary to work smarter, coordinate their efforts as a team, and make truly better decisions is "emagineering" management for operational excellence.

Every New Information System Needs to Be Developed Strategically

To make advanced information systems tools work correctly for individuals and for the maximum benefit of their organizations, such information systems must be implemented as part of a comprehensive corporate strategy. That is, giving individuals access to new tools may improve their own productivity but will not increase the organization's overall operational effectiveness unless such tools are deployed as part of a coordinated effort.

For example, installing a customer relationship management (CRM) system to use merely as a central repository for data detailing contacts with individual customers is of little value. True, individual account managers may now have a more accurate picture of the company's interactions with their assigned customers, but this alone does not create market value. What are the account managers and other members of the company supposed to do with this new source of customer information? What strategic goal is the CRM system intended to achieve? Technology executives have found that deploying technology simply for technology's sake without a plan for meeting the corporation's strategic objectives is a relatively futile exercise.

It is often tempting—especially for departmental mangers—to install stand-alone information systems. Such systems often can increase the capabilities of specific work groups, but if the processes that are being automated are important to the business, they should be integrated with existing information systems and allow collaboration throughout the company and its ecosystem.

Let's illustrate. A midsized company that makes a custom component for machine tools has a repair department. This repair department typically receives 10 returned items per day. These returns may either be under warranty, in which case there is no charge, or out of warranty, for which the company charges a reasonable repair fee. The department manager put in a custom-developed spreadsheet on a PC to replace the existing paper-forms system to track all the product returns received, account for the work performed and the appropriate charges, and log when the products were shipped back to customers. This allowed the manager to supervise the department more effectively. In addition, it showed excellent initiative and technology skills on the part of the manager.

However, what it did not do is collect data in a systematic way on which parts were breaking—and why and when. This type of information is critical when a new product is released and the design engineers need to learn which components have the highest probability of failure. Moreover, the same information is important for evaluating the quality of the company's parts suppliers. Note also that this return-parts tracking system could not allow customers to use the Internet to check the status of their parts—so customer service was not improved, and the returns department still had to dedicate several hours of labor per day to answering phone inquiries.

Yes, the departmental system was an improvement over using paper forms scattered throughout the repair area to track returns. However, because it was not integrated into the company's information systems infrastructure, it did not create the higher level of value for the company that it could and should have.

While many operational applications start small—at either the individual or departmental level—technology executives know that if they are important to either the company's customers or for lowering costs within other departments, they must at some time be integrated with the enterprise-level information systems infrastructure. Therefore, it is extremely important to "emagineer" how each operational system, no matter how seemingly peripheral to the business's most important processes, can be leveraged to help the company achieve operational excellence.

Measuring to Motivate

Once established, interrelated business processes can be improved only if there is a measurement system in conjunction with them that emphasizes achieving excellence and then improving on it. Key to the operational effectiveness of a measurement system is that it must monitor the same factors that most greatly affect the company's target customer base—not just its internal productivity. Operational measurement systems must be designed to measure those critical characteristics of an organization's outputs which are important to its customers or they will become meaningless in terms of directing the actions of managers and their staffs.

Technology executives must determine what attributes of their products and services delight their target customer base and arrange to have these attributes measured. They should then set specific objectives for these attributes and monitor outcomes against these objectives. As measurement systems mature, they should have the capability to use advanced-technology systems to correlate the most probable causes for both exceeding goals and underachieving.

For example, at check-in time, an airline's passengers may care most about the speed of the check-in procedure (nobody wants to wait in line for the opportunity to wait even longer at a counter), accuracy of seating assignments and baggage tagging, and helpfulness of gate agents. However, obtaining excellent ratings for all these characteristics for each flight may depend on events outside the control of the airline, such as weather delays or independent travel agents accurately entering passenger information at the time of ticketing.

A good measurement system takes into account events that are beyond the control of the company's staff and then also measures how they recover from such incidents to achieve their organizational objectives. One of the key tasks of "emagineering" management is to build operational measurements into business processes so that managers and frontline employees can use the results as a tool for improving their operational efficiency.

In the past businesses generally only measured one aspect of most processes. For instance, control systems are in place at nearly all major banks to measure how long a support representative takes to resolve a customer problem or in the plastics industry to measure the percentage of scrap created by each specific manufacturing task. Guidelines (or standards) often are assigned to these tasks for the purpose of reviewing the performance of employees and their managers.

With the use of today's information technology, corporations can and should both measure specific operational results and correlate these outcomes against their *numerous* (not just one or two) possible causes.

Many organizations are already using internally developed information systems to improve their management capabilities by correlating events with both their direct and indirect results. Recognizing the preference for purchased applications over those developed in-house, independent software vendors are developing a new generation of business decision-support applications that will sift through immense amounts of data to provide managers with possible reasons for both unexpected improvements in performance and unanticipated declines.

The key to using measurement systems effectively to gain operational excellence is to plan the measurement process as part of "emagineering" the operational efficiency of the company in the first place. Just as an airplane pilot must monitor the aircraft's speedy fuel consumption, weight, and altitude against wind conditions and temperature to achieve the optimal tradeoff between both fuel efficiency and on-time performance, so should a company correlate the causes and effects of its internal processes against external conditions.

For example, while the traditional measure of customer-support effectiveness may have been the number of customers served in a given period (the more customers served in the least amount of time, the better), the new basis for judging operational excellence may include type of problem, number of times the same customer calls about the same problem, training time for the support representative, amount of time since the individual had become a customer of the company, years of customer-support experience by the representative, length of time the supported product has been on the market, the customer-support representative's performance ratings, total number of calls received about a given problem, period since the product-problem database has been last updated, and so on.

Operational Measurements Are Not Cost Benchmarking

Customer-focused operational measurement systems should not be confused with industry-specific cost benchmarking. One form of cost benchmarking is to attempt to compare costs for various information system functions across companies in the same or similar industries. The objective of this exercise typically is to motivate information systems managers to become more efficient by lowering the corporation's total cost for data processing and communications. However, the unintended but actual result is often to encourage the information systems staff to concentrate its efforts on lowering its own costs at the expense of better supporting customers or increasing the efficiency of the organization's internal business processes. This is a terrible price to pay for measuring the wrong factors. Rewarding people for surpassing the wrong information systems objectives will decrease a corporation's market value.

To assist their companies in competing in the global marketplace, technology executives must focus on delighting customers, lowering internal costs and cycle times, and integrating the supplier-customer-ecosystem relationship as tightly as possible. These are the performance results that should be measured in conjunction with "emagineering" efforts to achieve operational excellence.

Less Obvious Tactics for Achieving Operational Excellece

What specific actions should a company initiate to increase operational effectiveness and efficiency using advanced technologies? Or more appropriately, if corporate executives believe that their efforts over the last several years have not been as productive as they could be, what new approaches should they pursue?

Technology executives have developed numerous tactics that help make their efforts successful. These tactics have been learned from both good and bad experiences. The following actions should be used to go from the stage of talking the talk to walking the walk. However, experience has proven that it takes technology executives—not managers and staff on opposite sides of the business-technology divide—to execute the following management tactics correctly.

- *Prioritize the business-process capabilities the corporation wants to be best in class.* Technology executives have learned that prioritization efforts must be based on increasing the company's market value. Obtaining this result is highly dependent on meeting customer needs better than the competition. Many traditional companies attempt to prioritize their information systems group's capital appropriation requests according to an individual proposal's projected return on investment without examining its strategic significance. This strictly-by-the-numbers approach all too often leads to lowering the cost of maintaining current information systems without achieving the technology executive's goal of increasing revenues and operational excellence for the entire corporation.

- *Appoint technology scouts to spend their time investigating and reporting on three key subjects:*

  - *The best new operational practices in any industry made possible by advanced technologies.* Technology executives learn from successes in other industries and apply them, with appropriate modifications, to their own unique needs.

  - *Competitors' customer-focused information systems initiatives.* Playing competitive catchup in the area of operational effectiveness when there is a requirement to install new information systems is extremely difficult, especially when there are intense time pressures. Knowing in advance what competitors are doing in this area provides technology executives with the time necessary to plan for a superior counterinitiative.

  - *Technology suppliers' latest and greatest offerings, the real ability of these offerings to perform as promised, and their potential for improving the company's operations if and when acquired for use within the organization.* Enterprise-level high-tech suppliers both evangelize their own ideas about how they believe their customers should improve their operations and also invite serious prospects to see how their other customers are accomplishing greater operational results. Even though these suppliers naturally have the ultimate objective of selling their products, they have proved over time to be an excellent source of innovative ideas.

- *Establish a strategic technology advisory board that includes outside experts on business and technology issues as well as the most senior corporate executives.* The purpose of such a group is to meet three or four times per year to review the results of recently completed or in-progress projects as well as to forecast key market trends and information-technology supplier dynamics. Outside advisors can evaluate most objectively how a company is progressing toward achieving operational excellence compared with other firms they work with as well as highlight emerging trends that may not yet be obvious to a company's internally focused management.

- *Implement a structured, collaborative information-sharing system to allow executives who are responsible for the planning, deployment, and management of new business processes to exchange opinions, information, news, and results.* The outcomes of this collaboration should be maintained in a format that allows review by senior and peer executives to better understand every active project's progress, quickly bring new members of a project team up to speed, and educate those who need to know about a project's objectives and status. The institution of collaborative systems can both accelerate and improve the quality of the changes being made within an organization to improve its operational excellence.

Achieving operational excellence through "emagineering" is doable by any company—no matter what the industry or geographic location. However, it first requires dedication and hard work—including a willingness to master new subject matter that may be outside an individual's areas of both expertise and interest—on the part of *all* the corporation's executives and managers. Second, achieving operational excellence requires a willingness to continuously change one's opinions and attitudes about how and when to improve business processes with the use of advanced technologies. Third, members of the management team from different departments must collaborate and work together toward mutual goals. And fourth, managing toward operational excellence calls for both leveraging the capabilities and staying within the constraints of the state-of-technology science and the organization's available resources—both personnel and financial.

Lessons Learned from Experience

Operational excellence today means first being able to achieve operational effectiveness in meeting the many needs of the company's target customers. Operational excellence then requires organizing the business's multiple production departments to work as unified whole to achieve operational efficiency in delivering what customers want cost effectively, quickly, and with the highest quality possible. On the other hand, traditional companies that equate operational excellence merely with superior internal manufacturing efficiency are missing a critical market-value-building "emagineering" perspective.

Operational improvements can and should be made at the personal, corporate, and business ecosystem levels. Today's technologies are most appropriate for assisting in the improvement of corporate business process operations, and this is where technology executives are achieving their greatest operational successes. However, in the future, efforts to increase operational excellence will be focused at the business ecosystems level, where there are even greater opportunities.

Corporations should prioritize the initiation of proposed operational improvement projects by their ability to increase market value as opposed to pure return on investment. By making judgments based merely on return-on-investment criteria, monies are too often invested in efforts that only lower the cost of operating existing information systems as opposed to those which can add market value by better servicing customers or improving the company's ability to participate more efficiently in its business ecosystem.

From its customers' perspective, all of a company's departmental business processes need to be consistent. Therefore, changes in one department's processes must be fully coordinated with all departments to be affected.

Company employees will fight for the best information systems tools available. They want to be excellent at performing their responsibilities within the business. However, operational line managers often will prefer to deploy information systems that optimize the performance of their department over those which are designed to provide the entire company and its ecosystem with a higher degree of operational capability. Technology executives have found that they must regularly remind internal managers about who the company's customers are, what these customers expect from the firm, and how competitors are challenging the company to focus their objectives on increasing overall corporate operational excellence.

Sophisticated measurement functionality that provides the capability to correlate actions and events with operational results needs to be planned for at the beginning of new information systems projects. The information gleaned from measurement systems can then be used as the basis for improving business processes systems in the future.

All companies have the potential to achieve the technology competence required to support overall operational excellence. Key to achieving "emagineering" excellence is dedication by the entire organization's management team. The team must be willing to grow its knowledge of the interrelationships between the business and technology issues the company is facing now and must manage over time. It must be willing to evaluate ideas for operational improvements that can be learned from other companies, high-tech suppliers, and industry experts. All the firm's executives must be willing to work collaboratively on improving their corporation's business processes to achieve the elusive goal of operational excellence.

Competency 6: Building the Best-in-the-World Ecosystem

TRADITIONAL PERSONAL AND CORPORATE productivity increases are merely the foundation on which the next evolution of industry-wide productivity increases are being built. *The megachange improvements in effectiveness and efficiency that technology executives are bringing to traditional commerce are the creation of business ecosystems.* Business ecosystems consist of independent businesses all of which are connected to each other through an information network that allows them to perform as a whole entity. Figure 6-1 illustrates the business ecosystem in which a typical consumer goods manufacturer, its suppliers, its distribution channels, and its customers participate.

Deploying advanced technologies at the corporate and personal levels to continuously increase the internal efficiencies and customer-support effectiveness of the ecosystem in which a company participates has become a critical factor for success. Why? Because multiple ecosystems are competing against each other for the ultimate consumer's business!

Figure 6-1 A business ecosystem: A consumer goods manufacturer.

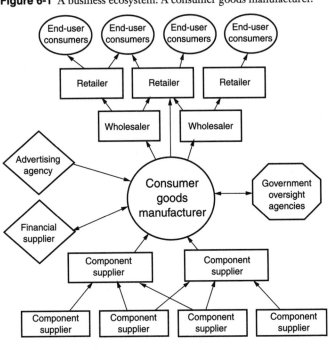

Think Ecosystem Operational Excellence

In the preceding chapter I stated why both corporate and personal operational excellences are so important for building market value. However, even more important over the long term may be achieving business ecosystem operational excellence. A networked ecosystem has the potential to obtain greater operational excellence than any one company as each member firm focuses on both its particular skills and the suppliers and customers with which it works.

Highly capable firms are encouraged by increases in their market value to focus their efforts on supporting the winner ecosystems in which they participate. An ecosystem can be extremely customer-sensitive and highly nimble as the executives of all the participating firms closely monitor the needs of the ecosystem's eventual end-user customers and proactively recommend and make improvements to better serve their common marketplace.

Why *now* are many corporations in our global economy focusing on the creation and management of business ecosystems to achieve operational excellence? Because they can through the use of advanced technologies, and they must do so before their competitors. Advanced technologies, such as instant messaging, high-speed communications, extensible markup languages, and very large relational databases, allow executives within companies to work together closer than ever before. For example, Wal-Mart can electronically tell every one of its trusted suppliers every day which of their products it sold in each one of its stores. It can request automatic vendor replenishment of its fastest-selling items, if it wishes. Its suppliers can reschedule their production runs, modify their orders to their suppliers, and reroute their shipments of finished goods based on these daily updates.

An example of the changing relationship between a supplier and its intermediate customer/distributor to the eventual end-user consumer is a leading video rental chain that is now collaborating closely with the entertainment firms that produce the videos and DVDs that it stocks. In the past, the video chain would buy what it projected to be the appropriate number of videos for each of its stores as soon as a new title was released. After the initial popularity faded, it would then sell the excess videos. The problem for the video rental company was that if it ordered enough videos to meet its customers' demands during the first few weeks after release, it lost money on many of the individual copies, which might be rented only once or twice. In addition, by overbuying, it caused a problem for its supplier, the entertainment firms, by selling too many used videos too soon—taking sales directly to consumers away from the producer. If, on the other hand, the rental chain bought too few copies, it could lose the loyalty and revenues of its most dedicated customers when they learned that they could not obtain the title they wanted when they wanted it.

The solution? Realizing that they had more to gain by cooperating than fighting, several of the video producers agreed to a revenue-splitting arrangement with the rental chain. Now the producers provide each store in the chain with what they believe will be enough copies of the movie on the day of release in order that it should never be out of stock. This quantity is normally four times what the video chain would have ordered. Each time the movie is rented, the producers are notified based on the point-of-sale transaction. With this advanced information system, they can track the rentals the same way as the rental chain's corporate executives. For each rental, the producers are paid an agreed-on amount of money. As time goes on and the store no longer needs as many copies of the movie as it did originally, it returns the videos and DVDs directly to the producer—taking them out of the used market.

Both the producer and the rental chain win financially by improving the operational effectiveness and efficiency of their ecosystem. And the producers and competitive rental chains that do not enter into such a relationship will lose in comparison.

As we can see from these two examples of Wal-Mart and the video rental chain, each firm in an ecosystem is focusing independently on increasing its value to the entire ecosystem based on its unique core competencies. Retailers use their competency in attracting end-user customers, and suppliers deliver products those end-user customers will want to buy. Since each company must add value to all the other members of the ecosystem *simultaneously*, this networked view of industrial organization goes beyond the old value-chain model, where companies would add value sequentially—each one highly dependent on the previous firm in the chain yet at the same time negotiating hard for the best terms possible even if the conditions decreased customer market share and total revenue for all.

Do not attempt to compare the emerging networked business ecosystems of the Competitive Economy with the failing *keiretsus* of Japan. Today's competitive ecosystems are nothing like the old Japanese *keiretsus*, where each *keiretsu* company had to do business with other *keiretsu* members. In today's electronically networked ecosystems, weak participants can and will be removed quickly and replaced with more efficient ones.

In a hypercompetitive economy, internal production efficiencies and effective customer-focused programs are created within ecosystems. Therefore, one key aspect of the "emagineering" process is for technology executives to envision the optimal ecosystem in which to be a key participant and then either create it with their organization at the center or, as a critical participant, join the ecosystem that it believes will be dominant.

Finally, I must note that the "emagineering" view of an ecosystem as a collection of collaborating, independent companies is different from how the multiple suppliers in many industries, especially those established in the first half of the last century, work with each other. For example, the U.S. automobile industry historically has been characterized as an environment in which each supplier-customer relationship throughout the food chain was fraught with distrust, selfish use of power, secrecy, and negotiating tactics that provided short-term wins for either the supplier or the customer but long-term mediocrity for each assembler's business ecosystem (in the United States, the "Big Three"—General Motors, Ford Motor, and DaimlerChrysler). In the past, these confrontational relationships have led business managers to believe that their company should be as integrated as possible. This led a company such as Ford to own its own steel mills at one time. However, corporate executives have since learned that they can increase their market value more successfully based on a collaboration strategy than an integration strategy. Now many of the participants in the U.S. automobile industry are trying to change their historic self-destructive relationships and move toward obtaining the benefits of a more efficient and effective collaborative ecosystem.

Using Advanced Technologies to Build Ecosystems

The operational underpinnings of today's fast-moving ecosystems are advanced technologies. And as the business case for establishing ecosystems continues to be built throughout industries, high-tech suppliers are developing and launching additional products to satisfy the needs and demands of technology executives. These technologies are focused on increasing the speed and availability of information throughout ecosystems. The companies that use these technologies are truly *networked* together.

Figure 6-2 illustrates the information systems that might be used to network a wholesaler-focused ecosystem, such as might be found in the hardware industry. As such an ecosystem develops, the information flows between companies increase, and data are updated continuously, the employees of each company will recognize that the competitive business battle is between ecosystems. Each participant in a company realizes that his or her firm's success is related directly to the ability of the other members of the ecosystem to provide superior goods and services at a lower price than its counterpart in competing ecosystems. The more proficiently members of an ecosystem can use advanced technologies to coordinate their plans and actions, the more effectively they can compete as a group.

In the Competitive Economy, the major battles become ones between different networked business ecosystems. Technology executives will be

Figure 6-2 Information systems in a business ecosystem.

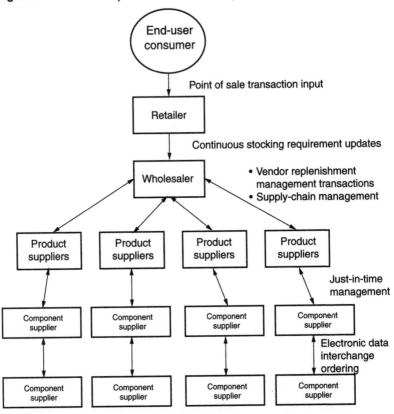

- Each consumer transaction that is automatically entered at check-out can generate changes throughout the ecosystem
- Additional marketing data are collected when consumers register in loyalty clubs in return for discounts
- Consumer and product sales data can be shared throughout the ecosystem to increase efficiency and effectiveness

the leaders in putting together the technologies and business processes that make these ecosystems work effectively and efficiently.

Ecosystems and Trust

Ecosystems are established based on trust. To participate in a successful networked ecosystem, the members must be willing to share some of their most valuable operating data and intellectual property.

The technology products that facilitate this sharing of highly sensitive information are mere tools. It is incumbent on the members of the ecosystem to use these tools properly to safeguard the data with which the others entrust them. Procedures for sharing information and maintaining the security of that data depend on the capabilities and commitment of the individual ecosystem members.

Trust becomes a particularly important issue when a company participates in several competing ecosystems. For example, a toy manufacturer will ship its products to directly competing retailers. Yet, for a newly released toy, each retailer initially wants a minimum quantity while it tracks the first 2 to 4 weeks of sales to determine if the item will be a success. At the same time, most retailers want their suppliers to also track sales by store and replenish their inventories when quantities drop below a predetermined level until they are directed to stop. [Vendor replenishment management (VRM) capability is one of the benefits of deploying advanced technologies properly.] Therefore, retailers provide their suppliers with daily sales and inventory levels. In this ecosystem, the toy supplier now knows which retailers are being successful with the new toy and which are not. The toy company also has the clearest picture of anybody in the ecosystem of sales and can make the best projections as to whether the toy is going to be a hit or a dud. What should it do with this information?

Obviously, the toy manufacturer should not give retailer A's sales figures to retailer B. More to the point, the toy manufacturer must safeguard each individual retailer's sales figures more closely than it protects its own confidential sales information. Of course, there is always the temptation for a toy supplier's salesperson to say to one retailer's merchandising managers, "Hey, your competitor is doing great with our new toy. It is going to be the hit of the season. Let me give you a few ideas on how to increase its sales in your stores." Does this type of statement breach the line of trust, or is it just good business for both the supplier and one of its major retail distributors? Or could the sales representative be bluffing in hopes of selling out the remaining inventory of a dud product?

While there are potential problems with sharing proprietary information, the benefits to the retailer of providing the toy manufacturer with its sales figures and have it restock when appropriate are great—each retailer will minimize both its capital assets dedicated to that supplier's products and its shelf and warehouse space devoted to each particular toy. This allows for better financial returns on individual items and the ability to carry a broader range of products to meet customers' requirements for a wide selection of toys.

Organizations that practice "emagineering" as part of their culture have found that the trusted sharing of data is a requirement for a successful ecosystem. Yes, there are risks—every firm has several individuals who will gladly dream up every possible reason about why it should never release business data to another and describe the potential problems that could be caused in all their gory details. However, experience has shown that the benefits of information sharing within an ecosystem far outweigh the costs. And the risks can be minimized when the participants in the ecosystems agree to abide by commonsense confidentiality rules and also implement and maintain prudent information system security procedures.

Security Fears and Resolutions

Yet, no matter what the opportunities and positive experiences of others, security fears are a major obstacle to building superior ecosystems and experimenting with intermember information sharing. Whenever professional information systems technologists do not want to implement a new system—even with business executives clamoring for it and all the financial projections making it look like a profitable investment—they are most likely to use the argument, "There are security risks and problems that you do not understand." How can a nontechnologist respond?

Security is a key corporate issue. A public company's outside auditors are expected to review the procedures the company has put in place to keep its records safe annually. There are continuous stories that come across the rumor mill about internal fraud or external hackers who have stolen corporate assets by breaking through computer system security defenses. Moreover, companies acknowledge that they do not want to publicly talk about such occurrences—only increasing the fear factor. Finally, it is difficult to put a price on the loss or theft of data stored on a corporation's enterprise-level computer systems. Sometimes the loss is merely an inconvenience; at other times, thieves and embezzlers can turn stolen data into real money, especially when they are company employees who have been entrusted with financial responsibilities.

The reality is that information flows within ecosystems need to be "emagineered," paying careful attention to trust and security issues at the outset. Advances in technology are just now resulting in the delivery of products that will allow companies both to share data with individuals in other firms within the ecosystem and to verify what happens to those data. Therefore, part of the "emagineering" process is

- To establish a security system that allows the corporation to authorize what information it is willing to share both with other companies and with what classifications of employee within those firms.
- Track the dissemination of any and all information.
- Log the receipt of information from other companies.
- Monitor to whom within the company information from other companies is provided.

Technology executives fully understand that problems will occur. Disgruntled employees may attempt to steal and sell highly valuable information. Computers will crash and lose sensitive information. Backup tapes containing important records may be misplaced. It is possible that some lower-level employee will publish another firm's confidential information on a Web site. All these incidents, however, will be minor in the long run when the corporation is flourishing in a successful business ecosystem and its competitors are not.

Technology's Answer to Esperanto

Creating ecosystems based on technology may sound relatively straightforward on paper, but the reality is that all companies have older installed applications on which they depend every day to manage their business processes. Most of these systems were developed and implemented well before the Web and when strategic planning executives never thought in terms of collaborative ecosystems.

Most older installed systems were designed to be closed systems. A closed system only passes information from one module, or function, to another within the same application. The question for technology executives building information networks for ecosystems is how to pass the data contained in these older, closed applications to other applications and how to upgrade these legacy applications in business-critical production systems to act on data received from others—and how to do so across an entire ecosystem.

The simple answer is to replace closed, legacy applications with new ones that can "talk" to each other in a common computer language—intelligently move information and data from one application to another. These new applications would be designed to be part of a flexible ecosystem information network. Such a desire evokes thoughts of Esperanto, an artificial language created in 1887 that was designed to be an international language. Although Esperanto never achieved the worldwide currency its proponents have hoped for, more than 100,000 people from a multitude of nations speak it today.

In the 1980s the Department of Defense tried to create an information world equivalent to Esperanto in a costly project called *Ada*. Ada was to be a universal language for computers, but in the same way that Esperanto has failed to become a true international language, so too did Ada fail to be adopted widely. The reality is that information sciences are still evolving and the way that corporations and individuals want to use computers also is changing continuously. Now is not the time to implement a static universal computing language based on the technologies of the early 2000s.

Having said this, when technology executives plan for ecosystem-connecting information networks, they still need to ensure that their technologists have the tools necessary to integrate data and functionality between different installed applications.

The Web browser has been the greatest integration tool ever. The browser essentially provides a common interface, or viewer, for all applications that support it. Therefore, an executive today equipped with a basic personal computer (PC) and Web browser (such as Microsoft's Internet Explorer) can, for example, review information about a new product's development status contained within numerous and very different applications. For example, the executive can access the results of a graphics-based computer-aided design (CAD) application that will display a visualization of what the designer wants the new product to look like. Next, the executive could go to a project management system to review the program leader's schedule and budgets for building it. Finally, he or she might run through the marketing sales slide show that will be presented to prospects by accessing yet another application. Just a few short years ago, to perform this same review, the executive would have needed a copy of each application on his or her computer. However, a basic Web browser is limited in functionality. It does not let different applications respond automatically to each other—functionally that ecosystem participants want. Organizations also need a way to exchange the same types of information automatically even though each might use dissimilar names for them. Since one application might label a product number as "product code" and another as "item number," there is still a need for a technology Esperanto.

The good news is that technology suppliers are continuously releasing advanced products to solve the data and application communication issues technology executives face when building ecosystems. The most recent example of such a key technology is XML (eXtensible Markup Language), which allows data types that are the same but have different labels in different applications to recognize each other more easily across the Web. Also, JAVA, another evolving technology, is being used to allow functional processes to be moved from one application and computing environment to another. However, these are merely technologies that are used as the underlying components of the much more comprehensive products that are needed to actually integrate an ecosystem's applications.

From Supply-Chain Management to Ecosystem Management

The successful ecosystem is the one that gets the right product to the right buyer at the right time while capturing the highest return on assets employed. One software technology that today helps companies within an ecosystem accomplish this is commonly known as *supply-chain management* (SCM).

Operational management software has followed a logical progression from the bottom of the production process up to the ecosystem level. The first scheduling software helped manufacturing companies maximize individual machine use; the next generation assisted in the scheduling of materials within a factory, followed by the extension of scheduling production across multiple factories. This was followed by enterprise resource planning (ERP), which helped facilitate the management of all of a company's resources, including staff and sales orders, within the organization itself. SCM assists networked ecosystem members with optimizing the flow of materials through each company's manufacturing processes. It then can schedule shipments to best meet the individual company's requirements through its distribution channels to the final buyer.

In theory, every time a buyer acquires a product, each company's production schedule in the entire ecosystem should be updated instantaneously. Unfortunately, the state of technology has not reached this high level of sophistication—yet.

However, what can be accomplished today is sending and updating information to the different participants within the ecosystem so that they can create their required scheduling plans. And then they can run optimization models to determine their most effective and efficient manufacturing, component-ordering, and shipping dates based on available resources. These new collaborative and optimization planning applications have been practical only since the late 1990s when computer hardware powerful enough to run such complex models became affordable—and could recognize the numerous interactions required. Once one company updates its shipment schedule and sends this schedule to another company in the ecosystem, that company will need to then update its schedule, which will affect both its suppliers and other customers, and so forth. No wonder the Holy Grail of SCM is to have one SCM system optimizing the entire ecosystem and all the intermediate points within it! When such technology becomes available, the industry might refer to the overriding management application as *real-time ecosystem management software.*

Since real-time ecosystem management software is not yet available, corporations must "emagineer" the processes with their suppliers and customers and, where possible, their suppliers' suppliers to orchestrate most efficiently the flow of materials into a final product that can be delivered to an end-user customer. In addition, each company in an ecosystem needs to do so in such a manner as to outperform competing ecosystems.

Different Ecosystem Focal Points

Creating "emagineering" consensus among all the participants in an ecosystem is fundamental to using its entire resources efficiently and effectively. Yet different industries have different focal points of power. The focal point of power is the corporation or corporations that have the clout to influence the goals the other participants must meet if they wish to remain in the ecosystem. The U.S. automobile industry and the global clothing industry are good examples of contrasting ecosystem structures.

The three major automobile companies (assemblers) in the United States are an excellent example of competing ecosystems that are attempting to increase their efficiency and effectiveness by building an electronic information network from the consumer back to the providers of the natural resources required for the various components that make up a car or truck. Each of the automobile assemblers—General Motors, Ford, and DaimlerChrysler—is the focal point for its ecosystem. Historically in the automobile industry, the technology issues for creating ecosystems have been easier to overcome than the business-policy barriers.

To take the lead in creating the best-of-the-three assembler-focused ecosystems, Ford is attempting to develop the capability to allow a buyer to order a custom car and have it delivered within a week—all by using tools widely available on the Web. This is an outstanding "emagineering" vision. However, the first barrier Ford had to overcome was integrating shipping firms into its ecosystem information planning system. They had been a forgotten part of Ford's older SCM applications. Moreover, since carriers typically compete on price, not speed of delivery, Ford's usual shippers had little motivation to participate in the previous generation of SCM efforts.

To fit into Ford's new vision of how automobiles will be ordered and delivered, the automobile carriers now have to be able to pick up the customer's unique car from the assembly plant at a specific time and then deliver it to any place in the United States relatively quickly and at the promised time.

Encouragingly, the upstream component suppliers already had invested appropriately in technology to integrate themselves closer to their automobile-assembler customers over the years, so they had no problem with incrementally expanding their information systems' functionality to participate in this extension of the ecosystem's capabilities.

It is highly probable that at some time in the near future a consumer will be able to go online and order the exact car he or she wants, be given a date and place to take possession of it at the acceptance of the order, and without knowing it, have created thousands of electronic data updates within an automobile assembler's ecosystem.

On the other hand, clothing retailers, especially those who are positioned in fashion markets, have one of the most difficult times building consensus about how their ecosystems should operate. Their suppliers' suppliers (especially those in specialty linens) tend to demand long lead times, whereas end-user buyers want to walk away from a store with their purchases in hand. In addition, it is extremely complex to forecast what items will be top sellers, average sellers, or duds, in what sizes, and in what cities. As a result, the clothing ecosystems are relatively inefficient, and the various members do not move in a coordinated and effective way to meet changing end-user consumer demand.

Yet some retailers have built their own captive supply chains through private labeling and have shown that it is possible to both lower the assets required to deliver fashionable clothing in their ecosystem and increase their return on those assets. However, independent firms in the fashion industry have not yet been motivated enough to form stable, more productive ecosystems.

The focal control points of ecosystems vary by industry. In the automobile industry, it is the car assemblers, not the individual dealers. In the clothing industry, it is the retail chains, not the manufacturers. Yet even though the focal control point firms are vital in each industry, they themselves cannot control the ecosystem information management backbone without the willingness of all the other members to participate actively. For a specific ecosystem to dominate its industry, it is critical to build a consensus on how the participants will work together before alternative ecosystems develop and race past it.

Internet Product Collaboration and Management

Most of a product's potential revenue and built-in costs are set during its design phase—well before it gets to manufacturing. This being the case, the design phase is the point where it is most important for different participants in an ecosystem to work together to ensure that new products have the greatest value possible. This is especially true for services and other nonphysical products, such as financial services offerings.

Product development requires tremendous amounts of input, experience, and tradeoffs within the sponsoring corporation and throughout the associated ecosystem. Moreover, after a product is released, the market feedback and market research reports of the benefits and issues users have encountered require vigilant management both for updating the product and for developing additional complementary and follow-on products.

Too often products are designed within a company by a dedicated team in one location. The product designs are then "thrown over the wall" to a group of manufacturing and procurement specialists in another location—often on another continent. The product prototype is then shown to marketing—which all too often will note that the new product looks little like what it asked for (or was told to expect by the product designers). Marketing must then communicate to the public that the new product will be available soon and build buyer interest before its release. Finally, the sales representatives are shown the new offering and told that they and their customers had better like it because they are being goaled on selling it in large quantities and at high margins. Of course, the vast majority of the target customer base (excluding select members of test-marketing focus groups) probably will see the product for the first time only after it has worked its way through the distribution channels. It is no wonder that 80 percent of all new products fail to meet their objectives—there is simply too little market-relevant input into the development process! Yet the reason product development is the responsibility of a dedicated team is that too much conflicting input is as bad as no input at all—be it from the visionary executive who demands a radical change or the stodgiest customer wanting to maintain the status quo.

One of the key principles of "emagineering" is that every concerned participant in the ecosystem must be able to collaborate during the entire product-development and ongoing life-cycle management process. Not only is this one of the great marketing capabilities of the electronic age, it is also one of the key means for all the firms within an ecosystem to increase their market values.

As part of the "emagineering" process for product development, technology executives need to identify all potential participants in the development process and do so by product-development phases. For example, they need to answer such questions as when and how should a company's most important customers be involved in the process. Should these high-potential prospects be asked to brainstorm at the beginning of the process with the product-development team—or should they first be involved when the product functionality, design, and cost are relatively well defined and the business is merely looking for a few small improvements before final release to production? Moreover, should an advisory group of customers be asked to provide feedback on their learning experiences with current products on a regular basis, just before launch, or after the product is made generally available to all? Should component suppliers be asked to design parts based on minimal functional specifications, or should they be given complete designs and told merely to bid on delivering a specific quantity?

Executives who are battle bruised from trying to manage the issues involved in meeting the changing demands and government regulations of regional markets around the world have found that Internet product collaboration development is critical to creating a comprehensive global-requirements source book for new products. Multinational corporations need, at a minimum, the ongoing input from regional product and marketing specialists, target customers located in different market environments, regulatory experts, and local distribution experts during the product-development process.

From a technology perspective, the principal requirement for Internet product collaboration is that members of the ecosystem—especially component suppliers to assembler customers—be able to view (or better yet, interchange) data in a secure manner. This is not a trivial matter. Typically, the different members of the ecosystem have dissimilar graphic design, computer simulation testing, and manufacturing bill-of-materials applications installed—all of which format data differently. Moreover, each company will format its specific product-management data differently. This makes information exchange relatively difficult. Luckily, most applications have had to be updated to allow for access across the Internet. This recent advancement finally permits viewing product-development information, including information-rich, detailed graphic designs, from different applications.

In a few years technology will allow real-time interoperability and updates between applications running in different companies. This is yet another reason why it is so important to "emagineer" the Internet product-development and product-management process within an ecosystem as it is being established so as to provide the participants with a technology road map they can begin implementing as soon as possible. When technology executives consider building ecosystems to last for the long term, they firmly believe that the ecosystems that can out-"emagineer" their competitors in the area of Internet product development and life-cycle management will dominate their industries within a decade. Such well-prepared ecosystems will have the tools in place to develop initial products that meet their customers' needs better than the competition. They will then be able to release successive generations of products that meet their customers' and prospects' needs rapidly (and obsolete their own previous products) so that the competition cannot exploit functional deficiencies.

Disposable Companies

In the battle of "my ecosystem" versus "that other ecosystem," competition and cooperation among different companies become key. Each participant must be more efficient and effective than its counterpart in competing ecosystems. And each firm must be prepared and able to cooperate with the other members to maximize the efficiency and effectiveness of the entire ecosystem. This can be an especially daunting task for companies that participate in more than one ecosystem—especially when the different ecosystems compete for the same customers.

Realistically, the individual participants in each ecosystem will represent a continuously changing set of values for the other members. An example would be two suppliers of packaging materials to the consumer products industry. Both could do business in numerous ecosystems. One, however, decides that its future lies in offering value-added services and actually outsourcing for its customers—consumer goods manufacturers—the task of final product packaging, matching packages to orders, and selecting the most cost-effective shipping methods to distributors. The other merely remains a supplier of packaging materials. With such a clear difference in strategy, each consumer goods manufacturer eventually will decide which packaging materials supplier will remain a participant in its ecosystem and which should be replaced.

The most common reason for disruption of an ecosystem is when a company is acquired and the new owner decides to either increase or decrease its commitment of resources to supporting a particular ecosystem. This is a major reason why an ecosystem must be flexible to respond to changes that are both unexpected and beyond its control.

One of the most important objectives of "emagineering" is to use advanced technologies to strengthen the ties between suppliers and their customers and expand those ties through an entire business ecosystem. However, it also must be pointed out that the same technology also provides corporations with the ability to replace any firm in an ecosystem more easily and quickly with another. For example, when Bridgestone/Firestone had a major dispute with its customer Ford Motor Company about the quality of its tires, it was relatively easy for Ford to replace Bridgestone/Firestone, its largest tire supplier, with Michelin and other tire manufacturers.

Technology also can allow an ecosystem participant to move from its current ecosystem to another—an event that occurs as best-in-class companies change their allegiance from weaker ecosystems to ecosystems with the information infrastructure necessary to win in the long term.

From a casual outsider's perspective, identifying ecosystem relationships can be difficult. For example, one generally has a hard time tracking the partnerships and alliances in the high-tech world—the full-time job of market analysts—because each firm tries to build the best new ecosystem possible to attack emerging market opportunities while maintaining ties within older ecosystems to market to its installed base of customers.

Only the Swift Survive

Managers who learned their skills in the manufacturing-dominated business world often are not prepared to recognize how quickly alliances can be created and dissolved in today's Competitive Economy.

Andy Grove, Intel's brilliant leader, put it right when he titled his book *Only the Paranoid Survive*. Intel, which brought standards to the chaos of competing merchant-market microprocessors for personal computers (PCs), finds that even its best original equipment manufacturer (OEM) customers consider it to be disposable if it does not meet the needs of end-user customers better than alternative microprocessor suppliers. Intel successfully created a business ecosystem, one that included Microsoft and all the major PC suppliers except Apple Computer, around its highly acclaimed marketing slogan, "Intel Inside," in the mid-1990s. Yet it never became a focal point—Microsoft earned that role with its Windows operating system and Office applications. In addition, when end users demanded the lowest-priced PCs possible and Intel did not comply with lower-priced microprocessors, the other members of the ecosystem quickly turned to Advanced Micro Devices, Intel's primary competitor, and invited it to join their ecosystems. Intel's lesson should not be lost on any technology executive: Every firm can be disposable if it does not change its products and policies to meet the newest demands of the ecosystem's end-user customers.

Firms must either work within their ecosystem to better meet the end-user customers' changing desires or risk being replaced with another. The alternative for a business that cannot focus on its current ecosystem's end-user customer is to find another ecosystem to ally with or face a decline in business opportunities and, relatively quickly, market value.

Lessons Learned from Experience

The newest evolutionary goal for technology executives is building, operating, and enhancing a business ecosystem in which all the participants are networked together. Ecosystems that can create a group consensus among their member companies about their target end-user customers and how to meet their needs will lead their industries. Working toward common customer-focused goals is critical.

Security concerns need to be faced head on when building an ecosystem information network. Corporations that freely share appropriate information benefit much more than those which restrict or micromanage data exchanges. "Emagineering" calls for monitoring information flows among companies, establishing reasonable (neither overly restrictive nor laughably lax) information security procedures, and implementing advanced security products as they become available. However, a basic trust between different organizations is necessary for the ecosystem to succeed.

Corporate applications should be integrated across company boundaries within an ecosystem. While this is desirable in theory, real-life integration can be extremely difficult. Therefore, firms that use "emagineering" need to maintain a core competence regarding the technologies and products that facilitate the passing of data between applications.

One of the next goals in the development of tools to assist executives will be real-time ecosystem information-management systems that go beyond internal enterprise resource planning and interenterprise supply-chain management. This widely anticipated advanced technology will initiate a transaction as soon as a customer's purchase goes through a point-of-sale scanner or a manufacturer fills a business customer's order and update all the ecosystem members' production-planning information systems.

Including all the key participants—from suppliers to customers—in product development and life-cycle management is necessary for long-term ecosystem success. With the use of Internet-based technologies, more effective collaborative product development is becoming a reality.

Although advanced technologies allow companies to build closer linkages between suppliers and their customers, they also allow an ecosystem to change individual participants as needed. Corporations must strive continuously to expand their capabilities—especially their competence based on advanced technologies to be the best in class in the area in which they add value—as well as improve their efficiency and effectiveness if they hope to remain important participants in an industry-leading ecosystem.

Competency 7: Initiating Creative Destruction While Facing Technology Uncertainty

C*REATIVE DESTRUCTION* IS AN EASY CONCEPT TO understand intellectually—but extremely difficult to execute personally. The economic basis of creative destruction states that market value is created when older products, services, business systems, physical facilities, etc. are replaced with newer ones that incorporate advanced technologies. While this is all well and good as an academic finding, it does not take into account the myriad issues that are raised when it is time for a business to destroy its own current assets—to make its existing products obsolete and change its organizational structure.

The handful of corporations in this world that have been able to increase their market value continuously over several decades have done so by judiciously managing the use of creative destruction as a strategic option. However, creative destruction in this context does not mean never-ending revolution and dramatic changes of course within a business. An organization that finds itself continuously in massive upheaval and uncertain about its future will be chaotic and unable to function properly. Individuals who never have time to master their tasks before they or their tasks are changed will never have the opportunity to provide the business with their personal best.

Creative destruction is applied intelligently when it is used to help a company evolve to better meet the needs of its customers. The management processes of creative destruction can and should be directed by a company's current executives whenever possible. Managers in charge of a successful business are the most knowledgeable about the best way to replace current product offerings with even better ones and how to increase the efficiency and effectiveness of current business processes by replacing them with even better ones. The challenge for corporate executives is to have the foresight and experience necessary to make the correct business choices for change, know when is the proper time to transform the business, and have the courage to lead in the destruction of a business they have worked so hard to build in order to replace it with an even more highly valued one.

"Emagineering" Equals Creative Destruction

Advanced technologies are today's tools for initiating creative destruction. Innovative technology executives spend considerable time "emagineering" how they can use advanced technologies to capture new customers and better meet the changing needs of their own target customer base. If the technology executives are located within an established company, they will focus their efforts on how to improve the market value of the existing organization by increasing its market share through revenue growth or increasing profitability by cutting costs. The creative destruction of existing processes is an option to achieve these goals that advanced technologies provide.

In the private sector there are always established competitors looking to take advantage of a company's developing weaknesses and entrepreneurs desiring to create their own personal fortunes by challenging the way customers think about entrenched suppliers. In the public sector there are oversight boards and numerous highly interested constituents who believe that their role in life is to criticize the agencies they are responsible for or interact with. Therefore, either an organization must learn how to manage and control the power of creative destruction on its own or others will force creative destruction on it in the never-too-distant future.

The best way to manage the positive aspects of creative destruction on a continuous basis is though planned, timed improvements in every critical aspect of the corporation. Successive releases of advanced technologies have made managing the creative destruction process vital to the success of organizations. Value-building creative destruction activities that should be initiated by the "emagineering" process include

- *Innovations in the products and services the firm delivers.* The home electronic gaming market was started by Commodore with its Amiga game console in 1985. However, when Commodore would not invest in replacing its relatively simple systems—because it decided the market was saturated by the early 1990s—with more advanced ones built on new hardware and software technologies, Nintendo, Sega, and Sony came into the market, put Commodore out of business, and then grew the market to a size more than ten times larger than the executives at Commodore had ever imagined possible.

- *Innovations in the way products and services are created.* A whole industry of electronic assemblers has been created as major high-tech companies such as IBM, Hewlett-Packard, and Compaq have found that while they may be skilled in designing, marketing, and selling products, other firms can manufacture, package, and ship these products better than they ever did.

- *Innovations in the way offerings are delivered to end users.* Magazines and newspapers now deliver their content through the Web. True, they may have lost some sales of their paper products, but they have increased the loyalty of their customers who want access to up-to-date stories and archive stories, and they have been able to extend their advertising offerings to include delivering ads in electronic formats to their readers.

- *Innovations in the way the organization manages itself internally.* Corporations that have deployed SAP's and Oracle's integrated enterprise resource-planning applications consistently report that these systems were used as a catalyst for reorganizing their companies to more effectively and efficiently make better, faster management decisions while doing a better job of delivering products and services to their customers.

- *Innovations in the company's partners and how they work together in its business ecosystem.* At one time automobile makers provided their suppliers of such parts as seats with a detailed description of what they wanted at the completion of their design phase of a new car. And then they would select three or four suppliers to produce the seats and every month pressure each of them to lower their price if they wanted orders for the next month—threatening that another supplier would get their anticipated orders if they did not make significant price concessions. Now automobile makers will bring one, or at most two, trusted seat suppliers into their development group and ask them to design the most appropriate seats for the car during the design phase. As business partners, the seat supplier and automobile assembler trade designs and feedback back and forth electronically until the car design is locked down. The supplier with the winning design is assured that it will be given the majority of orders—and these orders will be placed electronically to support the automobile assembler's just-in-time manufacturing processes—at a preagreed price. A second supplier is almost always contracted with in partnership with the primary supplier to assure the automobile assembler of the availability of seats in case the primary supplier runs into a serious problem, such as the loss of a plant or a strike. This insurance-supply agreement is always made with the assistance and full support of the primary supplier.
- *Innovations in how the business defines both its most important customers and its competition.* Procter and Gamble (P&G) is a great and wonderful consumer goods company that focuses aggressive, smart groups of product managers on maximizing the sales of their own specific products. The story is told that when Wal-Mart was growing but still just a regional retailer, Sam Walton, Wal-Mart's founder and president, wanted to meet with the president of P&G to discuss new ways for their two companies to work together. The president of P&G declined Mr. Walton's offer because Wal-Mart did not seem very important to P&G, and it was competing aggressively against those very companies P&G thought were its best customers. Luckily, a very smart executive suggested that P&G should determine who its most important customers actually were. This was a relatively difficult task

because all customer information was held by the multiple product groups and not consolidated at the corporate level due to P&G's reluctance to spend money on building its information systems' capabilities. As you might have guessed, when each product group manually sent its customer-revenue reports to the president's office and they were tabulated, Wal-Mart was found to be P&G's largest customer. The president quickly called Mr. Walton to schedule a meeting for strengthening the ties between the two companies and ordered his information systems group to immediately upgrade their capabilities to analyze P&G's revenues and profits by customers on a consolidated corporate level. And as P&G better understood Wal-Mart, it changed its strategy to better support its new-found best friend even at the expense of its traditional customers.

Recognizing When and How to Innovate

Experience shows that very few corporations take a disciplined approach to managing creative destruction. Most firms cope with change in a reactive mode. That is, they wait until their customers' buying habits change dramatically before they focus on making major innovations to their products, services, or policies—or they go on a crash renewal program only after competitors capture a significant share of their most important customers.

One of the reasons for this reluctance to change proactively—to implement creative destruction within an organization—is that senior executives rarely can comprehend when and what type of change is necessary until they are faced with an actual threat and already have experienced unexpected setbacks. Beneficial, proactive change that is made without a threat in sight and before the entire organization feels a need for urgent action is an unnatural act in conventional companies.

Since most market changes usually occur slowly, it is not until a glaring problem arises that traditional executives are motivated to act. The executive who calls for change early on is often branded an "alarmist"—somebody who is not in sync with the rest of the management team.

Yet overly cautious executives who see no reason to change are considered "frogs"—as biologists have shown, if a frog is put in a pot of water on a cold stove that is then turned on, the frog will remain in place until it boils to death because it cannot recognize a slow but fatal, rise in temperature. The same subtle changes in customer preferences make it very difficult for most senior executives to realize when it is time to institute creative destruction. This lack of awareness, combined with a natural reluctance to compete in a new and different environment, makes internally initiated change very difficult. This corporate inertia is why so many boards of directors believe they must hire chief executive officers from outside their companies both to gain an objective view of the current state of the business and to have in place a leader who is willing and anxious to engage in the creative destruction process.

The solution to the organizational issue of deciding what aspects of a business should be improved through the process of creative destruction is straightforward to technology executives. *Every aspect of a company's business operations should be evaluated against how it could be improved through the use of advanced technology.*

The first and key question a technology executive will ask when establishing a management process for creative destruction evaluation is simply, "When?" Should new versions of the firm's core products be released every 3, 6, 9, 12, 15, or 18 months? Should the internal accounting information system be overhauled every 3, 5, 7, or 10 years? Should the corporation's headquarters offices be changed dramatically every 10, 20, or 30 years? Should a team of managers be permanently assigned to the task of upgrading the company's revenue-producing Web site every day, week, or month?

Of course, the follow-on question to when is, "How?" Should the current product line be price-reduced, should additional functionality be added, or both? Should the new internal accounting system be based on Web technologies for ease of access or designed for integration among divisions and departments to provide a more in-depth but complex-to-navigate view of the state of the company? Should the corporation build a new headquarters office facility or renovate the existing one? Should the Web site be redesigned for flexibility in working with business partners or increased ease of use for helping customers and prospects find the information they want?

Organizations that have built competencies in "emagineering" will use these strengths as the basis for answering the questions of when and how. It is very important to recognize that acquiring a competency in "emagineering" is critical to also having competency in the management of creative destruction.

Starting with What Is Most Important

Organizational executives face three difficult choices when they first decide to formally initiate creative destruction processes within their companies. Should they begin by

1. Identifying additional ways to increase their organization's internal efficiency with advanced technologies? (This will lower costs and increase profit margins.)
2. Imagining potential new lines of business for their firm and creating plans for launching them? (This will put their company in potentially more exciting markets and invigorate the internal organization.)
3. Using advanced technology to better service their current customers? (This requires changing the rules of competition within the industry but can lead to greater customer loyalty and higher revenues and profits per customer.)

For most traditional executives, the first choice—increasing internal efficiency—is generally the most appealing. This approach translates into working smarter and has the least chance of causing failures that customers can see. And it will keep the company viable in even a highly competitive business environment—unless another participant changes the rules of competition dramatically.

On the other hand, there are always aggressive executives within an organization who want the opportunity to build businesses for the company. They view the ability to use advanced technologies as a foundation for quickly establishing additional revenue streams as a rare and golden opportunity to meet their personal desires for building a new business from scratch.

However, experience has shown that a company should start its efforts by focusing on what processes need to be improved to better serve its current customers. It needs to continuously analyze its current customer base's changing needs and desires to determine how it can delight its customers in its delivery of products and services. When it better supports its current customers, it also will have the capabilities to attract new customers—especially if it markets the advantages it can offer through technology-based initiatives to its competitors' customers.

More to the point, as was describe in Chapter 5, a company's internal production processes should be tuned to meet customer needs. Until a firm knows what its customers want and will pay for in the future, it cannot effectively increase the efficiency of its internal operations. Many companies that have completed internal efficiency-improving projects successfully found that they were very efficiently creating products that customers did not want or adding value to aspects of their business that were irrelevant to their customers.

Technology-Based Creative Destruction Is a Series of Risks and Rewards

Since today's management of creative destruction is based largely on the use of advanced technologies, we must recognize and deal with the uncertainty that is inherent is technology-based change. Let us face head on the fact that the deployment of new technologies of any type carries numerous risks. For many centuries, societies have accepted, often out of ignorance, these risks—including the proven risks to human life. For example, the naval technologies that allowed Christopher Columbus to sail to the Americas also carried the diseases that eradicated entire Native American societies. In more recent times, many pilots and navigators have sacrificed their lives unintentionally by helping society to learn how the latest aircraft technologies actually perform.

The financial risks to backers of new technologies also tend to be high. Venture capitalists willingly report that a significant number of their investments do not return the profits anticipated. As recently as 2001, aggressive investors in technology stocks lost staggeringly large percentages of their investments as the dotcom and telecom stock price bubble of the previous few years burst. Making and losing money through investments in cutting-edge technology is not new to the modern era—historians have recorded the successes and failures of new technology-based ventures and projects for centuries. In today's accelerated business climate, however, the few spectacular technology-based successes are also accompanied by the costs of a larger number of smaller failures.

With such a high frequency of technology-based failures, it is no wonder that most conservative, business-focused executives are reluctant to invest in the use of new information systems within their organizations.

Technology executives have learned that they must be both vigilant and comfortable with the possible negative consequences and failures of technology. Yes, there are abundant examples of how technology should not be deployed all around. Technology executives all can and should learn from the mistakes of others—and their own bad experiences. More to the point, it is important to ensure with "emagineering" that technology executives are knowledgeable about the problems that can arise from the inappropriate application of technology so that they do not foolishly repeat somebody else's failures.

The reality is that new technologies that have been deployed successfully on a large scale as part of the creative destruction process have created some of the most beneficial advances in our lifetimes. In fact, the successful deployment of many advanced technologies has created new employment opportunities for many and a higher standard of living for even more. Therefore, we must recognize that those who maneuver through the risks successfully will obtain rewards that are simply not available to those who will not even accept the challenge in the first place.

Technology Initiatives and Uncertainity Are Spread Throughout the Organization

What is different in today's corporations compared with those of yesterday is that the need to take technology risks has been pushed from the highest levels and specialized information systems departments all the way down and throughout the organization.

A good example of how the change in technology risk taking has expanded throughout organizations is 100 years old. One hundred years ago, the decision as to whether a shipbuilding company would stay with wood and sails or take up the challenge of mastering the technologies of steel and steam was the responsibility of the managing board of directors. Period. Vice presidents and other executives were not allowed to take any initiative on their own about the use of new technologies. Perhaps as a result of such restricted decision making, most of the builders of the great wooden tall-mast sailing ships of the late 1800s never made the transition to building transoceanic steel steamships. Move the clock up to today, and one finds that the decision to implement a company's dramatic new Web site may have been initiated by a director-level manager in the marketing department. Or the actual creation of the first generation of computer applications may be written by others outside the formal information systems group. For example, in western Australia, prison guards on the evening and night shifts who wanted to occupy their time wrote many of the core applications automating the administrative processes—creatively replacing the paper system—for the penal systems. Businesses now expect that even their newest employees will take the formerly perceived technology risks associated with entering data into and accessing information from computer systems. Even automobile mechanics working in car dealerships must know how to use information systems to record the services they have performed on a car for customer-billing and record-keeping purposes.

To realize the objective of making all its employees comfortable with today's information systems, Ford Motor Company in the United States is subsidizing the placement of a personal computer (PC) in and Internet connection to the homes of its employees—including and especially assembly-line workers. With this move, it hopes to make its employees more comfortable with using information technologies *and* provide a direct two-way communication source into their homes. No longer will communications among employees, their families, and Ford be restricted mainly to the workplace—it will available at all times and all places where there is a device that can access Ford's employee Web sites and e-mail. Yet, at the same time, the employees will need to take responsibility for maintaining, operating, and upgrading this technology—which will be new to many of them.

The reality of our new electronic information–based society is that those individuals who are willing to take the risks associated with adopting new technologies and can learn their power and limitations successfully before the competition have a greater probability of achieving superior rewards than those who want to remain in the status quo.

Moreover, those who are unwilling to learn how to use even well-understood older information technologies for basic communications and clerical tasks can look forward to dropping lower in the economic hierarchy. Not being willing to initiate change and embrace the uncertainty of using new technologies is the equivalent deficiency in winner corporations of somebody who could neither read nor write a mere two generations ago.

Technology Is Invisible

This brings us to the crux of the problem of managing advanced information technology uncertainty. Because information technology is largely invisible—the actual operation of information systems is hidden and only the results are visible—it is difficult or impossible for buyers to fully understand the capabilities and limitations of the products that are being marketed to them before they actually use them. In addition, users of technology cannot see all the functionality they have—or what is missing that they thought they had.

The invisibility factor in information systems products makes their acquisition and deployment radically different from the way equipment was purchased and used in the manufacturing industries. Unfortunately, the way capital goods were bought and maintained in the manufacturing world is the way traditional executives have been taught to direct the process of obtaining and managing information systems products. However, because these types of products are so different—you can see and touch the physical machinery required for manufacturing, whereas information-technology products are ephemeral—the management approach to each must be very different.

Most manufacturing companies expected to learn about new and advanced manufacturing, warehousing, and office products from their suppliers. If a company was considering buying a new piece of equipment, such as a state-of-the-art machine tool, conveyor, printing press, rolling mill, injection-molding machine, etc., it expected the supplier to describe the specifications and capabilities of the machinery accurately before it was purchased. In addition, these attributes could be verified easily when the product was delivered to the plant. With physical products, it also was relatively easy to see when a new product model had so much greater functionality than the machinery a company had installed—such as a new printing press that could print four times faster, cost 80 percent less to operate per year, and produce much higher-quality output—that there was no question about replacing the existing one.

Acquirers of advanced information technology, on the other hand, are dealing with very complex products whose critical components are essentially invisible to them. Buyers of complex processors can never see the million plus transistors opening and closing their switches, and users of commercial software programs are provided with code that is readable only by computers. While they can see what is on their screens, they do not know what is happening in the computer hardware on which the application is running or within the program itself. Moreover, unlike a machine tool that they could inspect physically to learn its functionality, they must explore and experiment with a software application in many different ways to determine what it can and cannot do.

Users have found that today's advanced technologies require an often far-too-lengthy exploration and learning period on their part to fully understand. And maintaining the knowledge in-house that the company's employees originally received from a supplier's training course is very difficult. Many technology executives have learned from experience that functionality in a technology component that is available but not important immediately is often forgotten quickly by the information systems specialists in charge of supporting it.

The invisibility of technology components means that managing their evaluation, deployment, and operation is a much more complex task for technology executives than for manufacturing managers who actually could see all parts of their equipment and machinery.

Technology Suppliers Continuously under Pressure

This leads to another key issue bearing on technology uncertainty: Many traditional executives want to know why technology suppliers do not provide the same level of accuracy and comprehensiveness of pre-sales information that they were accustomed to when they acquired such highly visible physical products as manufacturing equipment.

The straightforward answer is that despite their best efforts, high-tech suppliers cannot know how real-world users might employ the extensive functionality built into even their most basic products. For example, a word-processing application might be used for writing uncomplicated memos, well-formatted letters, legal briefs, medical records, newsletters, research reports, reference books, etc. The supplier's development team will add functionality for each group of users that it identifies and whose needs it wants to meet, but functions that meet one customer's needs may be totally irrelevant to others. Within a relatively short time, the supplier's own marketing organization can become overwhelmed with information about what the word-processing software can do and is not really sure about what it cannot do. Eventually, the marketing team leaves the onus on its prospects' technology evaluators to acquire the word processor, learn what it can and cannot do, and then decide whether it wants to purchase licenses for every member of the organization to use. While this is an example for a relatively inexpensive technology component, a PC word processor, remember that almost the same process occurs when purchasing multi-million dollar information-technology components.

The ability of any technology supplier to accurately and comprehensibly communicate what is possible and what is not with its products is limited—especially in the personal computing space. As any consumer can attest, their frustration about buying application software is that only after they have agreed to the licensing terms during installation can they find our from the documentation (which is contained within the program itself and can only be read after it is installed) what its capabilities and limitations actually are. Even in the professional world of enterprise-level computing, an old joke about many of the engineering-oriented pioneer suppliers in the information-technology industry is that they would sell the first versions of their latest and greatest products only to customers who would agree to write the manuals for them—and there may have been more truth than irony in this stab at frustrated humor.

Do not expect suppliers' press releases, advertising, and product descriptions to be overly helpful in fully explaining a product's capabilities. Because high-tech suppliers find themselves under tremendous pressure to meet the needs of the largest possible potential marketplace with their offerings, they often embellish the descriptions of the functionality available with their products while not mentioning the absence of key capabilities that many prospects would assume were included.

The pressures on a high-tech supplier that cause prospective buyer uncertainty are not just limited to marketing departments. Internally, product developers are working against tight time schedules and embarrassing-to-move deadlines while attempting to add to their products as much functionality as possible and ensuring that these features will work as promised. In addition, product developers may disregard the constraints of their company's marketing requests and requirements. They often will add functionality above and beyond the base-level internal product specifications because they believe users will find value in their bright new ideas. Or they may subtract promised functionality because they cannot create it in time or to the required level of quality. This occasionally will result in a high-tech supplier shipping a product with functionality that does not work as promised. Remember the "sleep" function on laptop PCs running Windows 98? It was shown as a choice on the shutdown menu and marketed widely, but it rarely worked on any of the generally available models.

Integrating Component Systems Technology Uncertainity

Experience has shown that while the uncertainty surrounding a single advanced-technology component is high enough, it increases significantly when different products from different suppliers must be integrated to create a complete information systems solution—either on a PC or for an enterprise-wide mission-critical information system. Sometimes the various components work together as promised—but often each needs to be modified in numerous ways to ensure that all components work as a unified system.

In addition, high-tech suppliers often have an attitude that if the current release of their product does not work as promised, especially for integrating with other technology components, this is not a fatal flaw. After all, they can always send their customers an upgrade or post a software patch on their Web site for downloading with the originally promised functionality. As a result, end users often find their suppliers inexplicably blasé about shipping products with missing functionality that they wanted and expected. However, the supplier is often happy just to be shipping a quality product on time that includes most of the functionality its most important customers are demanding. The software necessary to integrate the supplier's product with others to build the unique system a user was counting on often may be delivered well after the initial product release.

Technology Suppliers' Own Technology Dilemma

Technology executives understand that suppliers operate under a two-pronged market dynamic that makes their lives very difficult. One prong is the desire to support their installed base of customers. Supporting one's installed base should be a relatively profitable business. The problem is that installed-base customers tend to negotiate very sharply on price. This is especially true of customers who are using mature technologies that are well understood. They see themselves in a situation where forcing their incumbent high-tech supplier to lower its prices significantly every year is simply good business. The customer's trump card against its legacy supplier is to declare that it will be moving to new and more advanced technologies if its supplier does not provide major price concessions.

This is where the second prong comes into play. If and when the incumbent supplier announces that it is making a leap to a significantly new generation of better-performing, more reliable products, the underlying technology probably will be incompatible with the previous generation. That is, the supplier will be leaving its installed base behind without an upgrade path (or a limited one) as it too engages in the creative destruction process of abandoning an older generation of technology for the next new one. However, taking such an action—leaving customers without a painless upgrade path—quickly creates a business relationship that no longer includes the high level of trust required for long-term success. For example, Microsoft broke many trust relationships when it introduced versions of its Office suite of products that created documents that were incompatible with earlier versions. While this action forced users of older versions to upgrade more rapidly than they intended, increasing Microsoft's revenues at a greater than anticipated rate for several quarters, it also opened the door for Microsoft's competitors to come into corporations and win the next round of orders in emerging areas outside the PC marketplace, such as multiuser operating systems, databases, and tools for building Internet infrastructures, that Microsoft wanted to dominate.

Considering the pressures a supplier is under, the processes that it undertakes to develop its products, and the inherent complexity of the products themselves, it is no wonder that there is a great deal of uncertainty regarding what is being sold. Moreover, this uncertainty extends into how long current versions of a product will be supported and when the supplier will move to the next generation of incompatible products. These structural issues are accentuated by marketing efforts that are developed with the only objective being to increase revenues—not educate prospective customers.

Technology Marketing Puffery and Product Life Cycles

When a technology supplier—either a new startup or an entrenched competitor—introduces a totally new product or an updated version of an existing one, it needs to garner as much attention and generate as much excitement as possible throughout its target customer base. This often leads to *marketing puffery*—claiming functionality that alternative products do not have (but may still work poorly in the current version of the supplier's new product) or making outrageous competitive claims of product superiority without highlighting the special circumstances under which these advantages are demonstrable.

Then, as a product matures, it is more difficult to generate fresh interest from potentially new customer groups. Even after adding more functionality with new versions, the supplier finds that it must work harder and harder to convince users of its increased value. Yet it must attempt to do so both to maintain the highest pricing levels possible and to capture as much follow-on business as possible within its installed base.

During these last stages in the product life cycle, one of the most common marketing tactics is to promise significant future enhancements—soon. To meet this objective, large corporate customers often are asked to review the functionality planned for the next generation of product releases under strict nondisclosure agreements. While the futures look excellent, there is no guarantee that the next release of the product will perform as anticipated. However, such tactics do tend to delay company decision makers from undertaking the costly and disruptive effort of throwing out an older set of products and replacing them with newer types of technologies from alternative suppliers.

Figure 7-1 illustrates the product life cycle of a successful technology product. For some products, such as IBM mainframes and

Microsoft's Windows operating system, the life cycle from introduction to decline (including numerous version releases) can last decades—for most others, it is much shorter. The marketing programs that support the product are very different based on which phase of the life cycle the product is in at the time.

Understanding why high-tech suppliers market the way they do allows technology executives to make better decisions regarding the timing of their product acquisitions and to set realistic expectations for what will be delivered compared with what may have been promised.

Figure 7-1 Successful technology product life cycle.

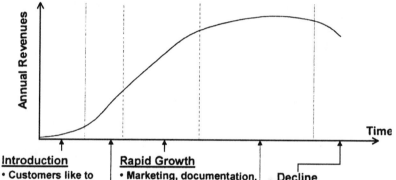

Introduction
- Customers like to experiment
- Supplier is learning from users the strengths and weaknesses of the product
- Documentation may not be accurate
- Marketing may be more hype than reality

Rapid Growth
- Marketing, documentation, and product capabilities become more closely aligned
- Experienced professionals are available to help new users
- Supplier buys complementary suppliers to add functionality
- Successful suppliers emphasize user support

Decline
- Supplier reduces R&D support for product
- Smaller competitors exit business
- Marketing and trade media coverage become insignificant
- Users stop acquiring upgrades
- Few new user projects include the product

Early Acceptance
- Supplier adds functionality as rapidly as possible with new releases
- Supplier establishes alliances with systems integrators and complementary suppliers
- User communities established to share common knowledge
- Trade media provides in-depth coverage
  - Early users report first-strike advantages gained

Maturity
- Customers are price sensitive
- Supplier is promising updated functionality in next release to compete with newer technologies
- Little interest to evaluate on part of media or industry watchers
- Oversupply of professionals skilled in product deployment and use

Technology executives who implement "emagineering"-based projects successfully have learned that they will have closer, better, and longer working relationships with their most trusted suppliers when they can differentiate confidently among the substance, the puffery, and the future hopes present in all high-tech product marketing communications. From a creative destruction perspective, understanding why high-tech suppliers frequently overpromise and underdeliver, such as in their inability to successfully provide the Internet-based two-way video-conferencing so many have promised for the last several years, forewarns corporate executives from taking revolutionary approaches to technology change when market-value-building evolutionary options are available.

Intimidating Print Advertising

Many high-tech suppliers' recent advertising efforts are offputting for business executives. To gain awareness, too many high-tech suppliers have begun running print ads that are unfathomable to most business-focused executives and almost all information systems executives. Their messages may have a hidden code for professional technologists who are on the "inside," or the intentions of the advertisements may be to educate business-oriented executives about the supplier's offerings and capabilities, but they are more likely to convince executives that all technology is risky and that whatever choices their organizations make will be wrong.

This is so despite all the high-tech marketers' hopes that through their advertisements in business print media they will impress the specific business executives who must sign off on capital appropriations requests.

Crazy, off-the-wall high-tech advertisements do more harm than good. They convince executives who want to remain focused only on business issues that they can never master even the basics of managing enterprise-wide advanced-technology deployment projects. Moreover, information systems executives cannot use them to explain the benefits the supplier's offerings might bring to the business.

Technology executives have learned that suppliers who waste their marketing resources on increasing the business-technology divide rarely can become trusted suppliers. High-tech executives are simply out of touch with reality when they believe that advanced-technology marketing means using outlandish advertising themes that do not communicate a product's benefits and only increase the risk and uncertainty levels of corporate executives.

Scalability and Reliability Are Business-Critical Variables

When evaluating technology uncertainty for enterprise-level information systems, decision makers realistically should assess the scalability and reliability of the advanced technologies they are considering. While many consumers take the scalability and reliability of information systems for granted, there is a real skill and talent to creating systems that can support thousands and millions of users (think America Online, Amazon.com, eBay, and Fidelity Investments) simultaneously without ever being shut down for repairs and all the while accurately maintaining their entire data set and running complex applications.

The biggest headache for large organizations that have implemented innovative business processes based on new advanced technologies successfully is that after the functionality is proven and the application becomes widely available, the hardware, software, or communications components often cannot scale up to meet the needs of very large numbers of users. In "emagineering," this is called the *failure of success.* That is, the information system that appeared to be able to give a business a competitive advantage running on a small compute server with a few demonstrators or in a controlled pilot situation slows down and fails to meet the needs of large numbers of production users—especially when the users are dispersed throughout the world. An excellent example of not planning for success occurred when Victoria's Secret attempted to conduct a Web-based fashion show of its newest line of lingerie—only to leave hundreds of thousands of potential prospects frustrated at their inability to access it. Most of those who did log on left laughing at the poor quality of the video and audio being delivered from overloaded systems.

Reliability must be maintained as systems support both more users and more applications. As both more users and more applications are added to a system, there are greater opportunities for errors to occur. In addition, even professional technology experts do not know how information systems really will work under conditions that have never been experienced before.

An excellent example of such reliability issues is found in the ubiquitous Windows-based PC. Microsoft attempts to make Windows as broad-based as possible. That is, it wants to be able to support all existing desktop applications and be the target platform for all future applications—from games to office functions to engineering design and analysis. At the same time, PC and add-on board manufacturers attempt to mold their products around Microsoft's Windows offering in such a way as to appeal to the largest number of potential users and to beat the competition by offering the lowest price possible—often by cutting quality and testing corners. Finally, end users load their Windows PCs with applications and add-on cards from any number of different suppliers. The final result is that many users experience the "blue screen of death" as their overloaded PCs encounter a fatal error that causes them to stop operating. Moreover, while all the suppliers involved tend to blame the others to a certain degree, the reality is that even the basic, commodity-like Windows PC has reliability problems when it is asked to scale up and support too many application tasks. No wonder Microsoft releases new version of Windows every 2 years or so with the claim that the new version is more reliable than the last.

In very large enterprise servers and applications, reliability becomes an even more critical issue. For example, early versions of Microsoft's enterprise-class operating system and database were claimed to rival the capabilities of more expensive IBM products. Yet, if Microsoft's products ran for too long without being restarted, they unexpectedly would crash. Such failures could both cause data to be lost and force users to remain idle waiting for their shared system to be placed back into operation. While IBM's equivalent products were more expensive in terms of acquisition costs, their superior reliability proved to provide lower operational costs. Even more worrisome, when a company's data records become corrupted or lost and cannot be relied on for billing and other critical functions, the business can be put in the precarious position of possibly failing.

When information systems professionals talk about the need for security, one of the key elements they are referring to is reliably preventing both authorized and unauthorized (hackers) users from unintentionally changing data or stealing information for their own personal gain. All prudent information systems executives know that mission-critical systems—those whose failure can cost the business measurable revenues, increase costs, or create legal liabilities—that lack reliability are a major potential liability for the organization.

Mission-Critical Certainty
versus Non-Mission-Critical Uncertainty

The deciding factor on how much a company is willing to pay in terms of monies and functionality for greater scalability and reliability should be whether the application supports mission-critical business processes or not. For example, when the online systems of E*Trade or eBay are down, they are out of business. When an unauthorized hacker downloaded Egghead.com's database of customer credit cards, the company incurred additional costs to notify its customers and work with the FBI to track down the hacker. In addition, Egghead.com's reputation among buyers was ruined, and it was exposed to potential liabilities if the hacker sold the credit card numbers, names, and expiration dates to thieves. Such problems can be fatal to a corporation—and I note that after this incident, Egghead.com declared bankruptcy.

On the other hand, when a shared department work server that manages file, print, e-mail, and communications services for knowledge workers who maintain most of their documents on PCs fails, the cost is not nearly as high. While such a failure is an annoyance to those affected, it is not a mission-critical problem that will have either a long-term or a significant impact on the organization.

Creative destruction initiatives require technology executives to differentiate between the deployment of advanced technology for mission-critical create-market-value applications versus non-mission-critical personal productivity and internal efficiency applications. (Figure 7-2 highlights the difference between mission-critical and non-mission-critical systems.) Technology executives always must be prepared to acquire mission-critical systems for those applications which must operate with certainty.

If many newer productivity applications for normal-sized internal work groups had to run on systems that could scale to support thousands of users and never fail, they would be prohibitively expensive to justify. Yet these applications can add significant value to an organization by running in what is commonly known as "just good enough"

Figure 7-2 Mission-critical versus non-mission-critical system characteristics.

Mission-Critical	Non-Mission-Critical
• Higher initial cost to acquire components	• Up to 50+% lower cost for systems components
• Much higher operation and upgrade costs	• Operations cost up to 80+% lower
• Full-time, professional technologists provide support	• Departmental and part-time personnel provide support
• Objective for planned and unplanned downtime is less then 6 hours per year — even with 7X24 operations requirements	• Any of numerous components may fail at any time and entire system may be down for up to one working day
• Corrupted data can be recovered	• Data that are lost may not be recoverable
• Can grow system over time to handle any number of simultaneous users and support any number of applications	• When system capacity in terms of users and applications is exceeded, system may fail. Upgrading system may not be possible
• Cost of systems failure can be measured in terms of lost enterprise revenue or higher internal production expenses — or both	• Cost of systems failure may primarily be annoyance to a few individuals and requirement to recreate work at the departmental level

mode. However, applications that are accessed by customers and suppliers or are required to operate to maintain continuous internal business operations—think of a bank's automatic teller machine (ATM) systems—must be supported with as highly reliable and scalable technologies as possible.

Selecting Technologies the Technology Executive Way

One of the most difficult management challenges for both business and information systems professionals to overcome is how to select among several competing technologies. Since advanced technologies are still works in progress, each supplier can both trumpet its product's unique advantages and credibly highlight the weaknesses of its competitors' products. Yet the buyer can only choose one. And even more important than the cost of the technology is the assurance both that it can do the task for which it is being specifically acquired at the moment and that its supplier will improve on it aggressively in the future so that the organization can depend on it for many years to come.

The best insurance against needing to make a major technology change—removing one set of systems on which employees are trained and highly dependent and replacing it with another—is to acquire products based on technologies that are also purchased by most others. For those executives who are uncertain about making technology choices, a prudent rule of thumb is to buy from the leader in the product market as long as the leader is growing (in unit terms) at a greater rate than its competitors. This is a cautious and safe approach for technology executives who want to *manage* the deployment of advanced-technology components—not be experts in every aspect of evaluating technology.

The rationale for buying from a fast-growing industry leader is best exemplified by the failure of IBM's efforts to convince PC buyers to take the revolutionary step of migrating to its OS/2 operating system. When IBM took lone ownership for OS/2 (OS/2 was originally a joint IBM-Microsoft project), Microsoft was showing industry decision makers the evolutionary upgrade path that it was planning to deliver to the marketplace with its market-share-leading, fast-growing Windows operating system. IBM was basing its claims that OS/2 was superior to Windows on the undisputed facts that OS/2 was more reliable and more stable than Windows and IBM's support was more professional for corporate decision makers, especially in the area of integrating OS/2-based computers into an enterprise-wide network.

These two characteristics—reliability and support—won IBM and OS/2 the affections, planning directions, and monies of many corporate-level information systems professionals—especially in the banking industry. However, Windows met the needs of a wider range of users (including home/casual users, mobile users, gamers, small businesses, and cost-conscious users), software developers, and PC and add-on component manufactures.

Technology executives who selected Microsoft's Windows over IBM's OS/2 made the correct decision. IBM never acquired more than a miniscule share of the market for PC operating systems with OS/2. OS/2's growth (in terms of units shipped and placed into production year over year) was much lower than that of Microsoft's Windows due to its limited customer appeal. Armed with just these two factors—OS/2 had smaller market share and lower unit growth—technology executives could make the correct decision to select Windows for their companies' PCs.

Eventually, Microsoft's Windows squeezed OS/2 out of the market. And what was the result for those organizations which had committed early to OS/2 at IBM's urging? First, they were forced to adopt one of Microsoft's subsequent versions of the Windows operating systems at great expense. Second, it took many of them years to catch up to the internal information system productivity levels of firms that started down the Microsoft operating environment learning curve at the right time and were not sidetracked by OS/2.

Technology executives also use the input of high-tech industry analysts to determine the most appropriate technology choices for the future and to evaluate which past selections have been proven to be correct over time. High-tech industry market analysts often are helpful in assisting companies in selecting the technologies that will have the longest useful life. Market analysts provide a tremendous amount of value in identifying alternative technologies; describing where early users have found them most effective; estimating size, growth rates, and market share of technology markets as they have (often too broadly) defined them; and analyzing the probability of longer-term success for specific products.

Market analysts, like weather forecasters, are not always correct in their projections. However, looking through their rear-view mirrors, market research firms generally can provide users with the relative sales levels of different technology products. Technology executives want to be either using the products that are gaining market share, as opposed to those which are losing it, or carefully monitoring when and why they should make the transition from a loser to a future winner technology to support the business processes on which their operations depend.

Continuous Relearning

For an organization to increase its certainty about the capabilities and quality of a new and advanced technology takes time, experience, and money. With the aggressive deployment of advanced technologies, one of the increased overhead costs for a company is the expense of accurately staying abreast of what suppliers' latest products can and cannot do and how they might improve the organization's business operations. This task is so important that some corporations designate a chief technical officer and staff to carry it out and report their findings directly to the board of directors. Many multinational companies have made it the key objective for their corporate chief information officer to focus on and then use his or her knowledge to guide the numerous lines-of-business management teams in their deployment of "emagineering" initiatives. While becoming savvy about advanced technology has a cost, it is also an investment for future returns and staying up with or ahead of the competition.

One of the more disconcerting issues traditional executives face when reducing technology uncertainty is that to be successful, they must learn new facts continuously and change their opinions on old knowledge learned well. This is a difficult assignment both organizationally and personally—especially in the fast-changing world of high technology and in the midst of unreliable supplier marketing. Yet winning with advanced technology and advancing to the level of a technology executive require continuous relearning. Creative destruction includes replacing old knowledge about what advanced technologies can and cannot do with new knowledge.

Experience shows that for technology executives, relearning technology realities is best accomplished through peer-to-peer meetings and discussions. As a result, many technology executives attempt to attend as many conferences and structured peer-to-peer meetings as possible. When done properly, such meetings allow technology executives to talk among themselves in a language that is incomprehensible to either their business-only or information systems–only peers. It is a time when skepticism about both trusted technology suppliers' current offerings and their promised next-generation product releases can be aired in a constructive, working environment—and experiences with offerings from relatively unknown suppliers can be raised and discussed objectively.

However, to make these peer-to-peer meetings productive for the organization and not just fact-finding educational experiences, the corporation's technology executives really need to know and fully understand how the company wants to transform its business processes. Armed with knowledge of the objectives that the corporation would like to achieve with advanced technology, the organization's best technology executives can learn better (and in greater detail) from others what the state of the science allows—and what it does not.

Gaining Certainity from Others

Another means of relearning is for technology executives to monitor the use of technology both within their industry and by other unrelated organizations because, over time, advanced technologies will migrate from one industry grouping to another. For example, the enterprise resource planning (ERP) applications provided by SAP (a major German-based software company) had their first successful sales to multinational oil companies. SAP's applications soon were acquired by global high-tech suppliers and then by other manufacturing industries, such as consumer products. Now they have been placed in such diverse organizations as utilities, banks, insurance companies, and government agencies.

While many corporations have competitive analysis functions, they all too often focus only on the product offerings and distribution strategies of rivals. To support planning for the creative destruction process adequately, a company's competitive analysis group also needs to monitor just as carefully how others in the industry are implementing advanced technologies. For example, at the beginning of 2002, "emagineering" practices would suggest that based on the current experiences of pioneering organizations in other industries and in other regions of the world, a firm's competitive analysis function should include a determination as to how wireless communications might soon be deployed by one's competitors to improve customer support efforts and internal business processes.

In addition, technology executives need to be assigned to meet regularly with high-tech suppliers to learn what advanced technologies they are offering, planning to offer, and are using themselves internally to replace existing operations. These meetings can be organizationally sensitive because the formal information systems organization typically wants all responsibility and control over supplier relationships so that it can manage them cost-effectively. (Remember, user organizations are much more cost-sensitive toward existing, mature applications that are installed and running than toward new and proposed productivity-increasing ones.)

Further problems may arise because supplier sales representatives often are directed to sell new end-user and organizational productivity applications around the company's formal information systems group. The company's information systems–focused managers and staff resent this because the difficulties and costs (the "warts" of the positive business case) involved with implementing new applications into the overall corporation's information architecture and then maintaining them over time are rarely brought to the forefront by the high-tech supplier's sales force. As a result, professional technologists typically wish to minimize or eliminate any direct contact between corporate executives and suppliers' salespeople.

Yet experience shows that the value gained by technology executives just by learning how their trusted suppliers themselves are actually using advanced technologies and what efforts they are going through to make "emagineering"-based business improvements to their own organizations is in itself immeasurable. Technology executives who meet with their peers in high-tech supplier organizations consistently report that these contacts both have made lasting impressions on their approach to technology within their own firms and have helped them learn the types of benefits from advanced information systems that are realistically possible for them to obtain.

High-level user-supplier conferences assist executives in achieving a greater degree of certainty in their understanding of the status of the many different and newly available technologies at any one point in time. For example, Motorola manufacturing executives who visited Hewlett-Packard in the early 1990s learned about the advanced information systems technologies Hewlett-Packard had deployed to cost-effectively build terminals and other commodity-level devices. They then implemented many of those processes (using Hewlett-Packard systems, of course) when they established Motorola's high-volume cell-phone manufacturing operation.

Moreover, experienced technology executives insist on meeting in person with their peers in other companies who are already using a technology they are evaluating and their trusted and potential supplier executives. They have found that face-to-face meetings are the only way to determine with certainty the truthfulness of the information they are being provided in an effort to persuade them to rely on a new advanced technology as the basis for initiating a project based on the principle of creative destruction.

Findings Need to Be Communicated

The results of technology executives' efforts to relearn what is possible and what others are doing with advanced technologies to increase their operational capabilities need to be collected in an online collaborative knowledge base. The relevant observations and findings then can and should be summarized as input for "emagineering" planning sessions.

The importance of this is twofold. First, it allows immediate dissemination of newly discovered information about advanced technologies throughout the organization. Second, it allows those actively monitoring advanced technologies to track over time both the maturing of specific products and the lessening of interest in older products that are being rejected for new applications.

The capability to maintain a collaborative reporting system has been instituted in all leading independent information systems consulting firms. This technology has proven to be a significant productivity tool and a key part of their own professional services automation efforts. A similar capability needs to be part of the information infrastructure of every corporation engaged in improvements through creative destruction based on advanced technologies, and it needs to be accessible to all the corporation's technology executives.

Advanced Development Groups for Primary Learning

There is yet an additional and key relearning tool used by many large corporations. While it is the most expensive, it provides these corporations with a window directly into suppliers' development laboratories. This tactic is to create a testing laboratory within the user organization itself. Such a laboratory, usually called an *advanced development group*, acquires promising new technologies from suppliers, creates "emagineering"-based applications that might benefit the business significantly, and then showcases these applications and the projected business benefits and costs involved to senior executives for possible enterprise-wide deployment.

The corporate benefit of maintaining an advanced development group is that it has extremely close contact with suppliers' developers. This means that it can both influence what functionally is included in new products and know with a great amount of certainty what those products can and cannot do at any point in time. The two disadvantages are that it is extremely expensive to run and that if it is not managed properly, it will not provide the significant returns possible.

The most important task of advanced development groups should be to increase the corporation's overall efficiency and effectiveness by assisting in the evolutionary enhancement of business processes. However, in the past, many corporations have transformed their advanced development groups into departments whose objective is to focus merely on lowering current information systems costs.

Other companies have allowed their advanced development groups to attempt to become software developers and technology integrators. This is often exciting for many senior corporate executives—especially those who have to communicate regularly with the investment community—because they believe that they are inventing a unique competitive advantage. Reality soon sets in, however, and it is seen that the total cost to create, integrate, support, and upgrade complex technologies is too high for even the largest corporation to manage comfortably for just one customer—itself. Such an operation usually will be shut down or sold off at some time in the future as the costs keep mounting and the rest of the organization expresses its dissatisfaction with what it considers to be the noncompetitive services provided.

However, a properly managed advanced development group can allow the company to establish a direct linkage for learning the breadth of advanced technologies the leading suppliers are able to deliver and how they can be applied across a wide range of the corporation's business processes ahead of the competition.

Buying versus Building Knowledge

Another key question whose answer technology executives need to be comfortable with is, "Why does the company need to develop and maintain this knowledge itself? Why should it not buy advanced technology insights from consultants and market analysts?" The answer is clear after one has been through the "emagineering" process: The technology executives *themselves* need to participate continuously in the relearning process to know how to evaluate the recommendations of third parties for their company's specific needs.

Consultants and technology-industry watchers analyze new developments with their own unique assumptions about their specific client base's needs—and different clients have dissimilar interests and concerns. To be successful, consultants have to make assumptions about what their clients are seeking to accomplish with new technologies.

While consultants and industry watchers are an excellent source of information for relearning, they rarely can provide a company with a customized, optimal solution for itself unless they are engaged full time—not occasionally called in on a sporadic basis simply to provide insights about current and potential trends.

Many technology executives attend conferences sponsored by industry watchers. These conferences offer access to excellent expert speakers and the ability to meet directly with high-tech suppliers. Yet the attendees consistently report that the most important knowledge obtained from a conference comes through informal meetings with their peers who have real hands-on experience with the technologies they are most interested in evaluating.

Since technology executives all know that learning is the starting point of action, the logical conclusion is that companies must relearn technology for themselves to create the executive and staff consensus required for initiating creative destruction–focused change.

Selecting Where to Be in the
Technology Uncertainity–Corporate Impact Matrix

All this leads to a fundamental strategic issue for technology executives to face and answer as part of the creative destruction process: How much technology uncertainty should they be willing to manage? Different industries treat technology uncertainty differently due to the nature of their business operations and products. And different firms within the same industry manage against technology uncertainty differently due to the impact their executives believe it will have on their market value. (No, organizations cannot eliminate technology uncertainty and manage with complete certainty.)

However, technology uncertainty is only one part of the equation technology executives must consider. The other part is what the impact of deploying new and advanced technologies will have on the company.

Traditional executives might believe that advanced technologies should be implemented initially to support business processes that only have a small impact on the business. Yet technology executives in such industries as financial brokerage and trading services have found that because the success of their firms is highly dependent on the competitively superior capabilities of their information systems, they must aggressively initiate high-impact projects that contain a large degree of uncertainty to stay ahead (or at least abreast) of their competition. Their product, money, is basically a commodity represented in electronic form that has a large number of alternative suppliers around the globe. They can be profitable only if their operations are more effective and efficient than those of their competitors—and the leading-edge deployment of advanced technologies in an effort to continuously improve on existing business process by replacing them with far better ones is a key means for achieving this objective. They must deploy high-risk technologies that will have an impact on their entire corporation to be successful. Therefore, winner financial trading and brokerage services companies maintain a high degree of in-house advanced-technology expertise because it provides them with the tangible rewards of survival and success.

Different companies choose different tradeoffs regarding the uncertainty of new technologies performing as planned versus the potential impact on the corporation's market value. Figure 7-3 describes the extreme positioning points that corporations might pursue on the technology uncertainty versus corporate impact matrix.

Just as financial brokerage and trading services firms want to be in the top-right corner of the technology uncertainty–corporate impact matrix, so do high-tech suppliers for running their own internal operations. High-tech suppliers are willing to deal with a large degree of uncertainty with the products they use to manage their own business processes because they believe that they have the core competencies necessary to deploy advanced technologies proficiently, their employees love experimenting with the latest and least-understood technologies, and they believe that they can sell the expertise they gain in working with advanced technologies to their current customers.

Figure 7-3 Technology uncertainty–corporate impact matrix.

	Low · Uncertainty of Technology Performing as Planned · High
High Potential Impact on Enterprise Market Valuation	Large corporations in mature industries seeking to cut costs and/or significantly increase customer support and satisfaction	Companies that rely on technology for competitive advantage and/or provide their target customer base with offerings that contain a high degree of information services
Low	Enterprises that are managing to the averages with the objective of avoiding being labeled an exceptional laggards	Firms experimenting with technology for the love of technology

**Uncertainty of Technology
Performing as Planned**

Note: Descriptions are for companies at the extreme corners of the matrix. Most orgaizations will be closer to the middle.

On the other hand, most government agencies and regulated monopolies (such as utilities and health care providers) tend to want to manage toward the lower-left corner of the matrix. Neither sector typically has the competition required to motivate the organizations within them into becoming the best in class, and in many cases the customers they serve are locked into them. Increasing their value based on competency with advanced information technologies in the protected economy is still the exception—not the rule.

In addition, the laws and regulations under which government agencies and regulated monopolies operate were drafted long before their oversight boards anticipated significant cost and productivity improvements from advanced information technologies. Individual risk taking is strongly discouraged—employees who make mistakes can expect to be reprimanded strongly, while personal financial rewards for individual achievement typically are miniscule. And both sectors require long, drawn-out planning, evaluation, and feasibility studies before the acquisition and deployment of advanced technologies can be accomplished.

The result is that while government agencies and regulated monopolies buy tried-and-true technology, it usually is obsolete relatively soon after deployment. Moreover, since most organizations in these sectors do not have vigorous continuous-improvement programs in place for upgrading their business processes and the information systems on which they are based, the information-based services they offer are often far from satisfying to the clientele they service and support.

One of the most public examples in the United States of managing to the bottom-left matrix is the air traffic control system. The technology used by air traffic controllers is acknowledged by all but a few diehards within the government agency that oversees air traffic control operations (the Federal Aviation Administration) to be antiquated compared with what is available currently. The agency seems to be continuously evaluating new technologies from highly regarded companies, such as Boeing, but delaying making acquisition and deployment decisions until the technologies stabilize and the certainty regarding how they will work in a production environment is higher. At the same time, airlines, passengers, airport authorities, and the air traffic controllers themselves are extremely frustrated at the limitations the current information system puts on the ability of airlines to add flights and operate existing flights more efficiently, safely, and on schedule.

By examining government agencies and other organizations that have similar management cultures, corporate technology executives have learned that by being too close to the bottom-left corner of the technology uncertainty–corporate impact matrix, companies increase the risks of being inefficient and ineffective in delivering services. On the other hand, businesses that have learned to manage much farther to the upper-right corner will create a tighter loyalty bond with their customers as they better meet their needs.

Let Pioneers Blaze Trails

Most technology executives have found that their highest comfort level with technology uncertainty is right after "bleeding edge" users have experimented with it. That is, they are willing to deal with high levels of technology uncertainty if the rewards also appear to be large—but they do not want to be the pioneers who first discover how the new technologies work.

Newly launched advanced technologies typically will be consumed first either by companies with special needs or desires that could not be met until the new technology was launched or by those few large organizations (including advanced military research laboratories) whose business strategies include technology adventurism. During and after deployment, the technology executives in these bleeding-edge firms will then provide their peers, through various channels, with their evaluation of the benefits their firms obtained and the offsetting problems inherent in the technology itself.

Profit-driven technology executives tend to want to be a quick second to adopt advanced technologies when the potential benefits far outweigh the intrinsic uncertainties. However, to be in a position to do so, they must monitor the advanced-technology landscape continuously to identify the appropriate opportunities.

Managing for Risk and Value

Based on the experiences of companies that manage according to the principles of creative destruction, technology executives have come to the counterintuitive conclusion that it is better to be higher on the uncertainty component of the technology uncertainty–corporate impact matrix for projects that touch the business's external ecosystem—customers and suppliers—and lower for projects that are intended merely to lower internal information systems costs.

The rationale for this conclusion is that a company increases revenues the most by being perceived as providing a higher level of customer care and support than alternative suppliers. To achieve this value position in the opinion of its target customer base, it must invest in deploying the latest advanced technologies properly—where the most technology uncertainty resides—before its competitors. Since most companies are constrained in terms of the number and types of technology executives they can put in charge of change-management projects, putting their best people on projects that have the greatest potential for gaining market share must have the highest priority.

Lowering internal information systems costs, on the other hand, is a sinkhole for valuable resources. Since vice presidents of management information systems often are evaluated with far too much emphasis on the percentage cost of information systems resources to revenues, they have a personal stake in assigning their best staff to internal departmental cost-reduction projects that have relatively low corporate market-value impact. The payback to the organization for these efforts is minor compared with customer- and ecosystem-enhancing improvements.

Therefore, for internal information systems efficiency-improving projects, it is better to use technologies whose capabilities the organization is relatively certain about and assign the deployment task to managers who are more technology-driven than business-savvy. For example, there are numerous examples of organizations, most publicly in recent years Oxford Health, a New York regional health care and insurance provider, that have attempted to upgrade their internal accounting systems using technologies beyond their competence level and inadequately planning for and implementing the necessary business-process changes. The results often have been an unexpectedly high negative impact on the companies (Oxford Health destroyed much of its market value) resulting from failed projects that would have done little to improve their market value even if they had been successful.

Lessons Learned from Experience

Organizations need to take a disciplined approach to the creative destruction of their own assets and business processes to build market value over the long term. The art of "emagineering" management is to know when and how to implement the creative destruction process on a continuous basis throughout the corporation.

Deploying advanced technology involves many risks. Every initiative combining new technologies with innovative business processes has the potential for problems from numerous and often unexpected causes. Technology executives understand that this is life in today's Competitive Economy—and get on with the efforts necessary to achieve success. Conversely, successfully mastering new technologies also can lead to great benefits.

High-tech suppliers do not always communicate their offerings' capabilities and limitations accurately to customers for many reasons—

including the positive reason that their products are often so feature-rich that they do not know what the products can and cannot do. Moreover, technology suppliers themselves do not always know how their products will work as individual components integrated with others in a larger information system. They often learn from the experiences of their early customers.

Information systems products frequently do not scale in terms of both the number of users and the applications they can support as their users would like. Only real-world operations can prove the scalability capabilities of most technology components.

Systems reliability is vital for supporting end users running mission-critical applications. Yet, when a technology component is pushed beyond the capacity for which it was designed, it often becomes unreliable. Information systems professionals understand that it is paramount for them to keep corporate data safe and secure so that users can rely on them. Achieving the highest levels of reliability for information systems operations means not corrupting data (the data entered will be the same as the data retrieved), not losing data, and minimizing the risks of data being stolen or misused by either internal employees or external hackers.

Never-ending relearning—accepting new answers to old questions as technology changes and improves—is paramount for remaining knowledgeable about the major technology issues that are critical to the long-term success of an organization. Technology executives' best source of information on what new information systems products can and cannot do comes from their peers in different companies. Technology executives need to continuously analyze their competitors' information systems–based initiatives, be knowledgeable about technology initiatives being launched by winner firms in other industries, and discover what applications and business processes their trusted high-tech suppliers are using to run their own businesses.

Technology executives must determine where on the technology uncertainty–corporate impact matrix they want their organization's different business processes to be managed before initiating new business-process improvement projects. Experience has shown that companies that are part of the Competitive Economy are most successful at building market value when they can successfully implement advanced technologies that have a major beneficial impact on their customers. While the risks inherent in such new technologies are high, the successful management of these risks can provide significant competitive advantages.

8

Competency 8: Enforcing Organizational Discipline

"E MAGINEERING" HAS DEVELOPED as a management technique to assist corporations in taking the enterprise-wide *actions* necessary to increase their market valuations. "Emagineering" is way more than an intellectual exercise for a small group of corporate executives and their staffs to refer to when identifying and discussing strategic options. "Emagineering" is a directive for technology executives to follow for successfully implementing the actions necessary to effect changes throughout their companies and across their ecosystems.

Technology executives in all industries have found that no matter how diverse their "emagineered" management strategies are, successful change actions are built on a bedrock of organizational disciplines:

- Agreement
- Common vision
- Planning
- Making decisions
- Avoiding analysis paralysis
- Build-review-improve-build cycle

- Acknowledging and correcting mistakes
- Technology timing
- Well-timed communications
- Leveraging change
- Education

The Discipline of Agreement

Experience has shown consistently that efforts to implement advanced technologies achieve their goals only when they are supported proactively by *all* of a company's senior executives. To be successful, these same senior executives must delegate an extremely high level of discretionary authority to managers lower in the organizational structure who are in charge of day-to-day implementation of changes so that they have the ability to make policy and tactical decisions quickly.

The double factors of proactive senior management support and delegation of authority give a clear signal to the rest of the organization that it needs to both actively assist with and follow the initiatives for change mandated by its senior executives. This means that management actions will be taken and business processes will be changed. Change will happen throughout the corporation.

However, if there is any dissension within the senior-management ranks, it will be communicated quickly down the organization. When there is undisciplined dissension at the senior-executive level regarding a technology-based initiative, the project probably will not be successful when success is measured in terms of the project meeting its original objectives. Why? In the past, organizations were built around the concept of long-term stability. Once a process or system was working, the organization learned to resist change and keep its standard practices working "as is"—no matter how imperfect—to meet the company's short-term objectives.

The invisible, or undocumented, rules and procedures under which organizations usually work define and limit the operational capabilities of a company that has not yet learned to take full advantage of information technologies to increase its effectiveness and efficiency in an evolutionary manner. When these undocumented rules are made inoperable due to senior-management directives, the organization is then forced to regroup and create new working patterns. The problem that operational managers must confront during change projects is that the organization itself does not work smoothly during the time it is regrouping to accommodate the new structure and procedures forced on it.

Over time, both the formal and informal leaders of most corporations' various departments have learned to develop defenses, often very subtle, against what they consider to be unnecessary upheavals. And one of these defenses is to test senior managers at every opportunity to determine how committed they and their peers really are to publicly announced changes. If the answer is that some of the senior-management team has reservations, the middle managers know that it is best to delay following any current change orders in the likely event that the corporate-level executives will alter their collective management course at some point in the not too distant future.

Technology executives understand that they must be part of the solution. They must coach others on why change is good and why the corporation is implementing changes in the most appropriate fashion—especially when faced with numerous tradeoffs. The presence of technology executives at all levels throughout an organization increases a company's ability to maintain the discipline of agreement.

The Discipline of a Common Vision

Another disruptive issue that arises frequently is that even if the executive team universally supports the change mandate, each member might have a different and individualistic vision of what the outcome should be. In this situation, middle managers throughout the organization can subvert change subtly by attempting to be helpful in telling the change-management team what, in their opinion, the company should be doing to improve its operations. Of course, every "suggestion" or "recommendation" will become critical to the success of the change project in the eyes of the middle managers involved—even if the different sets of middle-management-initiated guidance ideas are contradictory. In addition, the middle managers will be more than good enough to suggest extensions to the project that the original planners had never thought about in order to make sure the effort will maximize its return. This leads to well-intended expanding project scope.

As project scope creep gains momentum and lengthens the time to completion, increases the cost, and lowers the probability of overall satisfaction with the end results, the middle managers will in all honesty and sincerity argue, "If we are going to make these changes, we need to make them right." The result is chaos—the change project is now being planned as it is being implemented, and the discipline to maintain time, budget, functionality, quality, and documentation objectives quickly, even if accidentally, will be sacrificed in the confusion.

There is an old New England saying, "If you do not know where you are going, any road will take you there." The reverse of this is true in "emagineering." "If you do not know the road you are taking, you will never get there." What this means is that the organization itself should not be expanding its charter to create nice-to-have-but-not-necessary business processes at the same time that it is implementing new technologies. Middle managers who tend to encourage project scope creep cannot be expected to see the entirety of the evolution occurring in their company's customer base, fully understand how the entire corporation is being asked to transform itself (including and especially all the necessary and new departmental linkages) to meet these new market realities, and learn the capabilities and limitations of the new technologies on which the project is based.

In addition, it is unrealistic to expect 100 percent of a company's operational managers to be completely objective when recommending new business processes and organizational structures that certainly will affect their jobs and areas of responsibility. It is well understood within traditional corporations that during the course of any change project these same managers will be evaluated for raises and promotions based on their ability to run the daily operations of their departments—not on being the most enlightened advisors. However, in companies that do embrace "emagineering" and establish a culture in which managers collaborate across organizational boundaries, all executives are rewarded on their ability to assist successfully in the deployment of advanced technologies with a management-by-objectives bonus and higher potential promotional rankings in their personnel files. In this case, there is a strong incentive for managers to carry out the roles that have been assigned constructively as the organization makes the transition to achieve its new vision.

The Discipline of Planning

Technology executives conduct as much planning as possible and establish guidelines for how they want their organizations to change—with as much detail as possible—before start of the implementation phase of any new "emagineering"-initiated change project. As any good general knows, there can never be too much strategic, tactical, and contingency planning before a battle because as soon as the operation is committed to action, everything that can go wrong has a high probability of doing so. This does not mean that planning can go on indefinitely—it merely means that as much planning as possible should be done during the allocated planning phase (usually about 4 months, rarely more than 6) to help educate and prepare the change-management team before deployment.

Bringing the military lesson that whatever can go wrong will over to "emagineering," there must be an ability to act in a disciplined way to quickly put in place and communicate to others necessary deviations from the original plan. The key discipline is to change the plan when faced with the realities of implementation so that the resulting plan is an even better road map of how the project is expected to proceed.

The result of these two issues—first, plan extensively, but second, recognize that not every detail can be planned for—leads to a key aspect of the art of "emagineering." The corporation's senior executives must define as comprehensibly as possible the business polices they want the organization to follow. These policies must be captured in writing during the planning phase of any project. In addition, the responsible executives also should explain their business rationale for these policies so that the project-management team can make implementation decisions based on executive management's overall strategic objectives.

A typical business policy question for which the change-management team would need guidance might be, "Is it more important never to be out of stock of an item versus managing inventory to the most cost-efficient levels that occasionally will create out-of-stock situations?" The answer to this basic question will vary by industry for good business reasons. Greeting card manufacturers, for example, have 95 percent plus gross margins on incremental sales and sell thousand of units of the same type of card, so they never want to be out of stock, whereas power-supply manufacturers, to pick a counterexample, only have 30 percent margins and may never sell many of the product permutations they offer. A power-supply manufacturer therefore would be willing to be out of stock on its slowest-selling offerings.

Organizations whose most senior corporate executives clearly communicate throughout the organization what changes they are planning to make and how they are planning to use advanced technologies to make them before they start deployment actions have the highest track record of success. The time for making critical decisions about business policies, such as how orders will be entered or customer returns will be processed, is before the implementation process begins—not in the midst of the implementation effort when a team of high-priced programmers is in the middle of coding custom application software.

The Discipline of Making Desicions

Possibly the most important aspect of establishing a decision-making road map before embarking on any change process is that there has to be a clearly defined hierarchy of authority by business and technology issue area. The executives charged with making decisions must have a procedure in place whereby they are required to make business-process and technology-implementation decisions within 24 hours of the issue being escalated to the appropriate authority level. To paraphrase Harry Truman, in "emagineering," everybody knows where the buck stops—and when.

Implementing business and operational changes based on advanced technologies is a stressful duty for managers at all levels. Mastering the new systems is extremely nerve racking for frontline staff. All change creates uncertainty. And doing so with technology that is new to the organization increases the common anxiety level tremendously. This leads to many well-intentioned individuals freely giving their opinions about the entire project from their personal—and usually negative—viewpoint to relieve their own tension. In addition, these opinions can become more downbeat and spread throughout the organization if the project slows down (or comes to a screeching halt) due to the inability of team leaders to make decisions when faced with unexpected business issues or technology problems.

The solution is to ensure that each member of the project team is granted the authority to make decisions for his or her realm of responsibility. When an issue is raised to a team member with authority to make a decision, he or she must be required to specify exactly how the project *will* proceed regarding the issue within 24 hours.

The organizational additions that most companies will put in place to support their entire "emagineering" effort, but especially the 24-hour decision-making discipline rule, are illustrated in Figure 8-1. Key to the additions is the ability of the change-management project team leader to work directly at the direction and to the wishes of the company's operating committee without going through one or more intermediary layers of management. This ensures that the project team has authoritative answers to important policy decisions and that it can obtain guidance quickly on issues that it had not recognized existed during the planning phase. In addition, the chief information officer must have within his or her group the resources necessary to make technology judgment calls quickly.

I cannot emphasize enough how important the 24-hour decision turnaround requirement has been found to be as a critical success factor in project after project. The project team needs to know that it can expect hard decisions delivered quickly. If not, whenever there is a problem—no matter how small—and lacking a firm foundation on which to proceed, the project team will slow down and muddle along waiting for direction. If decisions are not made promptly and according to a process that everyone has the discipline to follow, the stress component of the change process can become overwhelming. Some key members of the project team simply may stop doing meaningful work until each and every issue is resolved—whether it involves them or not. In addition, the business organizations affected by the change effort quickly will lose confidence in the project team leaders and their corporate executives.

The Discipline of Avoiding Analysis Paralysis

At this point many traditional corporate executives may want to scream, "That is not how we implement change! We take our time and do it right!" Yet experience with companies that are taking advantage of advanced technologies to build market share and increase their efficiencies shows that "taking one's time" is a choice that often *results in* "not doing it right."

Figure 8-1 "Emagineering" organization additions.

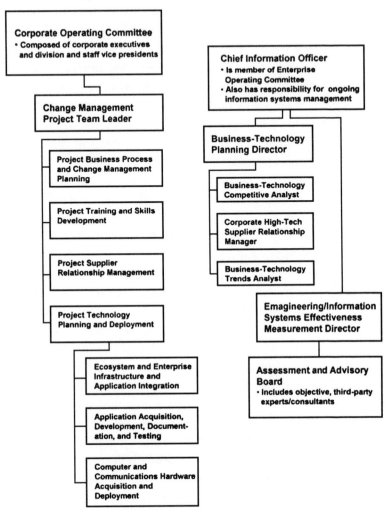

Executives in companies that are building market value through the deployment of advanced technologies find that they are continuously inventing the unfathomable future. Therefore, their implementation of new business processes actually changes the way their business ecosystems operate as well as their own firms. These technology executives neither know more nor are smarter than traditional executives in other companies. Technology executives' sources of information are no better than those available to others—which means that they too know that their expectations for the outcomes from deploying advanced technologies are a probability not an absolute certainty.

There is an excellent sports analogy to illustrate this issue and its solutions. A star major league baseball hitter can plan as much as he wants, but he cannot be sure what type of pitch an opposing pitcher will throw to him. He has to adjust his response in a split second as he sees the ball coming toward him. Nevertheless, he earns several million dollars a year if he hits the ball and gets safely to base more than one out of three times (a .333 average) he is at bat. This means that his team can expect him to fail two out of every three times he goes to bat. An executive who failed two out of three times in a conventional company would soon be let go. Yet a great batter is successful because he will be up at bat three times or more in a game, and as the game progresses, he will adjust to its tempo and the pitcher's style. In other words, the batter cannot plan for the pitch he will be thrown, but he can learn quickly from his mistakes, and then he has an opportunity to correct—either on the next pitch or at the next time at bat—his previous mistake quickly. If he never swings because he is still planning for what type of pitch might be thrown even after it has passed him, he will almost surely strike out. He must take action in the form of swinging at pitches if he wishes to remain a star player.

In "emagineering," technology executives are much more optimistic about implementing new business processes based on advanced technology successfully than about getting a hit based on an all-star baseball player's batting average. Experience has shown that each of the key planning assumptions in a change-management project has a 90 percent or better probability of being correct and that 98 percent or more of the tactical choices will be accurate. However, as any statistician knows, the total project success probability is a multiple of the underlying component probabilities. Moreover, it does not take the combination of too many planning choices that have a 90 percent probability of being correct and tactical choices at 98 percent probability of success before the odds of the total project's success deteriorate to under 50 percent.

The dilemma that technology executives face is that if they analyze and plan for too long a time, the result of their inaction is to make no decision and take no action. In a business world where the speed of communications has never been faster, key planning assumptions and industry norms will have changed before even one truly comprehensive analysis can be completed. Formal change plans based on excellent and thorough staff work are worthless if they are delivered after the business and technology environments have changed significantly.

Therefore, technology executives must be prepared to make decisions quickly on which they must act—just like a star hitter—and then *remake* those decisions if they can find a way to improve on them. Technology executives are more than willing to admit that they make decisions with incomplete information. However, they also will revisit those decisions if it becomes apparent that a mistake was made or a better choice could have been selected. Each time they "swing" at the same issue, they will increase their lifetime percentage of correct decisions.

An excellent example of how time can kill a project is the case of a leading insurance company that spent 18 months planning a new claims-processing and office-automation system for its 36 regional offices. To ensure a successful implementation of the system, the firm decided to have one very knowledgeable installation team deploy the new system in each regional office every 2 weeks. The information systems group considered this a stretch goal, even though it meant that it would take at least 72 weeks—almost 1½ years—to deploy the entire system. From the start of the planning effort to the last installation, this would be a 3-year project. From the perspective of a traditional company, this would have seemed a safe, conservative rollout effort for a major makeover of how the company would be conducting business for years to come.

Needless to say, the project was a failure. The regional business managers realized that the technology choices that had been made 6 months into the project and the business-process decisions finalized 12 months into the project were hopelessly out of date and behind the competition's systems by the time the eighth installation was completed. While this insurance company had analyzed, its key competitors had taken technology-based actions to gain leadership positions.

The common phrase for the state of companies that cannot transform themselves to meet the changing realities of their marketplace because they are caught in an endless planning loop is *analysis paralysis*. Once an organization is enveloped in analysis paralysis—and this happens within every company at some point in time—it has in effect made the decision to reject the change options available to it at the time and take no action. As you can clearly see, analysis paralysis is the opposite of creative destruction.

The more disciplined approach is to plan as much as possible before initiating the deployment phase of a change project. Then, during deployment, the change-management team must conduct regular, in-depth reviews that identify what is working as planned, what is not, and what actions that were planned earlier should be changed—and how. Before implementation, the change-management project team should do as comprehensive a planning job as possible in the time it is allotted. However, there is also a time at which the planning must stop and the battle—the deployment process—must begin.

Many well-respected business-technology consultants will not accept planning projects that the client wants to have drag on for more than 6 months—and most would prefer to complete the planning stage of such projects within 4 months or less. Their experience has taught them that all the essential planning issues and key evolutionary implementation solutions can and should be identified within 4 months. After this time, the planning document they have prepared for their client should become a working paper that must be improved on during the implementation phase as both the company's business environment and technology-product choices change and key planning assumptions are proven correct or not.

The Discipline of the 4-Week Build-Review-Improve-Build Cycle

For independent software suppliers who live and die by the success of their next product release—and their success is highly dependent on meeting their customer's expectations for timely improvements in terms of functionality and quality—the optimal build-review cycle is approximately 4 weeks long. This 4-week period allows the developers the time to create substantive executable code whose functionality can be demonstrated to project team leaders between reviews. Technology executives have found that this same 4-week cycle is well suited for companies in any industry.

"Emagineering" manages the implementation process of new enterprise-wide information-system functionality as a series of 4-week build-review-improve-build efforts. Teams of technologists and business-policy decision makers should work on a precisely defined aspect of a project with clearly defined objectives for a 4-week period. For example, if a team is charged with creating a Web site, the home page and first levels under the home page may be required to be delivered in executable code form, fully tested and documented, at the end of the 4 weeks between reviews. Initially, this is simply a *build* phase. The team shows the results of its first efforts to the leaders of the overall project team for an objective evaluation of where it has made progress against the overall plan and where it is falling behind.

During review meetings, implementation project leaders must communicate to project teams what assumptions were made during the planning process that have proven to be incorrect and new operational issues that have been identified and need to be addressed. At the same time, project leaders need to introduce to project team members additional functionality that must be added. In addition, they also must remove the requirements for planned functionality that is now regarded as unnecessary.

Backlog reports are often the basis for much of the review meeting's agenda. Backlog reports are the cornerstone for communicating to others in an organization what projects are in the process of being planned and deployed, what their status is, what changes are being made or considered from the original planning proposal, and which open issues need to be decided. A backlog report describes in the language of business

1. The projects and activities on which the information systems group is working
2. Their priority to the business
3. The currently projected completion dates with phase milestones and potential risks to success
4. The current resource use (people and money) and projected budget to completion
5. The tradeoffs that could be made in terms of functionality versus faster time to completion versus cost
6. Anticipated operational, competitive, and financial benefits

Publishing a backlog report throughout a company, just like manufacturing does, has been proven to be an effective means to get both business-only and technology-only managers to better understand the other's issues and develop appropriate corrective actions.

The five variables of information-technology projects that can be traded off against each other are time, quality, functionality, assigned staff, and budget. After a backlog report is distributed and comments are received from organizational executives, any of these variables may need to be changed to meet the company's current business priorities and to take advantage of new technologies that may have become available commercially since the last review.

After review meetings, the project team leaders have the opportunity to "improve" their solutions to the issues and problems that have risen during the initial build stage and realign their resources and deliverables to make the necessary fixes before the next 4-week review session. The discipline that successful software suppliers live by is that the review meetings must be brutally honest (leave office politics at the door, please), and they must be conducted on time and without fail. Meetings are not rescheduled even when a senior manager says, "We have to change the meeting because vice president so and so has a conflict." By removing politics as much as possible from the process, the development teams have the potential to gain significant efficiencies and productivity.

Of course, after each review meeting, the development team is expected to go right back into improve-build mode—not perform more planning analysis—based on the results of the review. This takes a tremendous amount of discipline. Typically, after review meetings, most individuals want to take several days (or weeks) to analyze the new inputs and reassess the dynamics of the project. Yet having "builders" sidetracked on analysis slows down completion of the project.

One of the key strengths of the build-review-improve-build cycle is that it avoids the slow torture development teams often experience as they continuously receive apparently random, uncoordinated change requests during the development process. By scheduling review meetings every 4 weeks, the build teams will know at what exact time in the future changes to the plan will be made. In addition, by doing so in a formal meeting, they also will know that the entire project team leadership understands and approves any and all changes. This disciplined development method is highly superior to the more commonly found "everybody is in charge of continuous redesign" approach that has a very high failure rate.

As project leaders gain more experience with the advanced technologies available to them, they can assess more realistically their technology-based capabilities over time to change the business processes of their companies and ecosystems. This competence will improve the productivity of teams working under the discipline of 4-week build-review-improve-build cycles.

The Discipline of Acknowledging and Correcting Mistakes

Technology executives' hard-earned experience only comes from actually working with advanced technologies—getting their hands dirty—and managing the work efforts of skilled information systems professionals. As in any learning experience, however, mistakes will be made.

It is no more realistic to expect an 8-year-old child to be told the multiplication tables in class, asked to study the tables overnight, and then come in the next day and answer all 100 problems on a multiplication test correctly than to expect energetic, bright technology executives to understand fully the capabilities of new technology products after a brief training class. The young math student learns and improves on his or her math skills from fixing mistakes after a teacher reviews the results of math drills, just as technology executives learn from each other at 4-week group review meetings.

Part of the discipline of the 4-week build-review-improve-build approach is to manage the process of identifying and correcting previous mistakes. Build-review-improve-build assumes that mistakes will be made and therefore establishes a mechanism to identify errors and correct them quickly. This requires a tremendous amount of trust on the part of both the company and the individuals working on project teams.

Many managers who have not had experience with enterprise-level information systems projects assume that new and advanced technology products will work as their trusted suppliers have promised. Yet this is not always the case. Unfortunately, members of implementation teams tend to be blamed when they cannot obtain the supplier-promised, management-anticipated functionality from new technology products in a simple and straightforward way. By conducting in-depth review meetings on a regular basis, the issues regarding the limitations of new products can be highlighted quickly, and the decisions concerning how valuable the anticipated functionality was to the organization can be assessed better. If such functionality is of very high value, the appropriate fix can be instituted. If not, the project build teams can get on with meeting their more important objectives.

Build-review-improve-build is very action-oriented. Moreover, while actions lead to both successes and mistakes, the mistakes must be acknowledged and corrected quickly to achieve success. Technology executives' experience with "emagineering" is that constructively taken actions—mistakes and all—that are reviewed on a regular basis are the foundation for building a core competence in business-technology-based change.

The Discipline of Technology Timing

Implementing advanced technologies requires true discipline in terms of timing. An organization that attempts to implement a vision too soon with immature technologies because the business case for change seems so compelling almost certainly will fail.

A great example of bad timing is the well-publicized failure of the Iridium venture. The Iridium concept was that a global wireless phone system could be created that would allow always-on communications through the use of a satellite network orbiting in space as opposed to the traditional land-based cellphone system. The business case seemed excellent. After all, what global corporation would not want to have all its executives able to communicate with each other anywhere and at any time?

The fatal flaws were that the Iridium phone itself was a clunky lunch-box-sized contraption that would be inconvenient for executives to tote everywhere and that it had to have a clear line of sight to an orbiting satellite—a difficult proposition to achieve from office buildings in the canyons of major financial centers. Simply put, the leaders of the Iridium fiasco wanted the end result so badly that they ignored the physics involved and the state of the science required to achieve their objectives. As a result, the project and all the company's efforts led to one of the single greatest technology-based venture failures of the last decade.

On the other hand, being too slow to move is also a problem. By understanding the Web and how it could provide excellent customer support and service, Dell Computer Corporation was able to gain a major advantage over its chief rivals in the personal computer (PC) marketplace by being the first in the PC computer industry to aggressively and properly build a customer-centric retail Web site—one where consumers and small business owners could custom configure the exact PC they wanted and order it immediately. Dell added to this first-strike advantage by building remarkable competence in how to use the back-end applications software required to manage its relatively complex build-to-order manufacturing system. The result was that its slow-footed competitors were forced to find other ways in which to compete as Dell became the leading provider of PCs to a customer segment that wanted to order online. Yet Dell's competitors had access to the same advanced technologies as Dell did. In addition, it could be argued easily that some of these competitors, such as IBM, Hewlett-Packard, and Compaq, had in-house more and better technology than Dell could acquire on the open market and easily could have gained a first-strike advantage ahead of Dell.

It takes real discipline not to start a technology-based effort too early or too late. Building competency in "emagineering" is a solid basis for knowing when to deploy advanced technologies as well as how to do so. And if you feel that your company is behind the technology curve today, a note of warning: Frequently, when a company starts after its competition has gained significant advantages, it makes imprudent choices in a desire to overtake its now-in-the-lead rivals.

The Discipline of Well-Timed Communications

The timing of when to make a technology-based change also must be linked directly with organizational communications about all the planned changes. The requirement to link the timing of deployment plans and the communication of these schedules is much more critical than most traditional executives may suspect at first.

The most commonly used phrase in technology planning meetings is, "We need to get to where the puck is going, not where it has been." This wisdom reportedly is the great hockey player Wayne Gretzky's contribution to corporate strategy creation. The reality when managing with "emagineering" is that senior executives need to communicate not only why and how they are planning to implement changes but also when. Adding the dimension of requiring the communication of time commitments to the decision-making process creates another facet of discipline. It makes technology executives think more clearly about their visions and requires technology suppliers and internal staff to establish realistic (and not overly optimistic) time-based planning targets. Communicating the timing of planned technology-based changes also instills confidence throughout an organization that its senior executives are proactively guiding the corporation to be a winner.

Many old-line companies rarely wanted to communicate realistically on substantive business issues with their employees. The idea of communicating a direction that could be modified every 4 weeks, based on build-review-improve-build cycles and new business or technology considerations, seemed inherently foolhardy.

Yet, by stark contrast, in winner corporations that participate in highly competitive marketplaces, key executives and internal coaches recognize that continuous change is simply a part of today's management environment. The fact that technology executives will communicate openly how they plan on taking advantage of new technologies is a reassurance that the necessary leadership for winning in the future is in place at the top. At winner companies that are continuously deploying new information systems based on advanced technologies, when employees are asked about their confidence in senior managers, they consistently say, "Knowing that top management is focusing on the right issues lets us know that our company is on the right track."

Proof of the value of open, time-based communications regarding planned technology changes can be seen in the way companies handled the so-called year 2000 problem. Most computer programs created before 1994 implicitly assumed that year dates would begin with a 19 forever. Few were able to handle the 20 prefix that would be required at the end of the 1990s.

Executives in both the public and private sectors found that the more they communicated with *everyone* within their organizations about both the seriousness of the year 2000 problem and the timing deadlines that had to be met, the more positively their organizations responded to the challenge. Many corporations created special independent year 2000 committees at the level of the board of directors to objectively review management's progress on solving this dilemma internally. Almost all created a year 2000 project-management office to identify necessary year 2000 remediation projects and monitor progress on a monthly basis. And many had independent auditors evaluate the readiness of the business for the date changeover and highlight potential problems. Since timing was important to success—from when the remediation projects began to when they had to be finished—executives were told that they could not engage in endless planning meetings.

These management directions ensured that knowledge about the problem and the company's status for fixing it were known throughout the organization.

Senior corporate executives consistently found that they obtained the best results when they openly and accurately communicated to the entire organization their multiple year 2000 remediation projects' actual status and issues on a regular basis. They did so without hiding the changes that had to be made from their original plans, unexpected problems encountered, and improvements to the corporation's business operations that resulted from often-sweeping changes in its enterprise-level information systems.

Constructive lessons from the year 2000 remediation projects clearly showed the positive value of timing one's technology choices and honestly communicating the objectives and issues encountered continuously throughout the course of the change project. The discipline instilled throughout organizations by the real likelihood of having a nonfunctioning business made possible the best of all outcomes—there were no corporate collapses or value-destroying calamities, as had been so widely feared.

Discipline for Leveraging Change

Business executives from many industries frequently believe that they should learn from the high-tech industry. How can IBM regularly remold its professional service offerings to meet the emerging needs of its most important customers? How did Hewlett-Packard convert itself from a supplier of test and measurement equipment to a printer company? How effective are the marketing programs that Microsoft and Oracle continuously slam against each other? What was the catalyst and insight that ignited EMC Corporation in the mid-1990s and blasted it past the entrenched suppliers of storage systems? How did Cisco Systems integrate its numerous acquisitions into the overall corporation? Why did Digital Equipment Corporation, Wang Laboratories, WordPerfect Corporation, Lotus, and scores of other technology suppliers that once were the predominant firms in their market spaces and to their target customer bases disappear as independent entities from the corporate landscape?

To learn how to leverage change firsthand from high-tech supplier executives, many customer executives insist on meeting and exchanging ideas with their counterparts at the most successful of the high-tech companies before placing a major order. These user decision makers consistently report that one of their most significant take-away from such meetings is learning how aggressively high-tech supplier executives must monitor changes in the way leading-edge customers are acquiring and using their products and how proactively high-tech supplier executives are willing to transform their organizations, redeploy resources, and establish new partnerships (even with current competitors) to exploit new opportunities. Making such dramatic changes quickly requires extensive discipline within an organization. Yet, in retrospect, the winner high-tech suppliers have had the discipline to refocus continuously on new opportunities over time—even while their current lines of business were doing extremely well—while those which have faded from existence did not.

One of the best examples of continuous successful transformation is Sun Microsystems. It started life in the early 1980s as a producer of inexpensive, relatively low-quality workstation hardware coupled with a free Unix-based software-development environment that it enhanced. Its first customers were computer programmers developing leading-edge software that generally was intended to operate on computers from companies other than Sun. It left the market for running compute-intensive analytical applications on workstations to other hardware suppliers who were much bigger and had more powerful and reliable hardware.

When Sun saw that its users were linking its workstations together and installing software on one of the workstations in the network to make it a dedicated file and print server, it aggressively began offering specialized products that could perform this function more effectively. Next, Sun's customers started to use its relatively inexpensive workstations (compared with compute servers from other suppliers) as communications nodes in a network. Recognizing the emergence of a new market, Sun attacked this opportunity with the zeal that has turned it into an approximately $15 billion corporation primarily known for supplying the computing nodes that are the backbone for running applications across the Internet.

Now Sun is in the process of attempting to position itself as the leading supplier of large computers, storage devices, and systems software for enterprise-wide, mission-critical applications that are based on the most recent advances in Web technology.

To even the casual observer of Sun's history, it is obvious that the company has only been able to make such dramatic changes through very strong internal discipline. Although some people (competitors and even employees within Sun itself) might claim that some of its successes were largely due to luck, one has to look at the results and be extremely impressed—especially when one realizes that Sun has always had to rely on internal discipline to change in order to compete successfully against other extremely capable high-tech suppliers.

One of the most unfortunate aspects of disciplined change across an organization is that individuals who will not assist constructively in the transformation must be asked to leave. Sun and other high-tech suppliers, for example, have a relatively high turnover rate among staff whose areas of expertise are being deemphasized or who are unwilling to commit to and execute on new objectives. One observes that this downside aspect of change has been disclosed publicly time after time at such current winner companies as IBM, EMC, Microsoft, Citigroup, General Electric, and others.

The mantra of corporate discipline for leveraging change is "Commit and Execute." Individual managers are asked to commit to goals that generally can be achieved during the next 4 weeks to 6 months, and then they are evaluated objectively on how well they have performed in comparison with what they promised, what resources they expended, and how others with similar goals performed. This all necessitates strong discipline—both individual and across organizational boundaries.

The Discipline of Organizational Education and Training

A very serious note of caution needs to be made at this point. Technology executives should never become overly enamored of the potential benefits of new technology by itself without taking into account the individuals who will use it. People, not the technology, ultimately determine the benefits that will be obtained from the deployment of new information systems. Every individual who is provided with access to new information tools must be well trained on both how and why to use them. It takes a tremendous amount of discipline within a company to spend the necessary monies on education and training—especially in conjunction with projects that are already over budget in terms of capital expenditures.

Education consists of presenting to the users of new technology what it is intended to do and how it will operate. An important part of the discipline of education is describing the strategic value of new information systems to executives and staff throughout the organization. Many technology executives believe that it is also very important to explain the decision-making process for selecting a specific technology and the tradeoffs that had to be made when selecting one technology over another.

Training is the process of instructing users and support personnel on the mechanics of how a new technology works. This includes what is required of them to make the systems perform as expected and how they are to use the new information that is being made available. Training also should include an explanation of how the system might fail and what users should do when a failure occurs.

Most executives who have deployed advanced-technology-based information systems *successfully* report that they spend over 25 percent of their project budget on education and training. They start the education process as early as possible. This allows them both to gain acceptance by the individuals who are going to use the new systems and to obtain feedback on what is important and what is not before the technology is deployed and when there is still time to make modifications at a relatively low cost.

In addition, these successful technology executives state that it is important to educate and train everybody who will either use or be affected by a new information system. This includes the end users of the system, their managers, and the technology staff that will support its operation. Not including any of these three key groups for budgetary or time-constraint reasons can lead to serious problems in obtaining the planned benefits.

Conversely, managers who have spent less then 20 percent of their project budget on education and training frequently report failures. In retrospect, these executives state that they believe that training should have started earlier, included a broader group of responsible individuals, and covered a broader range of topics. Managers in charge of failed projects consistently regret not having allocated more funds for education. And the reason they did not? The discipline of education and training broke down when the projects costs were higher than projected.

Strengthening the argument for greater education at the corporate level, senior information systems executives who have employed "emagineering" successfully insist that user education is the most critical aspect of technology transitions.

Yes, education and training cost money that chief financial officers (CFOs) are so often loath to invest in people. Conventional CFOs often resent training their current employees in skills that will make them highly marketable and allow them to leave the company more easily—often for a higher-paying job. However, the CFOs of the winner corporations in today's Competitive Economy have learned that even with these costs and risks, the successful deployment of advanced business processes based on information tools has paid off in terms of higher market valuations, which mean both lower capital costs (providing the benefit of allowing for even greater amounts of investment) and higher financial returns for the corporation and its investors.

Is Organizational Discipline Too Difficult?

Corporate discipline to implement "emagineering"-initiated change successfully requires cooperation among managers and staff throughout the organization to achieve common goals. The high-tech suppliers who have thrived over many years have taught technology executives that being able to change and improve their businesses in a disciplined manner is a key requirement for becoming and remaining a winner company. While the organizational disciplines described in this chapter may seem difficult to follow, there are many winner corporations in many different industries that believe that their competency in being able to follow these organizational disciplines is a major reason for their success in increasing their market valuations relative to those of competitors.

If there is any question as to why discipline is required to implement change based on advanced technology, note how organizational discipline has been proven to be so important to maintaining a corporation's market value from the financial side of operating a business. Companies that can project both their future revenues and expenses realistically are rewarded consistently with relatively higher market valuations than those which cannot.

Every manager knows that the budgeting and planning process is extremely difficult and tedious. It can only be done correctly at the departmental level with discipline by responsible managers and their staffs. Moreover, it certainly needs cooperation across organizational lines to be done correctly when rolled up to the corporate level.

Yet all winner corporations have the core competence to make relatively accurate financial projections and execute successfully against them. Publicly traded corporations that fail at this key but basic task see the negative consequences quickly reflected in their market values. Conversely, companies that promise and deliver accurately on their projected financials are rewarded with higher price-to-earnings (*P/E*) ratios.

The same high level of discipline that winner corporations demonstrate in their budgeting and accounting processes is also part of their attitude in the deployment of market-value-creating advanced technologies and innovative business processes.

Lessons Learned from Experience

To implement business processes based on advanced technology successfully, corporate executives must commit to a disciplined change procedure and way of thinking. This starts with establishing complete agreement among all senior executives to fully support the proposed changes and communicate their support throughout the organization.

For organizations that never before have engaged in "emagineering," it is critical that the beginning of the process be conducted in a focused and disciplined way. In addition, senior executives must proactively communicate and demonstrate their commitment to customer-focused change using advanced technology if they expect to obtain the full support of their employees, customers, suppliers, and other business partners.

Planning for "emagineering"-based change should be as comprehensive as possible—but not to the point of paralyzing the company. The priorities for the planning process include establishing the lines of authority and deadlines under which change-management leaders must make decisions about the project's implementation.

A 4-week build-review-improve-build cycle for implementing change tasks is the most effective approach to deploying technology-based business-process changes. Mistakes will happen, so technology executives need to employ the discipline of build-review-improve-build cycles for identifying and fixing planning errors and implementation mistakes quickly.

Mastering the art of timing when to implement new technologies is critical to success. Being technologically competent includes knowing the right times to acquire and deploy advanced technologies. Initiating major business changes with immature technologies can be disastrous. Being late leads to the urgent requirement to catch up to competitors who have already changed the rules of competition using advanced information systems.

People who can identify, adapt to, and leverage change within their business environments build winner organizations. Individuals who cannot adjust to significant technology-based changes within an organization should be asked to find opportunities elsewhere so that they do not eventually destroy the company itself.

During "emagineering"-based change, managers must be evaluated based on specific "Commit and Execute" objectives. Evaluations should include a review of the willingness and success of individuals to cooperate across organizational boundaries.

Education and training should be a major investment area for any change project. It requires strong discipline to invest in the people aspect of change, yet not doing so significantly increases the probability of failure. It takes tremendous corporate discipline to spend money on the appropriate levels of education and training when a project is already over budget—but these are often the most important investments that can be made.

Successfully instilling and maintaining organizational discipline is often the differentiator between a winner company as defined by market value and its lower-ranked competitors.

Competency 9: Charging Ahead of the Competition with Technomarketing

W INNING OVER THE LONG TERM is the result of evolving continuously over the short term to better meet customer needs. And short-term evolution typically is accomplished through marketing initiatives that align a business's offerings and policies more closely with the needs of its target customer base.

As leading-edge companies and consumers have themselves adopted advanced technologies to better manage their businesses and lives, executives have recognized that the art of marketing increasingly must be based on the sciences of technology. The resulting competence, *tech-nomarketing*, allows a company to take bold initiatives and differentiate itself in the opinions of its customers and prospects.

In many traditional companies, marketers are often one of the last groups that want to embrace technology-based business process change. Yes, they may institute the most obvious marketing efforts, such as registering their company's name as an Internet domain name (*www.ourcompany.com*) and create several Web pages that describe the company's offerings. They also may capture customer e-mail addresses with the intention of someday launching a well-thought-out electronic marketing campaign when its online customer base reaches sufficient size. But they are rarely willing or able (due to a lack of knowledge about the capabilities of advanced technologies) to take the bold steps of inventing new ways to market that have never before been attempted in their industry.

As the use of technology by consumers increases, no company can afford not to maintain a competence in technomarketing as an extension of its "emagineering" management practices. The success of technomarketing in increasing market value will come from the culmination of many customer-delighting initiatives launched by a business over many years.

Technomarketing to Build the Customer Loyalty Bond

In today's Competitive Economy, successful corporations use a combination of their marketing prowess and advanced technologies to make their customers feel that they are part of an ecosystem that is building and delivering products and services specifically for them. The objective is to establish a tight bond of loyalty between the customer and supplier while also making the inconvenience (and cost) of changing allegiance to another supplier extremely high. The *loyalty bond*, as it is called in "emagineering," is extremely important.

When Web technology was first introduced, many pundits assumed that there would be less loyalty between suppliers and customers and that the primary focus of competition would be on price. They could not have been more wrong—the basic principles of good business did not change just because of widespread use of the Internet. However, with the naïve encouragement of so many, hundreds of Web-based companies were funded that either sold products based on having the lowest price or gave information away for free in the hopes of obtaining advertising revenues. All but a few of these businesses have been failures. The reason is simple—without adding significant value, most could not create a loyalty bond with their customers.

The critical number of Web users required to make a site successful does not have the time or inclination to sample tens, much less hundreds or thousands, of alternative Web sites during a month. The typical user wants to go to the few sites that are recommended by his or her favorite Web explorers (who have discarded the real losers in their opinion) for a service, choose one for specific needs, and get to know it well. Such users only tend to change sites when the Web explorer community communicates the message over several months that their chosen site is not nearly as good as another. Most consumers can only maintain a loyalty bond with a small number of Web sites—and only Web sites with a relatively large number of loyal users will flourish over time.

The marketing goal of a company's Web site is to create a loyalty bond with the firm's target customers that no competitor can tear apart. Traditional marketing would call for merely providing basic product and company information wrapped in excellent graphics on a company's Web site. Technomarketing calls for more, however. The Web site must add customer value. For example, it must be the place where a customer can come and initiate a discussion with the company's marketing and support executives, find product maintenance instructions that were misplaced several years earlier, learn why the company believes its offerings are superior to those of the competition, order add-ons to the company's products that are not stocked by local dealers, etc.

In addition, the loyalty bond is extended with the use of a Web site when customers who visit obtain special offers and services. In the airline industry, these special services are focused on providing flight information and providing access to mileage programs. In the consumer goods industry, companies offer discount coupons. In the food industry, technomarketers may offer access to a comprehensive source of recipes and, for kids' foods firms, free games for children to play online or to download.

In technomarketing, continuous experimentation with a Web site is key. Good technomarketers use their imaginations to put up on their Web site what they believe their customers and prospects will be most interested in. They then monitor where visitors to their site go, how long they stay at each section, and what they download. When they feel confident that they understand how they are adding value for their customers, they then communicate to their entire marketplace the unique capabilities and value-adds their company's Web site provides.

Continuous Communications

For a business to create and maintain its customers' loyalty, it must engagingly communicate with them on matters in which they are interested. Now that the majority of customers have access to e-mail, this technology provides a solid foundation on which to change the medium of communications. However, most corporations have misapplied the technologies that can provide more comprehensive and productive customer communications.

In the past, supplier-initiated communications were through (1) advertisements, (2) one-dimensional paper mailings that allowed for no immediate customer responses, (3) telephone calls at the most inopportune time (e.g., dinner hour for consumers and 5 minutes before the next meeting for business buyers), and (4) occasional in-person sales calls depending on the industry and the prospective customer's buying budget.

Using advanced technology, e-mail allows businesses to initiate two-way communications with their customers and prospects cost-effectively. For example, when an individual registers an interest in a particular author with an online bookstore, that firm can store the information in its database and e-mail a short notice that the author is releasing a new book several weeks before it is published. The consumer now has the opportunity to preorder the book immediately for delivery on the date of publication or click back to a Web site to learn more about it.

Paper mailings, in comparison, are one-dimensional because they feature no capability on the part of the customer to interact instantly with the supplier. With paper mailings, the prospective book customer first would have to run across the advertisement for the new book accidentally among hundreds of others in a catalogue. Then he or she either would fill out the paperwork and mail it back or call to order the book. More likely, he or she would try to remember to go to a bookstore—any bookstore (so much for customer loyalty)—sometime after the book is available.

Effective technomarketing communications must be two-way communications, and each party must be able to respond to the other immediately—to carry on an electronic dialogue. Of course, the online bookstore customer in this illustration can click immediately on a Web address in the bookstore's e-mail, be transported to the bookseller's

Web site for more information about the book, and have the book sent to him or her on the first day that it is available. Most of us are familiar with numerous other examples where e-mail communications have proven to be so much more effective than paper mail or telephone conversations for conducting business transactions. This increased effectiveness is why e-mail has become the winner application of electronic business.

Valuable E-mail Marketing—Not Spam

From a technomarketing perspective, customers appreciate e-mail that gives them new information, provided that it is helpful, relevant, and perceived as factual rather than as marketing puffery. Well-crafted e-mail communications can both educate prospective buyers and provide a reason to move the buying process forward. In addition, as marketers have known for years, an advertisement that is relevant to a user can hold his or her attention for several hundred words—perfect for targeted e-mail from a trusted supplier—whereas an irrelevant one will not even get a full second's worth of attention before being mentally discarded.

Businesses need to have an "emagineering" e-mail strategy that includes providing links within every broadcast message to the Web pages that are specifically referenced. All too often, suppliers' e-mail marketing messages simply have click-backs that bring the recipients to the company's home page. The prospect finds that he or she has not been treated special for taking the effort to respond. And most frustratingly, the interested prospect must now hunt for where the offer that was made is hidden. Including reader-relevant links in marketing e-mail is simply a base-level requirement for marketing communications by technology executives.

The specific tactics used as the basis of a corporation's e-mail communications program should be shaped from feedback obtained directly from its customers. How does an organization obtain this feedback? The technology executive's answer is by conducting new and imaginative experiments of short time duration on a continuous basis. That is, technomarketers will send a small sampling of their customer base an e-mail to determine how they will respond. If the e-mail meets its objective, they will then send it to the entire customer base. If it does not meet their goals, they will either improve it or discard the idea all together.

Spamming—sending e-mails to individuals who are not interested in the supplier or the product being touted—has not been shown to create positive marketing results. Uninterested customers perceive spamming as a simple-minded misuse of technology and will respond negatively to the sponsor of the spam. In one instance, an online supplier of music CDs followed a spam strategy for several years by sending between two and four e-mails per week to anybody who had ever bought from or registered with it. Many prospects reacted with anger, filtering out the e-mails and taking their business to other sites. The retailer has since been barely able to survive. Its chief rival has more successfully sent e-mails to past customers that contain information about topics they have specifically requested. These e-mails are read and often are responded to positively. As this second company knows, volume is never a good substitute for quality and substance.

Companies have found that they can use technomarketing techniques to expand the effectiveness of their traditional marketing communications efforts. For example, businesses have found it increasingly expensive to send full-scale paper catalogues multiple times a year to all customers. Instead, many businesses, especially small and medium-sized specialty consumer-oriented companies, now send their target customer bases smaller, less expensive paper catalogues at the traditional times of the year when they are most likely to buy. Instead of showing all the supplier's products, the catalogues function as a large retailer's display windows— only showing those few items that are most likely to catch attention, such as tulip bulbs in the fall. The catalogue then encourages the reader to go to the firm's Web site to browse through its full and up-to-date line of offerings. This technomarketing approach both lowers the supplier's cost of catalogues and provides prospective buyers with an opportunity to view the up-to-date in-stock merchandise offerings that interest them—and all for a lower cost than would have been needed for a paper catalogue of the full inventory.

Successful e-mail marketing efforts spring from the creative imaginations of technology executives. Every company should challenge its marketing department to develop and deploy an industry-leading e-mail marketing program.

Online Support Is a Critical Technomarketing Function

The one Web-based capability customers consistently tell professional market researchers that really bonds their loyalty to a supplier is online support. Online support, when provided properly, can save a consumer the frustration of waiting on a telephone to talk to a representative. It also saves a supplier the considerable expense of staffing, training, and managing what often is a large and frequently complained-about customer-support department.

Online support has been pioneered by high-tech companies and is expanding rapidly to every type of organization, including government agencies, with positive results. Technology executives enthusiastically rate Web-based customer support as their most successful new customer-delight application.

There are two aspects of online customer support. The first is to meet customers' needs for *in-depth* information about products and services. Individuals expect to be able to find the level of information they need to make a buy or no-buy decision on their supplier's Web site. Many consumer goods companies from whom individuals only occasionally buy a product—from automobiles to personal computers (PCs) to watches—have found that the wired consumers who visit their sites have an unexpectedly great capability to influence others. Therefore, these presales support sites must be excellent—the messages they communicate quickly are retold and e-mailed throughout their prospect customer base.

The second part of support is to provide assistance in the maintenance of current and past offerings. In the consumer area, this might include instructions on how to maintain a small appliance, what components (such as lithium battery type) should be used as replacement parts, a description of add-on accessories (such as electronic games for specific game consoles), and where to send a broken item for repair.

The first supplier in an industry who can provide support effectively over the Web using the latest advances in technology will obtain a powerful advantage over its competitors. On the other hand, those who do not delight their customers with online support will have a serious problem getting customers who have a need for support to ever return to them. "Emagineering" a business's support processes and content over the Web to be superior to the those of the competition is critical to success.

At this time, the desire to beat, or at least never to be behind, the competition in the area of customer support is driving and funding many of the Web's most significant investments. For example, no brokerage firm wants to be behind its competitors in offering wireless Internet access complete with transaction-processing capabilities to its best clients' mobile phones—so all are investing in this capability. And many organizations are using inexpensive teleconferencing to permit electronic face-to-face (or monitor-to-monitor) meetings so that they and their customers can meet without making time-consuming and costly trips.

Expanding Customer Support to Include Product-Development Collaboration

While many technology executives are using "emagineering" to improve support for existing products, others are experimenting aggressively with building future products with the assistance of their customers.

The use of Internet product-development collaboration between a supplier and its own customers (and prospects) and its own suppliers is an especially promising capability for business-to-business ecosystems, as discussed in Chapter 6. However, it is also a powerful technology-based marketing tool.

Businesses can market to their prospects by inviting then to join in the ongoing collaborative product-development effort over the Internet. These prospects are now able to put their comments in a structured context, with additional input from both current customers and suppliers throughout the ecosystem.

The ability to market a product to a targeted prospect before the offering is fully developed and have the prospect feel that he or she is part of the development process creates a strong bond that a competitor will have a difficult time undoing.

In the future, technology executives will "emagineer" innovative Internet product-development collaboration processes for consumer products and services and will expand their deployment dramatically in the world of business-to-business commerce. This technomarketing tool may soon prove to be one of the most important ways for a supplier to establish long-term loyalty bonds with its customers.

Attracting the Next Wave of Customers

Technology executives have found that technomarketing can be used to cost-effectively and proactively build awareness of and a positive attitude toward their businesses among individuals who are likely to soon become their best prospects. Interestingly enough, the same technomarketing efforts that attract consumer groups that are on the verge of moving up from prospect to customer status also can reinforce the belief of current customers that they have made the correct decision to choose the company as their supplier. Since a company's most effective salespeople are its own customers, any marketing effort that increases their confidence in the decision to choose a specific supplier is a real benefit.

A great example of using technomarketing to attract prospects even before they can become customers is the promotion of upcoming movies. Movie studios consistently and with positive results advertise their upcoming releases in television advertisements that direct their prospective audience to the picture's Web site. There, potential theatergoers can learn more about the characters and plot as well as download games, screen savers, and money-off promotional merchandise coupons. This Web-based marketing effort then can create the buzz that draws audiences into the theater—often in the face of critics' disdain for the movie.

Ford Motor Company's Premium Auto Group uses similar electronic marketing techniques aimed at individuals it predicts will soon become its next wave of customers. It employs the same marketing messages for its upscale target customer base that wants reassurance that it has purchased a quality product and a moving-up group of consumers who soon will be able to afford a luxury-priced automobile.

From a marketing perspective, the Internet should be one of the most elegant of all media to capture prospects who are poised to become a business's next customer set. The structure of the Web allows it to cost-effectively educate about-to-be consumers regarding the new products into which they are growing.

In the world of business-to-business commerce, the Web has the potential to allow suppliers and prospects who do not currently know each other to seek out and discover the other and negotiate deals regardless of their size or geographic location. Suppliers who want to be found by new prospects—and that includes most of the world's corporations—should register the appropriate keywords with numerous search engines. In this way, when a prospective but new-to-the-market buyer enters that word to start a search, there is a likely chance of obtaining a match with the supplier.

An example of suppliers who should take advantage of this electronic marketing technique includes shredder manufacturers. There are many types of materials—wood, paper, rubber, and metal—for which shredders are used. However, most businesses only occasionally need to acquire a shredder of some type. For a purchasing agent assigned the task of finding a rubber shredder for the first time, using a search engine is a perfect way to find who in the world produces and sells such equipment. However, this will only work if the rubber shredder manufacturer takes the steps necessary to register its existence with all the major search engines and the content of its Web site assures the purchasing agent that it can be trusted.

While properly using search engines sounds simple—it is not. Experience shows that unless a company has technomarketing competency in-house, it will not take the proper actions required over time to ensure that it is using this highly pervasive marketing channel properly.

There are many technomarketing methods technology executives use to identify the next wave of potential customers—their target *prospect* base. The four most common are

1. Build a suspects list by sifting through data that can be acquired from firms that are in the business of profiling businesses and consumers for characteristics similar to the firm's newest customers. Advanced analysis tools then can help prioritize the company's most-likely-to-buy next wave of customers. For example, a supplier of minivans might search for couples under 40 years of age who have been married for 2 to 4 years with the assumption that they will soon be having children and trading in their sports car for a family vehicle.

2. Track the amount of time new visitors spend at a company's Web site, what pages they review, and what page they are on when they leave, and make an offer that is too good to pass up. For example, the Invisible Fence Company, a supplier of dog constraining systems, knows that it only has a limited time (usually

within 6 weeks of the purchase of a puppy) to reach prospective buyers. Thus it offers a free dog tag—an item every new dog owner needs—in return for a name, address, and telephone number from visitors to its Web site in order to make a follow-up sales call.

3. Attract prospects—pull them to the organization's site—using what is commonly referred to as an *associates program*. An associate of a company (usually business-to-consumer today) places hyperlinks on its own Web site that will send a visitor to the selling firm's Web site. The associate is paid a small fee for making the association between prospect and supplier and a larger fee if the prospect buys something on the first visit.

4. Place banner advertisements on other firms' Web sites that a company's next wave of customers is most likely to visit in order to pull them to its own Web site.

Banner Advertising

It is now time to discuss one of the most controversial of technomarketing tactics—banner advertising. Many industry observers believe that one of the major shortfalls of using the Internet for electronic business communications has been consumers' limited response to banner advertising. Banner ads are those small boxes, often with moving objects inside to catch your attention, which are scattered throughout most Web sites.

The vast majority of experienced Web users report that they simply find banner ads annoying. Yet the mistake has been to compare banner ads with print ads or outdoor billboards, rather than evaluating their unique position within a company's overall marketing programs.

Where banner ads fit into the technomarketing landscape is to make a company known to potential new customers who have not yet been motivated enough to perform a general Internet search to find it. And to work properly, they need to bring the viewer to a Web page designed to satisfy the information need quickly that attracted the potential *new* customer's attention in the first place—not to a generalized home page, as happens so often, that then requires the prospect to search for the offer promised in the banner advertisement.

The concept of banner advertising is reasonable. However, the execution of follow-up merchandising in general has been pathetically bad.

As a result, all banner advertising generally is lumped into the consumer category of "waste of time." Innovative technology executives are needed to dramatically improve the experience of those who respond to banner advertising. Until then, this medium will not be well accepted by consumers.

Embedded Advertising Is Next

From a technomarketing perspective, technology executives would most like to attract prospects to their business, either to their Web site or to their physical distribution channel, through positive reviews given by objective third parties. To obtain this capability for their clients, many media companies are investing intensely in combining advertising platforms.

For example, one objective of blending television broadcasts with Web access capability is to make it easy for consumers to purchase items they have just seen reviewed on a show. Wouldn't it be great if while a famous golfer is telling you why he likes a certain type of ball or club, you as a viewer could click on the remote control and access a Web site that provides you with more information? Wouldn't it be convenient for a consumer to be able to order the products he or she now wants with just a few more clicks? Or perhaps while reading an automobile magazine online, an article reviewing General Motors' newest model release has embedded in it a button that one could click to hyperlink to a General Motors Web site. And the General Motors site tells the automobile enthusiast more about the new vehicle and assists in creating a custom version online that would best meet his or her specific needs. And it could be ordered and financed from the Web site.

Technology executives are excited about the potential of new advanced technologies to create embedded advertisements. After all, the best motivator for moving potential purchase decisions along the path to completion is a satisfied user recommending to others that they should at least evaluate a certain product before making a final selection.

Will embedded advertising be appropriate for all product offerings? Answering this question is the responsibility of technology executives who know both their companies' marketing objectives and the true capabilities of embedded-advertising technologies.

Seducing Away Your Competitors' Customers

One of the most important missions of marketing is to take customers away from a company's direct competitors. Capturing this class of consumers is a double win for the business—it not only increases the firm's revenues, but it also makes competing more difficult for the competitor, who now has both lower revenues and lower profits.

The "emagineering" challenge is to first determine how advanced technologies can be used to disrupt the bond between competitors' customers and then what offer to make that will result in establishing a new relationship between your company and its most desirable prospects.

Many dotcoms started and stopped with lower price as their competitive disruptive factor. For this reason alone, they believed that they could capture and retain new customers. While having a comparatively low price is an important characteristic, consumers also understand the *value* of product availability, fast delivery schedules, accurate presales information, quality support services, and the many other dimensions of the supplier-customer relationship that lead to loyalty. Dotcoms that could not compete on dimensions beyond price found that they were disadvantaged severely and discarded quickly by value-conscious buyers.

The natural extension to pure price competition in electronic business-to-business commerce has been the creation of electronic marketplaces that bring buyers and sellers together in a structured and authenticated auction environment. In some cases, where commodity-like products are being put up for sale, these exchanges have been successful.

However, sellers of noncommodity products have been highly reluctant to join for many reasons. First and foremost, manufacturers who sell directly to industrial customers invest in presales and postsales efforts that they recoup in their final price. In an auction, the best-positioned sellers are those who have not incurred and do not plan to incur any support costs. Second, one-off orders between sellers and buyers do *not* allow for the long-term relationships that are critical to building successful ecosystems. Here again, a new market dynamic is developing in which it might seem that a corporation would be able to win customers away from its competitors purely on price only to learn that there is more to commerce than one-order bid pricing.

Companies that have been successful using "emagineering" to increase their customer base at the expense of their competitors have done so by widely communicating the advantages that implementing advanced technology has given their *current* customers. An excellent example of this is the way Charles Schwab innovated with use of the Internet to support its conventional discount brokerage business. When Charles Schwab added the ability for its customers to trade over the Internet, it advertised that Schwab customers could now work with brokers in its bricks-and-mortars offices as well as place orders 24 hours a day, 7 days a week—even when the brokers were not available. This was a value proposition that neither online-only brokers or, at the time, Schwab's traditional discount brokerage firm competitors could offer. It worked. And then Schwab quickly followed up by providing an immense library of equity research online—a capability that the other firms could not match. In short order Schwab convinced many of its competitors' customers that if they wanted to gain the benefits of advanced technology in the world of investing, they needed to open an account with Schwab. The result was that Schwab gained the largest market share among online individual stock traders.

For a company to capture its competitors' customers, it needs to first follow the basic principles of "emagineering"—start with front-end systems that better support the customer and then improve the back-end processes using advanced technology. When its experiments are successful, a company needs to market the benefits aggressively outside its installed base and place its to-the-point messages where competitors' customers cannot fail to recognize them. Whatever the business's new customer advantage—higher quality, faster delivery time, more comprehensive customer support, or some other feature—it will not be evident immediately to its competitors' customers. Therefore, a company needs to communicate effectively to its competitors' customers (today, often through e-mail and banner advertisements) the value it is adding by implementing advanced information technologies. The faster it can add greater value, the more likely it is to add to its own customer base by subtracting from its competitors' base.

Lessons Learned from Experience

The primary objective of technomarketing is to build customer loyalty bonds. The stronger the loyalty customers feel to a company, the more successful it should be. A successful Web site is one that creates a loyalty bond with the company's customers and Web visitors. Establishing customer loyalty is critical to applying advanced technologies productively to meet corporate marketing objectives.

The intelligent use of two-way customer communications through e-mail can build loyalty and revenues. E-mail is rapidly replacing one-dimensional paper mail and many other one-way marketing communications methods as the preferred means through which customers who consider themselves loyal to a specific supplier wish to communicate.

Technology executives must focus much of their technomarketing efforts on using advanced Web technologies to support their customers' needs for both presales offering information and postsales assistance. Well-designed support systems lower a company's total cost of providing support and the inconvenience customers undergo in obtaining it.

In the future, technology executives will initiate more Internet product-development collaboration efforts across their ecosystems. Product-development collaboration between suppliers and customers is one of the most powerful marketing tools available today.

Attracting the next generation of customers to a company before its competitors can is an important tactic for building a corporation's value for the long term. The Web now provides numerous capabilities to cost-effectively make a firm's prospects aware of its presence before they are ready to become customers. Sources of market intelligence used creatively also can contribute to an organization's ability to identify likely prospects for the purpose of conducting push-marketing campaigns.

Bad marketing communications are bad marketing communications—even when delivered electronically. And even potentially good marketing concepts based on new technologies, such as banner advertising, can have their reputations ruined if the follow-up merchandising effort is executed poorly.

Corporations that can provide the benefits of advanced technologies in such a way as to help their customers to also profit and then aggressively communicate these new capabilities can expect to capture their current competitors' customers. And capturing a competitor's existing customers is a knockout blow in the Competitive Economy.

Competency 10: Scrutinizing the Results of "Emagineering" Management

CORPORATIONS CAN ONLY BUILD their market-value-building competencies if they are able and willing to evaluate the outcomes of their "emagineering"-initiated actions objectively. Winner companies that deploy advanced technologies often are creating business processes unique to their industries. They are not following others. As a result, only they can truly recognize their successes and failures.

Technology executives are the only competent internal judges of how well a firm's "emagineering" efforts are succeeding. They have the holistic view of the company's marketplace, business strategy and priorities, and technology tradeoffs that is required to evaluate success accurately.

Information systems professionals too often will measure success by how smoothly a new technology was installed, how well it is operating, and how low the cost to support users is. While this is good information to know, it is insignificant compared with recognizing how new technologies and the business processes they enable are providing the company with unique competitive advantages that delight its customers.

Business-focused executives also have a very difficult time assessing the results of technology-driven evolution. They would like a direct correlation between investing dollars in information technology and substantive increases in the company's financial results. This does not take into account the central concept of "emagineering," which is that advanced technologies are merely tools on which innovative business processes can be built—but both the technology and new business processes must be implemented in a disciplined manner.

Having technology executives lead regular "emagineering" evaluation meetings attended by both business-focused and information systems executives is an excellent means to help bridge the gap between the two groups. In many corporations, the meeting notes, which are prepared by the senior technology executive in charge of the meeting, are distributed widely to other executives throughout the corporation so that they too can learn from the efforts of their peers—and better manage their responsibilities regarding the use of technology to achieve their management objectives.

Measuring Market Share Is Key to Increasing Market Value

"Emagineering" is predicated on the fundamental assumption that the corporation with the largest share of its target customer base and highest profitability in its industry also will have the highest market value in comparison with its competitors and others with which it compares itself. In addition, if it can maintain growth rates and profitability that are higher than the industry, eventually it will weaken its competition to the point that they must either focus on other customer segments or leave the business.

Since the starting point for an "emagineering"-based strategy is to increase market share continuously, the key indicator of the success of technology executives' efforts must be the results of measuring market share. The reasoning is simply:

1. A business that has the largest market share within its target customer base also should be the most profitable over the long term if its internal business processes are at least as efficient as those of any other supplier.

2. A business that has the largest market share within its target customer base also should provide the resources necessary to invest in growth opportunities.
3. A business that is more profitable and growing faster than its competitors will be rewarded over time with the highest market value.

Figure 10-1 presents a market valuation formula that should be framed and hung in every technology executive's office.

While having the largest market share does not ensure having the most efficient businesses processes and lowest production costs, it does give the company a major advantage in these two areas over competitors with smaller market shares.

If a firm that has the largest market share among its target customer base is not the most profitable when compared with alternative suppliers and must tell the investment community or its oversight board for too many financial reporting periods that it is still "buying market share against competitors," it has structural problems that "emagineering" may be able to help identify but probably cannot fix. Corporations with leading market share but low profitability need the business doctors from such firms as Bain Consulting, Boston Consulting Group, Cap Gemini, McKinsey, Mentor, and other winner strategic consulting firms.

If a company does not achieve the highest value among its peers

Figure 10-1 The "emagineering" golden equation.

**Largest share of
target customer base**

PLUS

**Highest profitability
of all suppliers to
target customer base**

EQUALS

**Winner corporation
with
highest-in-class
market value**

when it has the largest market share and comparably better profitability and growth rates, it needs either a better investor relations program or the investment community is making an important statement that management must take seriously with an appropriate response.

Both above-average profitability and above-average market value most likely are achieved by corporations with dominant market share. Therefore, market share is the primary criterion on which technology executives' efforts must be measured. Market-share changes are the early warning signals that market values will be going up or down in the future.

Measuring the Lines of Business on a Growth-Profitability Matrix

At the same time that a business is monitoring how its relative market share and competitive position are changing (hopefully for the better) within its target customer base, it also needs to manage its growth-profitability objectives. Technology executives need to determine initially where their business is in comparison with others on the growth-profitability matrix. (See Figure 10-2 for an example of three different companies and their relative positions on the growth-profitability matrix.) Then they must evaluate how "emagineering"-initiated strategies, tactics, and programs have helped improve on past results. Their feedback to the rest of the corporation should begin with what efforts are working and conclude with recommendations about what areas the business needs to improve.

Each corporation's financial group, in conjunction with the most senior executives, should set the minimum growth-profit objectives for each line of business. These objectives should be established for the purpose of increasing market value at a rate comfortably above the minimum that the board of directors believes the shareholders are anticipating. In addition, "stretch" goals—higher growth plus greater profitability—should be established and combined with an executive "beat the goals and take home more money" bonus plan in order to maximize potential increases in market value.

For-profit companies must measure growth in terms of revenue, whereas nonprofit organizations may measure growth in terms of constituents served, funds raised, or some similar key factor that quantifies constituent acceptance.

Figure 10-2 Growth-profitability matrix.

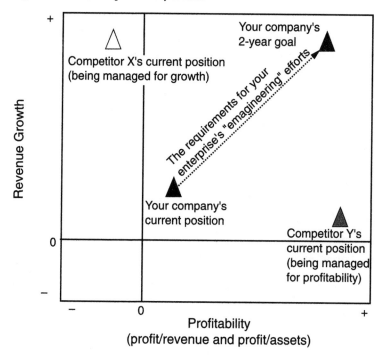

Note: A corporation's and its lines of business's positions on the growth-profitability matrix need to be graphed over time to determine changes in strategy and positioning

Profitability must be calculated based on both profit margins and return on assets. Companies need to measure their results against their competitors on both these key profitability measures to obtain a clear picture of how they are improving their value in the eyes of the investment community. Nonprofit organizations might use measurements that show how they are minimizing costs—such as budget money and head count per number of constituents served—in place of profitability.

The growth-profitability matrix is most valuable to technology executives when it is plotted over time and with the results of the deployment of advanced-technology projects considered. This is yet another way to measure the results of the organization's "emagineering" efforts.

As a planning tool, technology executives will create a time series (each at 3 or 6 months) of projected growth-profit matrixes covering a future period of 1 to 3 years. Technology executives then can project the benefits they must obtain from future "emagineering"-initiated projects to achieve their revenue and profit goals.

Since a key variable in the results of and planning with the growth-profitability matrix is product pricing, companies must perform the target customer feedback loop function to continuously determine if their prices are set consistent with the growth-profitability goals. Lower end-user prices should increase sales at the expense of profit margins; higher prices should increase profit margins but probably at the expense of lowering market share. Moreover, the impact on return on assets employed is highly dependent on the efficiency of the corporation's business operations in both cases.

Technology executives use the growth-profitability matrix within the context of "emagineering" both to identify potential opportunities for improvement and to compare themselves competitively against organizations whose financial results are available publicly. For example, many personal computer (PC) companies—or the PC lines of business of companies such as IBM, Hewlett-Packard, and Compaq—would compare themselves against Dell's financial results in the late 1990s. Not only did they find that Dell's information system–based direct-sales model in general was more profitable than their channel distribution policies, but they also found that Dell's internal manufacturing processes based on advanced technologies turned inventory into finished products more efficiently and more quickly. Needless to say, they recognized the need to deploy advanced information systems to make radical changes in the way they assembled and distributed product if they wished to remain competitive in the PC industry.

A corporation that has both the leading share of its target customer base and a higher position in the golden top-right quadrant of the growth-profitability matrix than its competition is a true winner. Measuring changes in the corporation's competitive position on the growth-profitability matrix over time and "emagineering" how to improve the position ahead of the competition are critical technology executive management responsibilities.

Weakening the Competition

The next measure of success with "emagineering" is to determine if the programs put in place using advanced technology are weakening the competition. Any examination of industry maturation clearly shows that weak competitors, no matter how large, either can be forced out of business or will be absorbed by a more vigorous organization.

Just as they focus on gaining market share by improving products and services and advancing their company's position on the growth-profitability matrix, technology executives also should monitor industry dynamics to find the vulnerabilities of competitors that can be exploited. In aggressive ecosystems, a firm's business partners will expect it to do its best to leverage any such competitive opportunities, and it is preferable to have competitors' ecosystem members become weak as yours become comparatively stronger.

Experience has shown that one of the most effective ways to quickly weaken a competitor is to use advanced technology to recruit its distribution channel and other intermediaries to your company's own ecosystem. This tactic is used in almost every industry by both established companies to stifle new entrants and new entrants seeking to take market share away from established firms who are losing the confidence of their distribution channel.

Another excellent tactic is for a firm to link itself extremely closely electronically through information systems with its suppliers that also provide components to different competitors. The company with the best electronic ordering and planning system typically gets better service, lower prices, and preferential shipments over other customers. This is a particularly effective tactic when critical components are in short supply and demand is high.

A longer-term method to weaken competitors significantly is to use "emagineering" to create the business processes necessary to rapidly bring out numerous well-designed products covering the broadest range of target customer base preferences before the competition realizes that the battle has switched from price to product innovation.

In contrast to the preceding methods, the worst way to attempt to weaken a competitor is to begin a price war. This tactic usually results in a long-term lowering of price-earnings ratios for *all* the participants in the industry caught up in cutthroat price competition. The U.S. steel industry is a perfect 40-year example of this phenomenon, to the detriment of all steel manufacturers.

"Emagineering" efforts to weaken the competition can be extremely difficult to plan for and execute, but if they are successful, they can confer on a company a large and sustainable value. American Airlines' pioneering creation of its online reservation system is an excellent example of one such successful effort. Not only did the electronic reservation system promote American Airlines flights ahead of its direct competitors, it also managed to keep low-fare upstarts off travel agents screens. On the other hand, companies such as Amazon.com, America Online, and Yahoo have attempted to establish auction sites in an effort to weaken perceived long-term competitor eBay. However, all have failed miserably—the market did not want more then one online flea market—and eBay's position actually was strengthened as a result. The lesson here is not to be a slow second with limited customer benefits (especially if the claimed benefits are in areas the consumer does not really care about) in today's environment of fast communications and realistically expect to weaken a competitor.

Corporations that use "emagineering" to specifically weaken their competition and are successful should see the results in terms of capturing their competitors' customers and a lowering of regard for the competitors' position among the target customer base as reported in their customer feedback interviews. These results can be measured quantitatively. In addition, media articles and security analysts' reports often will highlight specific issues that weakened competitors are facing that can be attributable directly to the attacking firm's "emagineering" efforts. While qualitative, these are excellent and highly public measurements of success.

The Value of Selecting
the Most Appropriate Advanced Technologies

When an organization slides off the mainstream technology curve, it is extremely difficult and expensive for it to get back on. Therefore, one of the key benefits of "emagineering" is to assist senior executives in making the correct technology choices at the proper time. When evaluating the results of "emagineering" efforts, technology executives should consider the benefits of not needing to throw out technology selections that would have been inappropriate and replacing them with more suitable ones.

A fundamental issue decision makers face when evaluating alternative technology choices is, "Which of these products is most likely to be deployed by others and be number one in its space over the useful life of the technology?" The long-term organizational investment in terms of training staff and creating new business processes that result from initially implementing a new information system is enormous—always much more than the cost of hardware, software, and implementation services. The costs (e.g., financial, lost opportunities, retraining, morale, confidence in leadership) to organizations that have rolled out information systems to their key employees but soon decided that they made the wrong technology choice and wanted to jump to an alternative technology are high. The disruption and loss of productivity of the affected employees as they attempt to unlearn the older information systems and master the newer ones are extremely expensive to the organization.

And the key "emagineering" value measurement? *Any time a company has to discard a technology product that has been deployed across the entire organization and replace it with a similar one, the "emagineering" effort has been applied incorrectly.* When a company can obtain many years of production benefits from the same information systems product, "emagineering" is adding real value. Tracking the number of technology replacements required by the corporation over time—with lower being better—is an excellent measure of the value of "emagineering" and the acquisition choices of technology executives.

Evaluating the Benefits of Upgrading Technology Components

Once organizations know they are on a winning technology curve, the next question is when to upgrade their internal technologies. For example, Microsoft has wanted corporations to upgrade to each new version of its Windows operating environment—both on desktop devices and on servers—over many years. At the same time, small businesses and home users have been urged to upgrade from Windows 95 to Windows 98 to Windows ME to Windows XP on their PCs.

Technology executives understand that while suppliers have every incentive to upgrade their installed base on a regular basis, there are only two reasons to do so. The first is economic—organizations should upgrade when there is a positive financial return that is greater than the corporation's cost of capital. In other words, installing the upgrade will result in measurably lowering costs even after the expense of implementation. The second is survival—the supplier announces that it will no longer support the version of the products and technologies on which the organization depends to run its mission-critical business processes.

The decision as to when and how to upgrade an organization's installed technologies with a new generation of products requires following a disciplined approach. Frustrated senior corporate executives report that all too often they are being urged by their trusted suppliers and best information systems technologists to spend monies on upgrades so that the organization can stay current with the state of the science—even when the projected economic benefits are murky at best.

On the other hand, technology executives would rather deploy their limited technical resources and budgets in projects that make the corporation more efficient and effective than to merely upgrade existing, working information systems. This is an ongoing conflict that can only be resolved by aggressive, knowledgeable technology executives who can manage the tradeoffs for the good of the company.

The basis for making optimal decisions regarding upgrades should be the "emagineering" planning process within the organization. In addition, the results of these decisions—how and when—can be evaluated in terms of costs and benefits within 6 months after an upgrade is completed. When scrutinizing the benefits of "emagineering" management, business executives should consider the value in financial terms of both implementing technology upgrades when they did and rejecting possible upgrades.

Evaluating Comparative Competitive Advantage

From a management perspective, evaluating how well "emagineering" has helped a corporation identify and leverage the benefits of significant new technologies before its competitors is a key measure of its effectiveness. Positive results from "emagineering" efforts to keep the corporation on the proper technology track may be significant only every couple of years—but the strategic importance often can be realized for many years into the future and radically change a company's relative market value within its industry.

For example, in the last 5 years, understanding the technologies and business implications of the Web as it relates to customer relationship management (CRM) has been crucial to increasing market value. Most companies that decided to wait until the technologies of the Web, CRM applications, and the business processes of using the Web to better understand and communicate with customers matured before acting aggressively are still trying to understand the implications and leverage them to their best advantage. By missing the first technologies—that were all too often dismissed as mere "toys for boys"—they have never been able to get on a beat-the-competition learning curve. It will take many years (accompanied by a slowing down of technology advances in these fields) before the companies who waited too long will be able to catch up to the leaders in those competitive areas where the correct use of technologies really matters.

Experience shows that key technology innovations in the past, such as PCs, relational databases, high-speed data networking, inexpensive multiuser compute servers, integrated client-server application suites, decision-support systems, automated CRM functionality, etc., that were adopted early by corporations managed by technology executives often created significant competitive first-strike advantages within their target customer bases. Competitors that attempted to follow the leaders at what they considered to be a prudent speed—often referred to by traditional executives as a "slow second" or "acceptable third"—might never reach the level of expertise of fully understanding the technology and its implications. Often they might deploy relatively less effective systems late in a futile follow-the-leader tactic. An excellent example of this was FedEx' first-strike launch of a package tracking system. The value this capability added to its overnight delivery of products created a barrier that others could not match for a considerable number of years. Only United Parcel Service (UPS) had the resources and determination to respond to FedEx' challenge. And it took UPS many years and management changes before it could claim parity with and in some aspects superiority to FedEx.

When technology executives scrutinize the results of their "emagineering" efforts, they need to identify objectively what technologies "emagineering" led them to acquire for the purpose of building a core market-value-increasing competency ahead of their competition. And if they missed key technology innovations that their competitors used to increase their own market values, they need to understand what went wrong in the planning process and correct it immediately.

The Art of Managing What You Do Not Measure

There is an old truism in professional business management that goes, "If you cannot measure it, you cannot manage it." As a result, many traditional companies often have attempted to measure every aspect of their information systems operations—from programmer productivity to cost per transaction processed. These corporate executives then pleaded with and bullied their information systems subordinates for year-to-year improvements against the metrics they had established.

Unfortunately, corporations that focus on measuring improvements in the productivity of their internal information systems organization rarely know what standards and goals they should set. For example, should a financial services firm spend 3 or 7 percent of its revenues on acquiring new technology in a year? Is it better served if 5 or 12 percent of its costs are budgeted for operating its information systems? Will a corporation's market value be greater in the next year if it spends more or less on implementing advanced technologies than it did last year?

Many corporate executives would like to answer these difficult questions simply and quickly by comparing their firm's costs against industry averages. Yet the correct answer usually is not related to what others are doing—the answers depend on a company's own strategic objectives. Benchmarking against industry averages, while doable, does not correlate with the levels of spending required to achieve the firm's unique strategy goals and increase its market value. More to the point, it compares the corporation's current position against a mishmash of objectives of other firms in the industry.

Technology executives have found that the proper measurement for their information systems groups is how they improve the organization's efficiency and effectiveness so that the traditional market-value accounting yardsticks, such as revenue growth, profit margins, revenue per employee, return on assets employed, days sales outstanding, and annual inventory turns, are improved.

Yet this approach leaves an uneasy feeling in the hearts of most traditional corporate executives that once the excitement and *esprit de corps* of pioneering new technologies wear off, they will be unable to measure excellent versus good versus mediocre information systems results on an ongoing basis. Therefore, they still want some type of continuing benchmark against which to measure their information systems group's performance.

Many independent consulting firms offer information systems benchmarking services. That is, they will rank a corporation's position in the use of information technology on any criteria senior executives want against any groupings of similar organizations. While this sounds scientific and logical and often does help both the company's technical and business executives better understand their relative competitive position vis-à-vis other firms, unless managed extremely thoughtfully, it also can muddle market-value-building efforts.

Independent cost-benchmarking efforts are similar to planning for the future while viewing the world from a rear-view mirror. A corporation's *current* information systems costs and capabilities often are highly dependent on decisions made longer than 5 years in the past. What is more bothersome about such benchmarking studies is that they rarely correlate a corporation's information systems costs and capabilities with its competitive business-process advantages and deficiencies—only with the estimated costs of others.

The bottom line is that managing an information systems organization while applying the principles of "emagineering" is different from managing a sales organization against quotas or a manufacturing department against standard costs and acceptable quality levels. It requires managing in an environment where goals often are more qualitative than quantitative and information systems efforts cannot be correlated directly and immediately with their results. (Again, compare the difference with the use of a machine tool in which each part that is made can be measured directly and immediately to determine if it accurately meets its manufacturing specifications.) Therefore, it is extremely important that corporate executives trust the members of their information systems groups to act as technology executives and professionals, and in return, the information experts must communicate openly with the organization's executives about why and how they are performing both their daily and project tasks.

How the Board of Directors Will Evaluate "Emagineering"

When a company has identified the correlation between the use of advanced technologies and progress on its strategic goals, its board of directors (or oversight board outside the private sector) should be able to evaluate the results of the firm's "emagineering" efforts both objectively and qualitatively. Since the board of directors represents the shareholders' interests and has the authority to hire and fire the company's top executives, it is extremely important that it too scrutinize the outcomes of the firm's "emagineering" initiatives.

Just as at the board level there is an art to evaluating the potential of executives to perform effectively in the most senior management roles, there is an art to evaluating the success of "emagineering" efforts. Much of the evaluation process at the board of directors' level is subjective, and ratings will differ from member to member. Yet skillful, dedicated board members can evaluate the benefits of "emagineering" for their organizations wisely and objectively without measuring the minutiae when the three key evaluation criteria are

1. How has the use of advanced technologies expanded the company's share of its target customer base?
2. How has the use of advanced technologies improved the organization's internal efficiency and external marketing effectiveness?
3. How has the use of advanced technologies increased the corporation's market value?

Properly conducted, "emagineering" assists a company in achieving its objectives by identifying the advanced-technology options available to it at any point in time to execute successfully against its strategic objectives. However, if the objectives are incorrect, such as building high-quality fountain pens for a target customer base that wants low-cost ballpoint pens, the results of the "emagineering" effort will be for naught. By evaluating the results of a business's "emagineering" efforts, the board will be able to better evaluate if the current strategic positioning is correct. When a company is pursing the wrong objectives in the wrong way, an independent board has the obligation and responsibility to point management in the right strategic direction and establish goals that will increase its market value.

Lessons Learned from Experience

The primary measure of success for "emagineering" and technology executives is growth in market share among the business's target customer base. Once a company has the number one market share position, technology executives will then continue to judge their performance based on how much they can increase this share and widen their lead over competitors with the innovative use of advanced technologies. The reward for having the largest share of the business's target customer base while also growing faster than the competition should be the highest market value in an industry.

"Emagineering" results also should be evaluated by how they assist a corporation in improving its profits. As we have discussed throughout this book, profit improvements can be achieved in many different ways through the use of advanced technologies. Technology executives should be assisting and challenging managers continuously within their companies to use advanced technologies to exceed corporate profitability goals. Senior corporate executives should then scrutinize on a regular basis how their organizations have used advanced technologies to achieve or exceed their profit goals by line of business.

"Emagineering" may help a company identify flaws in its strategic objectives, but it is not intended to solve fatal strategic problems.

The most effective way for an organization to use "emagineering" to weaken its competition is to deploy advanced technologies to support the other members of its ecosystem—customers and suppliers—in a superior manner. Superior support will result in increasing loyalty bonds and the use of best efforts to promote the company's interests ahead of its less technology-capable competitors. Companies that use the same distribution channels as their competitors have found that winning the loyalty of the distribution channel over their competitors though the deployment of cutting-edge business processes based on advanced technologies provides a strategic advantage that is difficult and costly for others to overcome. The worst way, and one that often misfires by lowering the market value of all companies in an industry, is merely to engage other firms in price competition.

Corporations that make the wrong technology choices or do not adopt new technologies at the proper time run a relatively high risk of falling behind their competition. Organizations that deploy new technologies and upgrade existing ones without a sound financial-return rationale will both pay too much for their information systems over time and devote technology resources to experimentalism when they should be improving business operations. Successful "emagineering" efforts will assist technology executives in properly and prudently managing the implementation of advanced technologies in terms of both the timing of new application deployment projects and optimization of the benefits obtained.

When evaluating the benefits of "emagineering" appropriately, technology executives must make an objective but often qualitative review of the business results of their firm's information systems group's efforts. Senior executives who attempt to micromanage their information systems group's performance against quantitative industry benchmarks are judging performance against the wrong metrics. Success in building market value is always the right measurement.

When "emagineering" is assisting a company in outperforming its competition in terms of market valuation to the satisfaction of its board of directors, the process is on track.

Index

About the Author

John Logan is founder and chairman of the Aberdeen Group, a consultancy that provides IT market intelligence, positioning, and market acceleration services to companies in order to identify new market opportunities, enter those markets successfully, and accelerate the adoption of new technologies. He is a popular speaker at venues around the world such as the MIT Leaders Forum and Gillette's Global Information Executives Annual Meeting, and a former associate with the prestigious Cambridge Research Institute.